"Both the lay and professional public is greatly in the debt of Dr. Maxine Boatner for her splendid biography . . . To her task she brings the industry of the historian, the graceful style of the narrator, but best of all the enthusiastic admiration of a devotee of her subject . . . she is able to write with rare understanding of the deaf and their problems. Unquestionably the result of her efforts will illuminate an important corner hitherto dark in the history of American education.

"That there are special schools for the deaf nearly everyone knows today. That these schools reach collegiate level hardly anyone knows. Much less does anyone know that at the collegiate level there is today only one such institution in the world and that that institution is located at our nation's capital.

"The founding and nurturing of this unusual seat of learning was preeminently the work of one man, Edward Miner Gallaudet. When one hears mention of the name Gallaudet in connection with the deaf, one is ordinarily minded to think of Thomas Hopkins Gallaudet whose name is indelibly written in the history of American Education as the founder of the first American school for the deaf in Hartford, Connecticut. But the identification of the name Gallaudet with the deaf did not stop with Thomas Hopkins. It continued with his illustrous son, Edward Miner. This is a fact far too little known, not only to American laymen but to professional educators as well." —*John S. Brubacher.*

* * *

"This volume has an exceptionally appealing story to tell . . . Dr. Boatner has told it well."—*Allan Nevins.*

"I have really had a wonderful experience and have done an amount of work of which I am not ashamed."

Emily.

Voice of the Deaf

A BIOGRAPHY OF
EDWARD MINER GALLAUDET

By MAXINE TULL BOATNER
Director of Historical Research,
Conference of Executives of American Schools For the Deaf

INTRODUCTION BY JOHN S. BRUBACHER

Public Affairs Press, Washington, D. C.

DEDICATED TO
EDWARD DENISON GALLAUDET
1901 - 1953

371.912092
B63v
105020
May 1978

Introduction

That there are special schools for the deaf nearly everyone knows today. That these schools reach collegiate level hardly anyone knows. Much less does anyone know that at the collegiate level there is today only one such institution in the world and that that institution is located at our nation's capitol.

The founding and nurturing of this unusual seat of learning was pre-eminently the work of one man, Edward Miner Gallaudet. When one hears mention of the name Gallaudet in connection with the deaf, one is ordinarily minded to think of Thomas Hopkins Gallaudet whose name is indelibly written in the history of Amercian Education as the founder of the first American school for the deaf in Hartford, Connecticut. But the identification of the name Gallaudet with the deaf did not stop with Thomas Hopkins. It continued with his illustrious son, Edward Miner. This is a fact far too little known, not only to American laymen but to professional educators as well.

Edward Miner Gallaudet not only gained recognition by founding a college for the deaf but he also kept constantly abreast of advanced methods for educating the deaf. Thus he early showed an interest in their oral education. On numerous occasions he visited Europe to study improved methods there. At home he was frequently visited by distinguished callers from foreign lands, sometimes even royalty. But most important his contacts in Washington enabled him to keep the cause of the higher education of the deaf constantly before those of wealth and influence who could advance it best.

Both the lay and professional public is greatly in the debt of Dr. Maxine Boatner for her splendid biography of this second generation of Gallaudet educators. To her task she brings the industry of the historian, the graceful style of the narrator, but best of all the enthusiastic admiration of a devotee of her subject. Connected herself with the institution in Hartford first set on its way by Thomas Hopkins Gallaudet, she is able to write with rare understanding of the deaf and their problems. Unquestionably the result of her efforts will illuminate an important corner hitherto dark in the history of American education.

JOHN S. BRUBACHER

Center for the Study of Higher Education
University of Michigan, Ann Arbor, Michigan

v

Foreword

When you are a little girl with all the senses God gave you and you have a friend with whom you play and love whose parents are deaf-mutes, it is an experience you never forget.

Helen was the epitome of youth and light and happiness. Her deaf parents, teachers at the State School for the Deaf in our city, loved their child and were profoundly grateful for her hearing. They gave her a happy home and welcomed her friends. Visiting her we learned to sign and spell on our fingers which became a tremendous game since the slightest symbol we made might bring forth candy, a banana, or even a toy from Helen's mother.

The superintendent and his wife in the school where Helen's parents taught were friends of my parents and from the time I entered college the superintendent began to encourage me to become a teacher of the deaf.

After college I pledged myself to a year's teaching experience in a small town public school in my home state. While there I again heard from the superintendent of the school for the deaf; this time he urged me to apply for a fellowship at Gallaudet College as the time was drawing near for the selection of Fellows. I wrote an application, thinking at the time "I might as well." To my surprise I was accepted by President Percival Hall and the following fall found me in Washington, D.C., studying and again enjoying the academic life. Aside from the fact that special methods were involved in their instruction, I found that young deaf people were quite the same as other young people.

Students entered Gallaudet College from all over the United States and many foreign countries; this was—and remains—the only college for the deaf in the world. Kendall School served as the "laboratory" for the Fellows; observation work and practice teaching were carried on in its classrooms. The Fellows were introduced to every academic practice on Kendall Green, assuming many and strange duties in order to become acquainted with the type of work they were entering. I taught Prep Latin—on my fingers!

We learned much about Thomas Hopkins Gallaudet, the father of deaf-mute instruction in the United States. In becoming familiar with his work we vaguely absorbed the fact that he founded the "mother school" in Hartford. As far as we were concerned that had happened a thousand years ago. Nothing was farther from my mind than that I would one day live in Hartford. I do not remember that I was taught anything about Edward Miner Gallaudet, the son who founded the College named for the father.

But my future was irrevocably tied up with the deaf, even though circumstances drew me from it for several years.

Within seven years after I finished my training at Gallaudet College, I was back on its campus teaching but it was not until I moved to Hartford two years later that the Gallaudet family came alive for me. Among the first persons I met in Hartford was Katharine Gallaudet, the "Kitty" of this book, who was Edward Miner Gallaudet's oldest child. Soon I met Kitty's cousin, Mrs. John Sparhawk, Jr., who had been Alice Gallaudet Trumbull, fourth child of Henry Clay Trumbull—Edward's lifelong friend. I became acquainted with Alice's sister, Katharine Trumbull Scoville, and met the widows of Denison and Edson, Edward's two oldest sons. Knowing these family members led to my meeting many of Edward's grandchildren and other relatives.

I soon began to feel that I had struck roots in Hartford and was becoming a member of the Gallaudet "clan." Although Katharine had closed the family home *Quiescas* she welcomed me in her apartment.

Mrs. Sparhawk lived in the Clemens' home, now called the Mark Twain Library and Memorial Commission, which housed a branch of the public library as well as several tenants. Once during World War II Edward's minister son Herbert came to my home. He was helping in the state civil defense program.

Eventually Mrs. Sparhawk introduced me to Edward Denison Gallaudet, the son of Edward Miner Gallaudet's oldest son, Dension. He and his charming wife Sally often visited my home and I met his sister Suzanne. It was Ed who really opened up the world of the Gallaudets to me for he had inherited the Gallaudet Papers from his Aunt Kitty at her death in 1942. Ed eventually asked me to undertake the task of writing about his grandfather. One bleak night in 1948 he arrived at my doorstep with cartons and boxes of Gallaudet material. He was so thankful to have gotten it out of his garage and into my house! The boxes contained most of the material that Edward Miner Gallaudet had so carefully saved and packed away when he cleaned out his desk and rooms on Kendall Green upon retiring in 1911.

The boxes revealed valuable papers once belonging to Thomas Hopkins Gallaudet which Edward had used in writing the biography of his father. Some of these papers were nearly one hundred and fifty years old. They deserved safekeeping and were put in the

Library of Congress under the watchful eyes of Mr. David C. Mearns and Mr. Robert H. Land. It became quite clear why no one knew much about Edward; all that was his I held in trust and it had never been used for publication.

During the many months I spent in writing about E. M. G. I lived among great stacks of Gallaudet material all about me—on my chairs, my table, and my bed. I have fallen asleep with his reports in my hands. I feel that I have come to know him personally. My friends have shared my gleanings and his relatives have sat perplexed while I discussed their family history from its roots. Often I have wondered how Edward might feel had he known a woman was writing his life. The fact that I am a graduate of his Normal Department, (it is now known as the Graduate Department) might redeem any prejudice he held.

The fact that Edward Denison Gallaudet passed away before this book was completed has been a source of deep regret. He, more than any other Galludet of the past fifty years tried to hold high the banner of his grandfather's and his great-grandfather's work. To him this volume is dedicated.

Edward Miner Gallaudet's diaries will now find rest at the Library of Congress. His papers, citations, and family matters will be turned over to Gallaudet College where Mrs. Lucille M. Pendell, Librarian, will arrange them in the beautiful new Edward Miner Gallaudet Memorial Library—started by the fund put aside on his seventieth birthday and increased by his loyal alumni and by the Congress of the United States.

MAXINE TULL BOATNER

Trinity College Library
Hartford, Connecticut

Acknowledgments

The names of some of the prominent deaf men and women who have encouraged this biography of their benefactor are mentioned in the body of this work. There are still others who have sent me letters and made helpful suggestions.

Teachers of the deaf include Dr. Elizabeth Peet of Washington, D.C., and Dr. Robert S. Brown, Superintendent of the Mississippi School for the Deaf. President Leonard M. Elstad of Gallaudet College, a Normal Fellow in 1923, has given my work considerable support, and has also been very helpful.

Two men who have done much to promote interest in my work among the Gallaudet College Alumni Association are David Peikoff, '29, National President of the Association, and Loy E. Golladay, '34, National Vice President in charge of Chapter Projects. Gordon W. Clarke, '35, Miriam Rockwell, '20, Ethel M. Giett, and Marie M. Szopa, '26, have assisted in various ways.

Alice Tiegal Hanson, '93, widow of Olof Hanson, and the first woman graduate of the College, has written me several times, and loaned picture albums belonging to her late husband. Her daughter, Mrs. Homer Jones, of Washington, D.C., has provided me with helpful correspondence. Francis C. Higgins, '36, Leon Auerbach, '40, and Alan Crammatte, '32, of the college staff, have written me. Emma Neumann Folckemer, Ex'12, contributed reminiscences, as did H. Lee Clark, Ex'02, and James A. Sullivan, '18. Benjamin M. Schowe, '18, Wesley E. Lauritsen, '22, Winfield Scott Runde, '01, George M. McClure, Hon. '96, Boyce R. Williams, '32, and Irving S. Fusfeld, N '21, have all shown a keen interest. Michael Lapides, '13, has also been quite helpful.

I shall never forget the entertaining interviews with Alice G. T. Sparhawk, Edward's niece, who helped me identify many family pictures. She recently slipped from this earth at the age of ninety-one. She dearly loved her family.

I have corresponded with Margaret French Cresson, daughter of the sculptor Daniel Chester French, who executed the statue of Thomas Hopkins Gallaudet, and also with the late Helen Nicolay, whose father was Lincoln's Secretary. Henry E. Lippitt, II, great nephew of Jeanie (Jennie) Lippitt, a pupil of Alexander Graham Bell in Boston, furnished material about Jennie written by his mother, and his cousin Frederick

Lippitt of Providence sent me data about Jennie. I have also corresponded with Bern Budd, Edward's nephew, now a New York lawyer and a trustee of Trinity College. My thanks go to these people and to Virginia W. Somerville, artist and etcher, who made the geneological chart of the Gallaudet family for this book.

A. F. Pabst sent me a book on *Representative Deaf Persons* which has been a useful source of information, and Mrs. Percival Hall, widow of Gallaudet College's late president, loaned me pictures. There are others who have helped me in numerous ways, as the late John Marshall Holcomb, Jr., who sent original Gallaudet letters with pictures, and Miss Inez A. Hull who helped with early suggestions.

The Library staff at Trinity College in Hartford has been most attentive: Mr. Donald B. Engley, the Librarian, furnished me a study for my writing, and Mr. George W. Adams, the Reference Librarian, helped me find many obscure facts. I would like to give my thanks to the whole staff.

Allan Nevins of Columbia University read portions of the manuscript and made pertinent suggestions, among them being that I should do my work on these valuable papers at the Trinity College Library where they would be safe. Mabel Collins Donnelly has read the manuscript and made some invaluable suggestions. J. C. Furnas, and Kenneth Stabler, an editor of Public Affairs Press, read the work in its early stages and gave me points for which I am grateful. My sincere thanks also go to my typist, Hazel B. Dingle. To various members of the Faculty of Yale University I am indebted for advice on historical details and trends in higher education. Particularly do I wish to mention Dr. Clyde M. Hill, Dr. John S. Brubacher, and Dr. Mark A. May. Mr. James T. Babb, Librarian at Yale, gave me several helpful interviews. And I should thank earlier professors who showed interest in my work: the late David M. Key, Milton C. White and H. Ellis Finger, Jr., present President of Millsaps College.

The American School for the Deaf in Hartford has generously furnished me with books and old records, and its staff has given me every consideration, particularly J. Pierre Rakow and Alfred J. Hoffmeister, '37. The school has been an inspiration to me, making me feel that I have walked with Thomas Hopkins Gallaudet and Laurent Clerc, as well as with the young Edward, who went from its doors to broaden the outlook for the deaf of the whole world.

M. T. B.

Contents

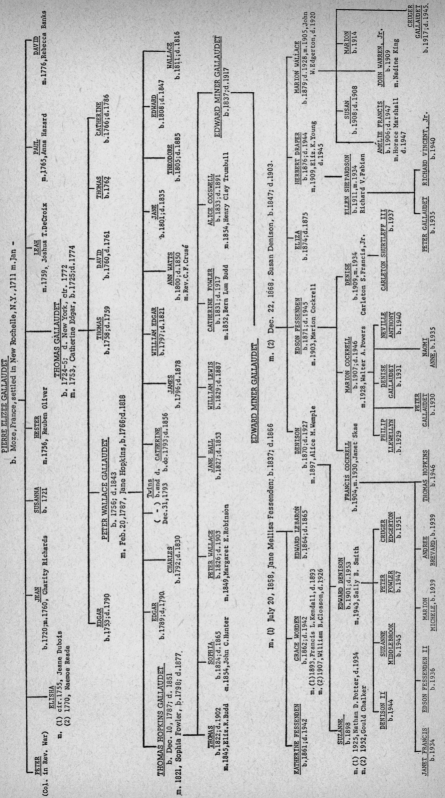

GENEALOGY OF THE GALLAUDET FAMILY *(prepared by Virginia W. Somerville)*

Beginnings

When Richelieu succeeded in taking La Rochelle in 1628 and the French Huguenots became a desperate people, there was one family among the fleeing hundreds, destined to go to the new world and make a name for itself on the pages devoted to the history of philanthropy in America.

Joshua Gallaudet and his family lived at Mauzé, just twenty miles east of La Rochelle, at the time of the Revocation of the Edict of Nantes. His wife was Margaret Prioleau, a daughter of Elisha (Elisée) Prioleau, minister of Exoudun.[1] Their son, Pierre Elisée Gallaudet, a doctor, came to New York and was one of the founders of New Rochelle in the early 1700's. The records of Westchester County reveal very little about him. Two land deeds—one made to him and the other by him—are recorded at White Plains, dated February 11, 1726.

Pierre Elisée and his wife Jan had several children—among them a son Thomas, born in 1724, who married Catharine Edgar of Rahway, New Jersey, in 1753. Her father, Thomas Edgar of Edinburgh, Scotland, and her mother, Janet Knox, had come to America and settled in New Jersey in 1718.

Thomas and Catharine Gallaudet had six children, all born in New York. Their second child, born April 21, 1756, was named Peter Wallace Gallaudet. At an early age he settled in Philadelphia. One of his uncles served in Lee's Legion during the Revolutionary War, and an older brother also served in the Continental forces. None of the name of Gallaudet espoused the side of the Crown. Another uncle, Elisha, became a well-known engraver and may have been the die-cutter for the first United States coin; in any case, it is definitely established that he engraved the paper money for New York City in 1774 and the paper money for the Colony of New York three years earlier.[2]

Peter Wallace Gallaudet eventually went into the mercantile business. His earliest activities in Philadelphia are not recorded, except for one fact found in a grandson's diary:[3] he once acted as private secretary to George Washington. Early in 1787 he was married to Jane

Hopkins in her Hartford, Connecticut, home. Her mother, Alice Howard, was the great-granddaughter of the Reverend Thomas Hooker, Hartford's famous first minister. Her father, Thomas Hopkins, was captain of a vessel engaged in West Indian and other foreign trade.

Twelve children were born to Jane and Peter Gallaudet. The first eight were born in Philadelphia and the others in Hartford following the family's move to Connecticut in 1800. The first child was Thomas Hopkins Gallaudet, born December 10, 1787. Thomas was thirteen years old when his parents settled in Hartford, where they lived in Prospect Street among a group of families of varied characteristics but united by the ties of a common heritage. Here lived the wealthy and cultured Daniel Wadsworth, and Dr. Mason Fitch Cogswell, who was to play such an important part in the life of young Thomas, was a neighbor.

Peter Gallaudet and his family made their home in Hartford for fifteen years before moving to New York City, where his wife Jane died. After a brief stay in Philadelphia during the early 1820's, he moved for the last time, in 1824, to Washington, D.C., where he lived for almost a score of years, occupying a position in the Register's office in the United States Treasury until his death in 1843.

Thomas Hopkins Gallaudet, the eldest son, attended the Hartford Grammar School until he entered Yale College as a sophomore in 1802. Three years later he won his A.B. degree. Written reports, from him and from his children, have come down through the years concerning his fragile health. References to his limited energy are to be found in a biography of Thomas written by his youngest son.[4] Because of his poor health Thomas did not seek an active career immediately after leaving Yale; instead he stayed in his father's home and pursued the study of English literature and law. He then returned to Yale as a graduate student and tutor, staying two years and winning a master of arts degree. But during this period he experienced frequent misgivings about his spiritual values and was often despondent.

Still far from strong, Thomas decided to try his hand at becoming a Yankee trader. He stocked up with materials in New York and rode South on horseback as far as Kentucky, selling his wares and hoping that life in the open would bring him more robust health. When he returned to Hartford in 1811 he decided to enter the newly opened Andover Theological Seminary to prepare himself for the ministry.

Trained in his undergraduate studies by such men as Timothy Dwight, straightlaced Congregational minister; Benjamin Silliman, geologist; and Jeremiah Day, mathematician, Thomas combined the

Dr. Thomas Hopkins Gallaudet.

Coat-of-arms of Gallaudet family.

FRIEND
TEACHER
BENEFACTOR

A statue commemorating the efforts of Thomas Hopkins Gallaudet among the deaf.

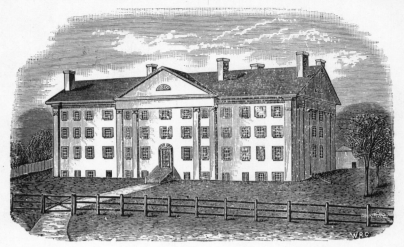

The American School as it looked when erected in Hartford in 1821.

The American School, also known as the Old Hartford School, occupied these buildings until new quarters were opened in West Hartford in 1921.

Abbé de L'Eppée who founded the
Paris school for the deaf in 1760.

Successor of Abbé de L'Eppée, Abbe
Roch - Ambroise - Curran Sicard
taught Thomas H. Gallaudet in 1816.

Monsigneur De
Hearne, noted Bel-
gian clergyman who
did much for the
deaf, was hospitable
to E. M. G. when
he was abroad.

A photograph of Mrs. Thomas H. Gallaudet taken in early 1850's.

Jennie F. Gallaudet, first wife of E. M. G., and daughter Grace.

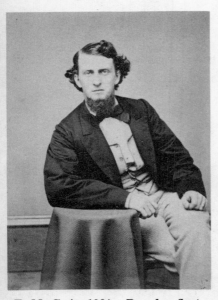

E. M. G. in 1864. Beard reflects "Lincoln" influence of period.

A picture of E. M. G. taken in 1875 by photographer Brady.

best qualities of his varied education and inheritance in preparation for the work he was about to enter. In 1814 he graduated from the Seminary after giving himself to intense study.

It was about this time that he became interested in the daughter of his Hartford neighbor, Dr. Mason Cogswell. Alice Cogswell was a child of nine who had lost her hearing earlier as a result of a fever. His first visit with her was in his family's garden, where she was playing with his younger brothers and sisters. It intrigued the young minister to communicate with her, particularly since she showed a marked aptitude for learning. Her father had ordered a book from Paris written by the Abbé Sicard of the Royal Institution for Deaf Mutes, and he let Thomas practice its contents with Alice. Thomas showed ingenious aptitude in communicating with the child, and he taught her many simple words and sentences. A local poet, Lydia Huntley Sigourney, also had been able to gain Alice's confidence and had given her lessons. The success of these attempts made her father more painfully aware that not only his daughter but other deaf children should have some means of obtaining an education.

An eminent surgeon and lecturer on the Yale faculty, Dr. Cogswell had already made some investigation of the situation of deaf people in Connecticut. In examining a report compiled by the Congregational clergy of Connecticut in 1812, he found that in the state there were 84 deaf and dumb persons. On this basis, he estimated, the New England States contained at least 400 persons "in this unhappy situation." In the United States it was estimated there were at least several thousand such persons; and in all the country there was no means of educating these deaf people.

In 1815 Dr. Cogswell called a meeting of a group of prominent Hartford citizens to consider this situation. He also invited the young minister, Thomas Gallaudet, who made a decided impression on the assembled group when he described the eagerness with which Alice had learned the word "hat," and even her own name. Following the meeting Thomas was surprised to learn that the distinguished men with whom he had talked in Dr. Cogswell's parlor wanted him to undertake a study of the education of the deaf, proposing that he visit Europe to learn this teaching art.

The proposal of such a venture was startling. It would require both money and time. Moreover, suitable arrangements could not be made easily. Dare he accept? Was this to be the future for which he had prepared himself so laboriously? Would he not, after all, take a pulpit, but instead devote his talents to the school room? What about his health—could he depend on it? He begged for time to consider. At twenty-eight it was certainly time to make some vital decisions. Such confidence as these men showed in him made him humble and he sought guidance through prayer. Soon he gave them his answer: he would go.

In three short weeks he obtained his passport, packed, tidied his affairs, and was ready to leave. His passport, signed on May 1, 1815, by Secretary of State James Monroe, described Thomas as "5 ft. 6½ in., darkish complexion, dark gray eyes, thin in person, forehead not high, but retreating, straight nose, of the common size, large lips, and teeth very visible when speaking."

He visited his family while in New York, then sailed on the tiny vessel *Mexico* on May 25, 1815, venturing with the true spirit of the pioneer. One can picture his slight frame silhouetted against the far-away skyline of an 1815 New York, bound on this unusual mission financed by his Hartford benefactors. He was one of the earliest in a movement then gaining momentum—the exodus of American students to foreign shores. A month before Edward Everett had sailed from Boston with George Ticknor and two sons of John Quincy Adams. Everett was to study at the University of Göttingen, where he became the first American to receive a Ph.D. from that institution in 1817, the year in which Thomas Gallaudet was to see his efforts crowned. These early years of the nineteenth century were to be characterized by awakening humanitarian interests which included the problems of the physically handicapped.

On his month-long voyage, Thomas had the opportunity of becoming acquainted with Washington Irving, who was making his second trip across. There were also British army officers aboard, and others who made shipboard life interesting. Gallaudet wrote home describing situations and his reactions.

He had taken along the book by the Abbé Sicard on methods of educating the deaf.[5] As he studied it and thought about his assignment, he marveled how quickly Alice had been able to learn. She had acquired words by watching him write them in the sand while she played in the garden. Words, words, words! They were to occupy the remainder of his life. He was to fill books with them; better still, he was to put them into the heads and hands of children and young adults who had never known the meaning of words. Perhaps this voyage abroad would lead him to realize his hopes and dreams of helping others to help themselves.

From his Journal one is able to follow Thomas' path from the moment he landed in Liverpool in June, through London, Oxford, Birmingham, Edinburgh, and finally Paris. In England and Scotland he was bitterly disappointed to find that the teaching of the deaf was a monopoly confined to the Braidwood family; and there was neither the money nor the time to serve the years of apprenticeship required. Fortunately, while in London, he met the Abbé Sicard, who invited him to Paris as a guest of his institution. Thomas had already seen enough of "method" in English classrooms to realize that the English concentrated on teaching the deaf to speak; from Sicard's textbook he knew that the French teachers relied upon the Abbé de l'Epée's creation of a system of signs in which a "sign" stood for a word.

When writing to his friend Dr. Cogswell, Thomas stated: "I should wish, and I yet hope, to combine the peculiar advantages of both the French and the English modes of instruction, for there are considerable differences between them." It is interesting to note that here for the first time he used the word "combine" in connection with the two methods.

In London Thomas had attended the Abbé Sicard's lectures and witnessed the exhibition of two star pupils of the Paris institution, Jean Massieu [6] and Laurent Clerc. [7] The lectures had created great interest and drawn members of the English nobility.

In August of 1815 Thomas boarded the smack *Buccleuch* for the 400-mile trip to Edinburgh. Upon arriving he presented his letters of credit but again encountered the Braidwood monopoly, which he characterized in his Journal as a "Sad monopoly of the resources of charity!!"

In letters to Cogswell, however, he told of new friends in Scotland. "Here men of science," he wrote, "have taken an interest in the instruction of the deaf and dumb." He dined in the home of Dugald Stewart, the celebrated Scotch philosopher of the University of Edinburgh.

His new friends were intrigued by the frail young American and listened with admiration and respect when he outlined his mission abroad. Dugald Stewart aired his views of teaching a deaf person to talk, comparing one so taught with a parrot: the bird could be trained to imitate speech, but did he understand what he was saying? Stewart could see no reason in making speech the object of a deaf person's education. He held that the methods of de l'Epée, as developed by the Abbé Sicard, were of a higher nature than strict oralism and capable of more extensive usefulness inasmuch as they could not only benefit the largest number of the deaf and dumb but could provide for the gradual and thorough evolution and discipline of all the intellectual powers.

From August until the following February Thomas waited in Edinburgh while the political situation in France quieted down. He felt the need of more study, particularly in the French language, and pre-

pared himself to read the Abbé's treatises on the instruction of deaf
mutes. His plan was to familiarize himself so thoroughly with Sicard's
language and philosophy that when he arrived in Paris his complete
attention could be given to the Abbe's instruction. He fully realized
that he could not finish his training in either England or Scotland. He
attended lectures at the University of Edinburgh by Dr. Thomas
Brown, Professor of Moral Philosophy, whose subject was the philosophy of the human mind. He also found time to visit libraries and
acquire a few good books in the shops. Thus he spent his time until
the spring of 1816.

Thomas returned to London before sailing for France. While there
he met Major-General Macaulay and his brother Zachary, father of
the historian Thomas Babington Macaulay. Zachary Macaulay was
editor of the *Christian Observer,* and interested in peace societies.
Thomas' mind was open to the world of ideas, enveloping politics as
well as religion; and when he sailed on March 5th he carried a letter
to the Abbé Sicard from Zachary Macaulay. He arrived in Paris the
ninth of March and Sicard received him with open arms. All facilities
of the Paris institution were put at his disposal. The Abbé arranged
to give him lectures three times a week; he attended classes at all
times, observing, and learning the sign language from the expert Paul-
mier. Thomas considered Thursday, March 21, as the real beginning
of his work.

Because of his interest in various affairs, and the fact that he was an
ordained minister, Thomas was invited to give a series of discourses on
various points of "Christian Faith and Practice" in the Chapel of the
Oratoire in Paris. During these stirring times abroad his letters home
referred to Napoleon and to the effects of war in France and Russia.
In answer to one of these letters, Professor Silliman congratulated him
for being able to meet so many people of interest. "The iron reign of
the Corsican prevented me from becoming personally acquainted with
the men and things which now surround you," he commented. Silliman
had been barred from Paris because of his political remarks.

When Thomas prepared for his homeward journey, the Abbé Sicard
yielded to the entreaties of Laurent Clerc, who asked to be released
from his position in the Paris institution to return and help Thomas
Gallaudet found the first school for the deaf in America. Clerc was to
be the first educated deaf man to walk the streets of this country, and
his presence encouraged the establishment of the French method of
signs and finger spelling that became the basis for the democratic
Combined System of teaching this specialized work subsequently
practiced by the residential schools for the deaf in the United States.

Thomas Gallaudet combined the voice, the eye, and the hand, to found America's own system.

These two pioneering spirits sailed from Le Havre June 18, 1816, on the *Mary Augusta*. Clerc learned to write English during the month's journey, and was capable of answering any question put to him upon his arrival in the States. He and Gallaudet spent the next seven months speaking, raising funds, and getting the American Asylum for the Deaf and Dumb ready to receive its first pupils. The doors were opened April 15, 1817, and at once attracted outstanding visitors. James Monroe, then President of the United States, paid his respects to the institution when he visited Hartford in 1817. Henry Clay, Andrew Jackson, and Charles Dickens made the American Asylum a part of their itinerary; when Mrs. Anne Royall wrote her travel book after touring the States, she referred to the school as "the glory of Hartford, and indeed that of America."[8]

The strength of the school's foundation came in part from its benefactors. Life subscribers to the institution were such men as Daniel Wadsworth, often referred to as "the original Maecenas of Hartford"; Charles Sigourney, French Huguenot descendant and wealthy manufacturer who corresponded with Thomas Jefferson on matters of education; Nathaniel Terry, banker; Stephen Van Rensselaer, founder of the Rensselaer Polytechnic Institute; David Watkinson, philanthropist and book collector; and John Jacob Astor. Through the leadership of Henry Clay, then Speaker of the House, the United States Government made a land-grant to the Asylum of 23,000 acres of Alabama lands, the sale of which formed the first permanent endowment for the school. The acts of such men made possible the success of the mother school which would eventually train teachers to take the initiative in starting similar schools throughout the country.[9]

For thirteen years Thomas Gallaudet remained the head of the American Asylum. His duties exhausted his frail body almost beyond endurance, and he asked for retirement. He was spared for his writing and for his contributions to the mental and spiritual growth of his community and state, and his influence reached to many foreign countries.[10]

THOMAS' ROMANCE

There is no record of romance in Thomas' life until after he became Principal of the American Asylum. The tender passion was in the offing, however, from the moment he went to New Haven to interview a father who had two deaf daughters he wished to enter in the school. Miner Fowler and his family lived in Guilford, Connecticut. Their

daughters, Sophia and Parnell, were among the first students to be
entered on the school roster. Sophia was nineteen and had never received any formal schooling. When the thirty-one-year-old Principal
was introduced to this amazing child-woman, he marveled at once at
the grasp of her mind.

Before Sophia Fowler had been three years in the school Thomas
had given her his heart completely. He consulted her parents and
asked that she be allowed to live in the city so that he might conduct
a true courtship. Sophia, now twenty-three, was happy in her mentor's
promise to continue her instruction after their marriage, which took
place on August 29, 1821. They went to Saratoga for their honeymoon.

The next twenty-three years were exceedingly full ones. Offers of
other positions were coming to Gallaudet. He was asked to organize
high schools, to promote industrial schools, to found a department of
education, to return to the pulpit, to participate in educational gather-
ings in other states. He preferred to stay with his growing family, and
to have time to write, while participating occasionally in civic affairs.
The honors he passed on to others, standing by to lend counsel when
needed. Young Henry Barnard was appointed Connecticut's first
Secretary of Education when Gallaudet declined the position; yet Gallaudet went about the state with Barnard to help him organize his work.

In retirement Gallaudet turned to writing, using this ability to encourage the establishment of seminaries for training teachers. He was
invited to organize such an experimental school [11] at Princeton University. He had helped Catherine E. Beecher in founding the Hartford
Female Seminary in 1825, but he would not accept the invitation to
leave Hartford and establish the New England Institution for the
Blind, which became Perkins Institute. He preferred to devote his
talents to his home city and to the home school organized for the purpose of educating his own children. He and his charming wife created
in their home a social life of delicacy and charm. Their guests included Horace Bushnell, theologian and minister, who consulted
Gallaudet on his sermons; Henry Barnard and Horace Mann, educators; Lydia Huntley Sigourney, the poetess, who might call and leave
her latest book of poems. Sophia's quick perception and colorful personality made deep impressions on visitors. Yung Wing,[12] an early
Chinese student at Yale, never forgot her. Later, Sophia Gallaudet
was to grace the home of her youngest son, Edward, in Washington.
When he stood before an audience in 1864 to make his Inaugural
Address as President of the National Deaf-mute College, Edward paid
high tribute to his parent's romance. He said: "Dr. Gallaudet gave to
the world the most convincing proof of his belief that the deaf and

dumb could through education be made the social and intellectual equals of those possessed of all their faculties, by taking one of his own pupils as his wife. . . . She, my mother, whose ears have ever been closed to the sound of her children's voices, whose tongue could never sing a lullaby to calm their infant fears, now sits before me an intelligent and joyous participant in the exercises of the day." [13]

In 1837 Thomas Gallaudet accepted the Chaplaincy of the Hartford County Prison, at first giving his services. It was an innovation that appealed to him. He served in this capacity for the next eight years, and is said to have worked miracles with the men. Beginning in 1838 he performed the same service at the Hartford Retreat for the Insane. Samuel B. Woodward of Worcester, Massachusetts, who was on the staff of the Hartford Retreat when it was founded in 1822, invited Gallaudet to work with him at the Worcester Asylum for the Insane. But he had found his niche in Hartford and continued at the Hartford Retreat under Dr. John S. Butler. This was the position he held when his death occurred on September 10, 1851, fourteen years after the birth of his fourth son, who was to become his greatest link with the future.

II

A Son's Inheritance

On a bitter cold Sunday, the fifth of February, 1837, Edward Miner Gallaudet was born at No. 30 Chapel Street in Hartford. He was the youngest of the family of eight children.

Edward grew up in a household where no one could take another member for granted. He learned early that one must deserve the good things that came his way. Manual work was never scorned. Although sister Sophia taught Edward, he recited to his father, who made it a rule never to allow Edward more than three hours a day at his studies. But during that time not a moment was to be wasted. Study became a part of Edward's daily program, and to look forward to the privilege of learning was implicit in the day's routine. This was the culture of the "whole being," for Thomas Gallaudet placed great emphasis on education as a continuing process. He once stated his belief that "the waste places of society can be reclaimed, and many abodes of penury, ignorance and vice can be converted by education, economy and industry, into homes of comfort, peace and joy." When Edward was five years old he was allowed to attend his oldest brother's graduation at Trinity College, walking in the procession with Thomas and holding his hand with the greatest confidence. He belonged there; this first step toward higher education was for him an omen.

Later, in his diaries, Edward reviewed many of his childhood experiences. Because he had been the "baby," wanting to tag along with his father on frequent short journeys, Edward was closer to him than any one of the other children. He reminisced about trips to Springfield, where he and his father visited "the dictionary maker Merriam," and to Norfolk and Stonington, or to Amherst, where they climbed Mt. Holyoke. He enjoyed many opportunities for long talks, in which he could absorb his father's ideas and be exposed to his philosophy of life. Edward became inculcated with his father's threefold aims which were the importance of the home as basic training; the dependence on guidance for action, and the culture of the Whole Being. The elder Galaudet knew both the importance of religion and the needs of the body.

Edward never forgot his father's gentle jokes and tricks, or the sweet ways he had with the young. He once wrote that his father never used the rod "as he found other methods of punishment just as effective."

These "other methods" Edward knew. He was high spirited as a youth, often needing reprimands for slipping off and coming in late. He did this once too often when he was twelve. His father waited for him, engaged him in a game of backgammon, and kept him awake until midnight. Let Edward ache for his soft bed! But never a harsh word. Music was taught to the children as each one came along. Thomas' spirits had been so uplifted by the voice of Jenny Lind that he sent his three youngest children to New York to hear her though money was scarce.

Edward recalled that in his "intellectual infancy" he had lived largely on *Robinson Crusoe,* the *Rollo* books, *Sanford and Merton,* and Hans Anderson's *Fairy Tales,* with occasional "surreptitious feasts" on the *Arabian Nights* in the house of a friend, where the literary censorship was not as strict as under his father's roof. But he quickly added that one must not infer his father's rule to be a hard one, for he never imposed the shorter catechism on his children, allowed Edward to read his Sunday school books in church, and, though opposed to novels, gave Edward permission to read the newly published *David Copperfield* although the boy was then only thirteen. This was Edward's favorite story until *Uncle Tom's Cabin* caught his imagination.

Edward was about as handsome as he was precocious. His wavy chestnut hair, that tumbled over his collar, formed a high pompadour above clear blue eyes and a well defined brow. It is no wonder that Mrs. Eliza Goodrich, a family friend, wanted to adopt him. A daughter of the wealthy General Champion of West Chester, New York, she could have given Edward many advantages. But he was happy not only in his family but among his many friends. His early playmates, both boys and girls, stamped themselves forever in his memory. He was always able to recall faces and incidents from his childhood.

Hartford was beginning to boom in the late 1840's and early 1850's. Stage coaches and water travel were giving way to railroads. Joseph Morgan, who had operated a coach line and tavern in Massachusetts before opening the Morgan Coffee House in Hartford, became a director in the railroad company which ran its cars from Hartford to Boston, via Springfield and Worcester. The Hartford and Springfield Rail Road Company was chartered in 1835, but did not begin to run until 1844. The New Haven Railroad, which came to Hartford in 1839, was completed to Springfield in 1844, thus connecting Hartford and New York with the line of the Boston and Albany road, and diverting freight and travel from the waterway.

Barely two months after Edward's birth, John Pierpont Morgan was born to Junius Spencer Morgan and his wife Lucy Pierpont. Grandfather Joseph was already able to give young John the worldly enjoyments. He was sent to private schools and then to Hartford High School for one year. It was then, during 1849-1850, that Edward came to know John Pierpont Morgan, called by his intimates "Pip." After this year John was sent to private schools again. His future lay in building a money empire, while Edward would found a college unique in educational annals. Edward, however, would first experience a deep personal loss.

In the beginning of his high school days his father had talked to him seriously about his future. Thomas Gallaudet suggested to Edward the idea of eventually entering upon the work of educating the deaf. He spoke at some length, Edward remembered, of the joy he had in doing what he believed was his Master's work, and said he believed Edward would never be sorry if he carried out the suggestion. This impressed Edward greatly, but at twelve he replied to his father that he believed his future lay in business, since he was determined to roll up a great fortune. When his father asked him about college Edward answered that his future did not lie in the academic direction—that he was eager to enter into business as soon as he completed his high school course. His father's only reprimand was "go ahead and be a business man, but never a banker for his work is too narrowing."

Edward's immediate career was determined, just as he finished high school, by the sudden death of his father, which made it imperative that he seek work at once. Any further schooling would be the result of his own activities. Within a week after his father's death he accepted a clerkship in the Phoenix Bank of Hartford. This bank included among its officers men who had long known Thomas Gallaudet, many having been on the original Board of Directors of the American Asylum: Charles Sigourney, Daniel Buck, Ward Woodbridge, and David Watkinson. What more natural than that they should help Gallaudet's son? It was not long, however, before his father's words came back to haunt him. His mind began to crave a "pabulum of a higher order than the counting of bank bills and the reckoning of discounts." He lamented that his father had not lived to send him to Yale.

Nine months after his father's death Edward began to keep a diary. It was a small red-bound book about six by nine inches, designed with a tooled effect and lettered in gold. The word "Records" graced its spine, and "E. M. Gallaudet" was stamped under a heraldic design on its face. On the fly leaf was inscribed: "Occasionals—E. M. Gallaudet, Hartford, Conn." From 1852 until 1884 Edward was to confide in it his loneliness, his disappointments (with himself and with life), and his aspirations. Into this book went his awakening to the religious experience, and evidence that he felt bitterly the loss of his father, whose influence he needed during his formative years.

He was ripe for a genuine friendship when Henry Clay Trumbull came into his life. Seven years Edward's senior, Henry Trumbull began to fill Edward's need for an older companion. Henry had worked in a bank in Stonington before taking a position with the Hartford, Providence and Fishkill Railroad. He then lived in Hartford with his older brother, James Hammond Trumbull, State Librarian and later Secretary of State of Connecticut. So great was Henry's influence on Edward that he joined the church with Henry, and accepted a gift of a Bible which was the first one he had ever owned. "I used long ago to have the promise of one from my father," confided Edward to his diary. "He used to say: 'Eddy, when you want one, I will give you a beautiful one.' . . . Alas! Alas! during his life I never did want a Bible and so never had one." But he now owned one given to him by his dearest friend—"more than friend, one whom God in his special providence seemed to give me that I might have some one in whom I could confide and one whom I could respect and love." He hoped they would be spared to each other and always be friends.

Edward, nevertheless, continued his self-doubts, but Henry's friendship was beginning to direct his thoughts toward helping others. The Congregational churches of the city had organized the Young Men's Mission Society in November of 1851, following the suggestion of Thomas Gallaudet. In addition to other activities the Society opened a Mission Sunday School, and young men from Center Church were invited to help in the Morgan Street Mission. Both Henry and Edward volunteered their services. Henry was eventually appointed superintendent and Edward became clerk and librarian.

Edward began to save carefully, for now he was determined to go to college. Nearby was Trinity College and it was possible to attend by holding a part-time job, perhaps teaching at the American Asylum. In 1854 he felt that he had saved enough to make a start, and he won admission as a Junior. In the meantime he had cultivated the friendship of a number of young ladies—including one whose letters he kept for the next sixty years, along with those of the girl he eventually married. Several of these girls attended the Hartford Female Seminary and others went to Miss Julia Draper's School on Pratt Street. He visited as far afield as Farmington, Connecticut, to serenade the young ladies at Miss Porter's School.

There was in Edward a great capacity for love: he strove toward beauty, youth, and achievement. He loved physical activity—a ride up Prospect Hill on a fine horse to survey the city spread out below. And who knows but that he dreamed of becoming governor, or a famous minister? Yet he had his doubts. He sang in the church choir and he belonged to the Undine Boat Club. It troubled him that he was so drawn to the "worldly life." Would it be his downfall? He was repeating exactly the pattern his father had followed at the same age, when, as a student at Yale, he had been sadly torn in his love for and distrust of frivolity. Edward, however, was willing to face temptation.

VERDICT ON COLLEGE

During his college days Edward sought solace in his *Occasionals*. He had been lucky to find employment at the American School under the Reverend W.W. Turner, and had been invited to continue his teaching upon leaving college. He planned to accept the offer, considering it Providential; but at the same time he was ambitious to do more for the deaf than merely teach them, or to become the principal of a school. He began his teaching six months before graduation from college, and in order to do it he had to recite daily at six in the morning and four in the afternoon. Trinity College was then located where the State Capitol building now stands. Edward was living on Buckingham Street with his mother, in the home his father had enjoyed only seven months before he died. The college was between this street and the school, the school then being at the top of the hill beyond the Union Station on Asylum Avenue.

In April of 1856, shortly before his graduation, Edward was visiting his sister Alice at the Trumbull House, where she had lived since her marriage to Edward's friend Henry Trumbull. This hotel was owned by Edson Fessenden, who had come to Hartford from Vermont five years before Edward was born. The Fessendens had a daughter Jane, eight months younger than Edward. He enjoyed visiting Alice and her husband, especially since Jane, whom he called "Jennie," was often invited in to make a foursome.

On this particular day, however, he found himself alone in his sister's rooms, and sat down for a while at the piano. The eyes of his father in the portrait above the piano caught his attention. Edward's diary later recorded the strange experience. His recent actions seemed to have come under the scrutiny of his father, and the eyes told Edward that he was disappointed in him. This gave Edward a jolt and he moralized distractedly. What he saw was a mingled expression of sadness and warning. He promised himself—and his father—to change his ways.

Edward never once referred to Jane by name from that time until their marriage. She was an only child, having lost a small brother, and had grown to young womanhood in her father's hotel where she had been born. An indifferent student at the Female Seminary, she preferred to travel and be away from home as much as possible. It was probably lonely for her, even more so than her letters revealed. Slender and dark, with her hair worn back in Spanish fashion, Jane was striking in her brunette beauty. She would go to Boston to shop, and often visited as far away as Pennsylvania.

It is through the letters Jane saved—written to her by friends—that we know how much Edward was in her heart and mind. When she was away they wrote to tell her what "Mr. Gallaudet" was doing! Reticent, seldom betraying her feelings, she was as reserved about references to Edward as he was loathe to mention her. Once he let himself expand enough in his *Occasionals* to refer to a "pair of dark eyes" which seemed to bind him to Hartford.

As the school year ended in Edward's nineteenth year he was again overwhelmed with the desire to become a minister. He even contemplated leaving for the Western wilds to become an itinerant preacher! But he suffered from indecision and morbid thoughts about his unfitness to become a minister, and began to lay the blame on the college influence. Such surroundings had seemed to shake his fixedness of purpose, and he prayed to grow more pure and holy in his feelings. This mood stayed with him for several days, until he took a buggy ride with one of the young women teachers. Then the scenes became "elastic and buoyant—the air sweet and bracing—the scenery picturesque." In a better mood he again thought of the ministry, but wondered if he should make a definite decision while still so young. In such a frame of mind he had a short vacation in New Jersey, visiting relatives, and amazed himself by practically falling in love with a twelve-year-old-girl! He poured out this facet of himself into his diary and quoted a long passage from Longfellow's "Hyperion" relating to success: "doing well whatever you do, without a thought of *fame.* . . . if it come at all it will come because it is deserved not because it is sought after." He claimed these were his sentiments, and stated that long since he had determined to win distinction for himself if he could do so without setting aside his Christian principles.

No one knew better than he how "alluring, seducing, enticing and pleasant" the world was—to one so young and cheerful and full of vigor, with temptations thick about him. For nearly a month after his graduation he wrote nothing in his diary, then finally delivered in its pages his ultimatum on college life. "College life for me is over," he began. "Sad on some accounts and happy on others are my feelings at the severing of the pleasant tie that has bound me here for two years. The temptations have been many and great and I have too often yielded—I hope I have gained some good by coming here but I fear I have received much evil. My testimony is that four years of life in an American College is a terrible ordeal which few can safely pass. It is the rock on which many a noble man has made shipwreck of his soul and his hopes."

Edward went to the Convention for Instructors of the Deaf, in Staunton, Virginia, travelling some 2,000 miles before his return. He went sight-seeing in the Thomas Jefferson country and met a great-grandson of Jefferson's while visiting Edgehill. This young man was Thomas Jefferson Trist, a deaf-mute, who had attended the New York School for the Deaf and eventually taught in the Pennsylvania School.

Refreshed from his travels, Edward returned to begin his first full year of teaching at the American School. Another position had presented itself but had not materialized. Through a fellow teacher, Jared Ayres, Edward was put in touch with the Reverend Mr. Samuel W. Bonney, on the American Board of Commissioners for Foreign Missions, who hoped to interest the right person in establishing a school for the deaf in China. Edward was in the mood to go if Mr. Bonney would send him five hundred dollars and guarantee him a thousand or fifteen hundred more after his arrival. He went so far as to plan his procedure. He would obtain letters of introduction and recommendation from the President of the United States and several members of the Cabinet to the Government of China, and his first efforts would be to secure the patronage of the Emperor. Failing along these lines he would enlist the aid of European merchants and also look for aid in the United States. He felt it was important to *start* right and with plenty of means—not promises! Such a journey might satisfy his irresistible longing to travel, and might be a good thing before he entered upon the "real activity of life."

However, after such rationalizing he would fall a victim to a case of "blues, blues, blues," which made him disgusted with deaf and dumb teaching and with himself. His *Occasionals* discussed life in relation to Edward, and he made no move to bring about a situation while he waited for results from without. Mr. Bonney had suggested that he get in touch with Samuel Colt of Hartford, the manufacturer of fire-arms, who might give the thousand or fifteen hundred dollars "without being any poorer." There is no indication that Edward followed this suggestion. Instead, he went to the Parthenon Society at Trinity College and heard some fine speaking. His diary then echoed with his thoughts of becoming an orator himself. "Oh for the power to electrify an audience," he exclaimed. . . ."Shall I ever be able to speak in public with any success?" At the moment it was a toss-up whether he would be a writer or an orator.

The year 1856 closed with Edward living in his little worlds, filled with contradictions and doubts. A misunderstanding had arisen concerning his status as a teacher, and by April of 1857 he addressed a letter to the Board of the American School stating his case. His agreement had been services for a salary of $600; exemption from Chapel duties, as was customary with beginning teachers, with a salary raise in the beginning of his second year, which required Sunday Chapel duties. However, in the beginning he did assume week-day Chapel duties in order to relieve the Principal, who would have had to take them upon himself, since the teacher who had resigned (and whose job Edward was filling) was a third-year man.

The Chairman of the Committee thought Edward should not receive an advance in salary until he had completed a full year on the $600 salary. Edward had been told upon his appointment that his knowledge of signs and spelling was equivalent to a year's actual experience as a teacher, and no special instruction had been given him. Luckily the Principal agreed with Edward; and attached to Principal Turner's letter, as Edward kept it, is a receipt for the difference in his salary! He had won his first victory in a battle for his rights.

A Decision at Twenty

· On Edward's birthday, February 5, 1857, he entered in his diary: "It is my birthday, and I am no longer in my teens. . . . If I thought that the remainder of my time in this world was to be spent in as unprofitable a manner as these twenty years have been I should long for death." He asked God to visit with favoring showers and life-giving sunbeams whatever good seed had been sown in him during the springtime of his life—and cause it to bring forth an abundant harvest.

As much as he still desired to become a minister he felt that his "mental outlook" was not sufficient to make him acceptable; but by this time he had formed the habit of planning, whether he felt the project feasible or not. He toyed with the idea of going to a seminary for one year, returning to teach, and then finishing his studies privately. If he succeeded he would devote himself to the ministry; if not, he would work faithfully in whatever position Providence assigned him. He deplored his meagre college education and had a horror of being only a half-educated man.[1] No other letter had come from Mr. Bonney. However, he had received an offer from Mr. A. G. Hammond, formerly of Hartford but now of Chicago, who wanted Edward in his firm. He was seriously considering this, for it offered a way to earn money for his seminary studies; but it was followed closely by a second letter which made any previous offer of no importance to him.

It was a coincidence that produced the letter sent to Edward by Amos Kendall of Washington, D. C. Edward just "happened" to take a ride in a stagecoach with H. P. Peet, then head of the New York Institution for the Deaf, shortly before Amos Kendall wrote the New York school hoping to secure the services of Peet's son, Isaac Lewis Peet. The son, desiring to succeed his father as head of the New York Institution, declined Kendall's offer but, acting on the suggestion of his father, who had once taught under Thomas Gallaudet in the American School and who had so recently seen Edward, proposed Edward's name for the place. There began an exchange of letters between Edward and Amos Kendall. In due course the latter offered Edward the superintendency of the newly organized Columbia Institution for the Instruction of the Deaf and Dumb and the Blind, recently incorporated in Washington by an Act of Congress.

Kendall explained that this Act allowed out of the Public Treasury $150 per annum for every indigent pupil belonging to the District of Columbia, and permitted the reception of pupils from all parts of the United States. He told Edward of the living situation: that a two-acre lot of ground and a house of respectable size had been presented to the Institution (Kendall presented this himself)[2] and that the liberal disposition of the citizens left no doubt there would be ample support. He predicted the District would furnish twenty deaf and dumb pupils and ten blind, and that the adjoining state of Maryland, which had no institution, would furnish pupils. With the aid of Congress a suitable building would be furnished.

Kendall then put in his major stroke: "Much, however, will depend on the ability and skill with which the Institution may be managed in the outset," he ended his letter to Edward. Kendall's letter also insinuated that several had already applied for the job but were all strangers to him and he did not want to make a hasty decision. He also alluded to Edward's youth but said that objection had been modified when Mr. Peet had said that Edward's mother might assist in her counsel and efforts.

Edward took Kendall's letter to his fellow teacher, Jared Ayres. Since they had often discussed a school for the deaf that would give

An 1869 photo of
E. M. G. and his
second wife, Susy.

Daughters Grace and Katharine on their English tricycle.

Amos Kendall, close
friend and adviser.

Yung Wing, life-long friend
of E.M.G. He served as
an official representative of
China in Washington, D. C.
(Courtesy of Yale Library)

the pupils more than an elementary education—even proposing to organize a college, once they had found a millionaire to back it—the idea now took shape that a school in Washington would be the ideal one to develop. Why not create a college under the patronage of the federal government? Ayres advised Edward to accept the offer, assuring him that it gave him a rare opening to do a most important work for the deaf of the whole country. Within four days Edward had answered Kendall's letter, asking for more details of the institution: the present conditions; the plans and prospects for the future; and particularly what amount and kind of labor would be required, and the salary offered. He enlarged upon the important place the work occupied in his heart because of his father, and then proposed a personal interview.

Kendall's next letter stated specifically what Edward's duties would be. They were many—to wit: to advise as to repairs, alterations, and additions necessary to prepare the house now owned for the accommodation of the Institution; to employ the necessary teachers, digest plans for instruction, and superintend the teachers; to provide suitable food and clothes for the children, and employ servants and laborers, the means being furnished; in fine, to perform every executive duty indoors and out as well as to advise the Board of Directors in reference to the regulations necessary to advance the interests of the Institution. "To obviate any difficulty which may be apprehended from want of funds," he added, "I will guarantee the payment of your salary for the first year."

Kendall understood that the Principal of the Pennsylvania Institution received $1,600 salary, and as the District of Columbia Institution was comparatively small and in its infancy, he supposed the salary would be considerably less. If under Edward's management, however, the Institution should expand so as to be of national importance, a commensurate increase of salary might be expected. He hoped Edward would state the lowest amount that would be satisfactory for the present. He invited Edward and his mother to visit him in Washington when arrangements could be consummated.

Edward went but his mother did not accompany him this first trip. He had his reasons for wanting to know what was expected of him. He had a vivid memory of what his ailing father had endured at the American School because of division of power, in the school management, between the academic, the household, and the faculty. The Board had not seen fit to give the elder Gallaudet the reins of the school he had founded. The household manager, called the Superintendent, had equal power with the Principal who was a learned scholar and minister of the Gospel. The Faculty members went their way with no coordination—although they were all fine, educated men. The Board members considered themselves the arbiters of management, being more concerned with household matters than academic problems.

Edward was determined this would never happen to him. He made the initial trip for his interview, accepted the Washington position, and hurried back to Hartford to settle his affairs. He was back in Washington by June 13, 1857, ready to begin the work that would consume his energies for the next fifty-four years. He had at last come into his inheritance.

A Change of Climate

Edward was cordially received by Amos Kendall's family. They made him welcome in their home until the Institution was ready. Mrs. Kendall, a second wife, was twenty years younger than her husband. She was kind to the young Superintendent, and showed the pupils many small attentions. Kendall's personality impressed Edward greatly. Here was a man already in his sixty-fourth year, with hair and side whiskers perfectly white. He looked frail in body but had brilliant, vivacious blue eyes, and an unusually fresh complexion. His manner to Edward was courteous and cordial, and as if a mutual sharing already existed. The young man seemed to have won his confidence completely. He soon let Edward know that notwithstanding his youth the internal management of the new Institution would be entirely in his hands; that he believed in the one man in power. He frankly told Edward that if he proved not capable of managing the Institution another man would be found who could. "This did not frighten me," wrote Edward, "for I was possessed of a fair amount of self-confidence." Someone had told Edward that Kendall would be a hard man to please, but he did not find him so. It was Edward's habit, too, to be frank and discreet, and to be sure he was right before he went ahead. In such matters Kendall and Edward saw eye to eye.

In 1857, when Edward arrived in Washington, James Buchanan had been in the White House only four months and the city had a population of about 60,000. During the first month good weather prevailed; flowers bloomed in profusion, and it was warm and fair. But a thunderstorm burst upon the city on July 8, and Edward was introduced to the mud and mire of the city's streets. From Kendall's mansion he commanded a sweeping picture of the scene, with the domeless Capitol visible a little over a mile away. As he gazed he asked himself: "For how many years will this be my home prospect?" Surely he did not then think of the year 1911.

Like the thunderstorm, Edward's troubles burst upon him suddenly. On July 12 he made the first entry in his *Occasionals* since the previous March in Hartford. "That I should be," he wrote, "at the age of twenty the head of an Institution seems to me a wonder. It far surpasses my wildest dreams and hopes." He felt he had barely "emerged from boyhood's years," and he asked for strength and discretion to maintain himself in the position, putting away all "unholy, ambitious, worldly feelings." He prayed that he might spend himself in the cause of deaf mute instruction without a thought of applause of his fellow men, of amassing wealth, or of the pleasures of the world.

But trials began to fill his days: troubles with the servants and with the pupils. They weighed down his spirits and discouraged his heart. His prayers became more humble, asking for tranquility of soul, evenness of temper and an amiable disposition. He asked for that "maturity of paternal feeling—so necessary in the head of a family," which would make him cool-tempered when he was apt to be petulant and hasty.

It was years later, in his *Memoirs*, that he found time to reminisce about his physical surroundings of the year 1857. He then described the twenty-five acres of land—in the original tract set aside by Amos Kendall from the hundred acres of his estate—which was cut up into a dozen two-acre lots, on each side of which was a frame house. These houses were painted on their fronts and white-washed on the other sides, and they were situated on the land nearest to Boundary Street, now Florida Avenue. Around each lot was a rather high white-washed picket fence, and a lane separated the six lots on Boundary Street from those to the north. A number of trees, mostly poplars, were protected by slatted tree-boxes, white-washed like the fences. In contrast, Kendall's home presented a pleasing relief to the eye.

Edward described how the city looked between Kendall Green and the original Government Printing Office; how the streets were ungraded and ungravelled, and how the open commons furnished grazing for cows, horses, goats and geese. He recalled the visitors to the Green: Mrs. Toucey, the wife of the Secretary of the Navy and his mother's old Hartford friend; Mrs. Ledyard, daughter of the Secretary of State, General Lewis Cass. Gail Hamilton, who wrote under the name of Mary Abigail Dodge, walked out with Senator John P. Hale after her busy day as governess to Gamaliel Bailey's children. She had taught English in the Hartford High School between 1853 and 1858, and was the niece of Senator James G. Blaine's wife. Gamaliel Bailey edited the *National Era*, in which first appeared *Uncle Tom's Cabin.*

Other friends called on the Gallaudet family, including Mrs. David W. Mahon, wife of a Pennsylvanian who was Chief Clerk in the Office of the Auditor. Like many others, she brought gifts for the deaf children.

AMOS KENDALL'S FRIENDSHIP

As Edward became better acquainted with his duties he also learned to know and admire the man who had imposed these duties on him. It is doubtful that Edward knew anything about Amos Kendall before he began correspondence with him in May of 1857. However, at the time Kendall came into Edward's life, Kendall's greatest activity was past. He had risen from a farm boy in Massachusetts, through hard study and graduation from Dartmouth, to the study of law under William Merchant Richardson of Groton, Massachusetts. When he decided to follow the Western path of other young men he went as far as Kentucky where he tutored a year in the home of Henry Clay. He finally settled in Georgetown, Kentucky, and practiced law, acting also as the postmaster and editor of two struggling newspapers. In 1816 he moved to Frankfort where he had larger fields for his work.

While Kendall was working out his destiny, Thomas Gallaudet was studying abroad to gain knowledge about the deaf, and his son was destined to cooperate with Kendall in establishing the first college for the deaf in the world.

In Frankfort, Kendall took charge of the *Argus of Western America*. It was said about him as editor and writer that his keen analysis, trenchant style, and aptitude in controversy speedily won for his paper additional prestige. Long a follower of Henry Clay, Kendall broke with Clay in 1826 after developing a deeper devotion to Andrew Jackson. It was this devotion that led him to Washington where he immediately identified himself with the Jackson administration. His devotion won Kendall a place in government affairs when he was appointed fourth Auditor of the Treasury, where he served from 1828 to 1834. He was so ardent and sincere in this capacity that he was made Postmaster General, doing a really remarkable job in an administrative way. It was during this time that Edward Gallaudet was born.

For eight years Kendall was counted as one of Andrew Jackson's closest associates. The group surrounding Jackson became known as Jackson's "Kitchen Cabinet." Kendall's influence grew steadily, and he is said to have brought about a welcome reform in the Post Office Department. His writings continued to be his great asset, and many feel that he helped Jackson considerably with his state papers. In 1830 Kendall was instrumental in bringing Francis Preston Blair to Washington to organize the *Globe* as an auxiliary paper to the *United*

States Telegraph, each serving as administration organs. But Duff Green, editor of the latter, finally showed too much partiality to Calhoun and Jackson adopted the *Globe* as the organ of administration. The *Telegraph* became defunct after 1837. For a while the *Globe* did the public printing for both Houses, which it lost early in 1833, but the next year it began the publication of the *Congressional Globe*— which furnished daily proceedings of Congress.

When the United States Bank was attacked by the newspapers in the late 1820's, and became the chief issue of the campaign of 1832, newspaper warfare was intensified. An *Extra Globe* was issued, and it continued to act as a Jackson mouthpiece. Kendall resigned as Postmaster General to edit the *Extra Globe* in 1840. Edward Gallaudet was two years old when Kendall returned to journalism. The next few years were trying, for between 1840 and 1844 Kendall was low in both health and finances. He became an agent for collecting claims against the government and his fees enabled him, in his fifty-fourth year, to purchase a farm of about 100 acres on the boundary street of Washington. He called his farm Kendall Green. Finally free of financial obligations he entered upon a new phase of his career, around 1845. Edward, then a child of eight, had begun to hear tales about the telegraph line. It was this invention that was to bring money to Amos Kendall. He became interested in the Magnetic Telegraph and was made the business agent for Samuel F. B. Morse, serving on a percentage basis. He defended Morse in law suits pertaining to patent rights. He had met Morse while working in the government claims, for Morse was then endeavoring to get an appropriation from Congress to extend telegraph line from Baltimore to New York. Kendall's quick mind pictured Morse's project as a private enterprise, and when Government funds were not forthcoming Morse and Kendall signed a contract in March of 1845 whereby Kendall was invested with full power to manage and dispose of Morse's interest in his patent-right, according to his discretion. This relationship lasted twenty-five years, making Morse and Kendall wealthy men.

Again Kendall turned his mind toward something vital, for now he had the money with which to indulge a long latent desire. He made possible the erection of the original and, subsequently, the present Calvary Baptist Church in Washington, giving money to, and participating actively in, the Sunday School and mission work of that church.

Into Amos Kendall's life in 1856 walked a man who pretended to be interested in a philanthropic project, to which Kendall quickly made donations. When looking further into the matter Kendall discovered that this man, P. H. Skinner, seemed to be an imposter. He had taken

possession of a building in the First Ward in Washington and fenced
it in like a prison with a high board fence.[3] He had then gone about
the city collecting all deaf and dumb children he could find, adding
them to several he had brought from New York City, calling it a
school, and claiming to be conversant with the methods of instructing
deaf mutes.

It so happened that Kendall's friend, James C. McGuire, had a
washerwoman whose son was in the so-called school. Noticing that
the conditions there were miserable, she reported the situation to Mr.
McGuire, who relayed his information to Mr. Kendall. Together these
two men visited "the school" and found conditions even worse than
the woman had pictured.

Kendall was appalled, for at a meeting he had called to organize this
project Mr. Skinner had been present and had acted as Secretary.
Kendall immediately called a special meeting of his newly organized
Board, which included David A. Hall, James C. McGuire, the Rev.
Byron Sunderland, William H. Edes, Judson Mitchell, George W.
Riggs, Jr., and William Stickney, a son-in-law of Kendall. This meeting took place on November 10, 1856, about the time Edward in Hartford was working so hard at the Morgan Street Mission; and Kendall
presented his report which convinced the Board that Mr. Skinner was
not a suitable man to manage the property or the pupils of such an
institution.

While the group was assembled a communication was received from
Mr. Skinner, explaining his conduct and offering his resignation as
Secretary. It was voted to file these papers, and the Committee unanimously agreed to continue its labors and to inquire after suitable persons who might be procured to teach the children. William Stickney
was appointed Secretary at this meeting, and William Edes and
Judson Mitchell were named to confer with Mr. Skinner about trans-
ferring his school to the supervision of this Board. Mr. Kendall's donations had already been accepted and plans were made to apply to
Congress for an Act of Incorporation of the Institution.[4]

Kendall felt that the deaf and blind of the Federal District had as
well-founded claims on the bounty of the general government as the
insane,[5] so acting in accordance with his views he framed a bill incor-
porating the proposed institution, and making some provision for the
support and instruction of the indigent blind and deaf children of the
District of Columbia. After learning the true status of Mr. Skinner,
Kendall went at once to the Orphan's Court of the District of Columbia
and had the indentured children removed and put under his legal
guardianship, obliging himself for their support until the organization

of the Columbia Institution was completed. Congress then appointed
Kendall president of the Columbia Institution for the Deaf and Dumb
and Blind.

By December of 1858 the Board had resolved to give public notice
in the papers that the Institution was in formation, and by January of
1857 when Edward was approaching his twentieth birthday, Kendall
presented his draft of a "Petition to Congress for Incorporation," as
well as a draft of an "Act for the Consideration of Congress." On
February 23 he called his Board together to "assent to and adopt for
their future direction and management" the Act of Congress to incorporate the Columbia Institution, approved February 16th. It was also
resolved at this meeting to send out a circular to the several Justices
of the Peace in the County of Washington, calling their attention to
the duties imposed on them by the Act.

At a Board meeting in Kendall's residence on April 20, he was authorized to open a correspondence with Mr. Isaac Lewis Peet of New York
City, or other suitable persons, to secure him or such other persons to
take the superintendency. Kendall was given authority to get a man to
assist temporarily in taking charge of the children.[6] Immediately he
was to take steps to put the children on the charge of the Government
for their support.

During the latter part of April the correspondence between Kendall
and Peet took place, and when Peet refused the position Kendall wrote
to Edward Gallaudet. By May 30 of 1857 the Board met to officially
appoint Edward the Superintendent of the Institution, and his mother
was appointed Matron. Edward was to appoint his own and his
mother's assistants.

On his first visit to Amos Kendall, Edward had made clear his purpose in accepting the position: plans for a college would be his aim.
Kendall and his Board had accepted him on this basis and, in Edward's
words, "were pleased with the idea of having what they had conceived
of as no more than a small local school grow ultimately into an institution of national importance and influence." He stepped into his new
position with enthusiasm.

THE YOUNG SUPERINTENDENT

Edward was authorized to employ necessary servants, purchase a
horse and carriage or light wagon, and take appropriate and effective
measures to raise funds for the support of the Institution, as well as to
procure donations of furniture, groceries, dry good, articles of food,
and whatever might be useful in its management and support. All
funds were to be handled by the Treasurer, who would furnish money

to the Superintendent. Edward would render to the Board quarterly accounts showing detailed receipts and expenditures, and would account for all property donated to the Institution and the disposition made of it.

He attended his first Board meeting on October 5th of 1857. Before him sat the Rev. Mr. Byron Sunderland, pastor of the First Presbyterian Church of the District, who would be serving on the Board until his death in 1901. Between them there would be an estrangement, but it would pass. Next to Mr. Sunderland sat George W. Riggs, Jr., the well-known banker, who was to fill the office of Treasurer until his death in 1881. Other members of the Board were William H. Edes and Judson Mitchell, who were to give generously of their time and money until their deaths in 1865; James C. McGuire, a prominent business man—and long a personal friend of Amos Kendall, who was to serve until 1888, the year of his death; and David A. Hall, a lawyer, who was to serve for fourteen years, until his death in 1871.

Edward was appointed Secretary pro-tempore. He was called on for a report of conditions up to the present, and was authorized to prepare his first Report for the Secretary of the Interior, under whose Department the Institution functioned. This was the beginning of Edward's many negotiations with the various government departments. Jacob Thompson, then Secretary of the Interior, was the first government official with whom Edward established relations for his Institution. His talent for meeting people was to take him a long way up the road to success. Men found him personally attractive, enabling him to form friendships where he entered their social, as well as their business and political lives. This was a vital attribute that stood him in good stead in his undertakings.

At the third Board meeting, in November, he was asked to present plans for permanent buildings designed to accomodate fifty pupils and their teachers, and to draft a petition to Congress for appropriations. At once he was initiated into the mysteries and means of persuading Congress, a talent which would become most useful in his work. Kendall and Stickney were put on the building committee, and while Edward's petition awaited congressional action, Edward got busy with the renovation of the two houses that stood on adjoining lots. These fronted Boundary Street, opposite the northern end of Eight Street East. Kendall had donated one; the other was rented from Stickney. The latter contained about ten rooms, and Kendall's house had nine. Both were of wood, loosely built—and far from comfortable in cold weather. Mrs. Thomas Gallaudet began her work as Matron. She had with her a maid from her Hartford days, Sarah Grady, a devout Catholic who had served in the Gallaudet family for many years.

The school had opened with nine deaf-mutes and five blind pupils. Edward had three assistants and three servants, altogether a family of twenty-one persons. The assistant matron was Mrs. Maria M. Eddy—of Worcester, Massachusetts, and James Denison of Royalton, Vermont, was Edward's assistant. Edward later recalled how the presence of his dear mother—and of good Mrs. Eddy—gave to the establishment dignity and distinction "which were, for the time being, lacking in its youthful male officials."

The fall and winter passed, and it came time for Edward to enter upon his duty of raising funds for the school. Early in 1858 it had seemed desirable "to excite the interest of Congress and the public" in the Institution by giving an exhibition of the progress of the pupils. A request was granted by the House of Representatives for the use of the old Hall, out of which it had just moved, This Exhibition, held on the night of January 21, was the last public meeting in those historic chambers. The *Washington Union* of January 22 reported that "E. M. Gallaudet, Esq., the Principal of the Institution, delivered a brief, sensible, and eloquent address. He reviewed the gradual creation of institutions for the education of the deaf and dumb, and of the blind, in the various states, and then urged the claims of the institution here, which has been founded, and sustained by individual liberality, and now asks the aid of Congress."

Amos Kendall was in the chair, and the Honorable Jacob Thompson, Secretary of the Interior, sat at his side. Members of Congress, clergymen, and distinguished citizens were in the audience. The reporter for the *Washington Union* wrote a good account. Edward briefly recorded the event in his *Occasionals,* which he had neglected for months. He said the address was printed and circulated widely among Members of Congress and the friends of the Institution.

A YOUTHFUL MARRIAGE

Other pressures were now being brought to bear on Edward, aside from his official duties. The Directors' action in placing a very young and unmarried man in charge of the Institution had been criticized in some quarters. Learning of this Edward made trips to Hartford to further his interrupted romance. Family letters reveal this; he wrote nothing about it in his *Occasionals.* Sisters Alice and Sophia wrote him letters in praise of the young lady Jane Fessenden; and it was soon settled that Edward was to take a wife.

Ten years later Edward was to write about himself: "I have just read in a review of Gen. de Trobriand's 'Four Years of the Campaign of the Potomac' the following critique on Gen. Sickles' character which I copy here because I think that it portrays some of the points of *my* character: 'His characteristics are an active brain, an ardent temperament, a quick and supple intelligence, and a stubborn will. Ambitious by nature, he enlists in the service of his ambition a keen perception, a practical judgment, and a profound knowledge of the law of expedients. Obstacles do not discourage him, although he will never struggle fruitlessly against an impossibility; but as he has always a number of strings to his bow, when one breaks he will simply replace it by another.' "

It is rather unflattering to think, much less to say, that Edward married because it was the expedient thing to do. But the account he wrote of his engagement, under the date March 14, 1858, makes one feel that it was only *one* of the events of 1858. He said: "The past winter has been truly an eventful one to me. In December 1857 I was betrothed to Jenny M. Fessenden of Hartford." Turning the page of his *Occasionals* one finds the next paragraph cut away, and the passage continues with an account of the address delivered at the Capitol, previously mentioned, to which he devoted almost a full page. The continuing page and a half he devotes to the running of the Institution and he makes no other entry until January of 1864. In his *Memoirs* he states that he felt solicitous to do all he could to better his position with critics of his bachelorhood, and that he was married July 20, 1858, to Miss Jane Melissa Fessenden, of Hartford, Connecticut, whom he had known from his boyhood, and brought her to Kendall Green before the opening of the second school year. [7]

The house in which the officers lived was handsomely painted in honor of the coming of Edward's bride, and the rooms for their use were tastefully prepared—and most comfortably furnished, by his wife's father. Edward added a mite to this information in his January 30, 1864 entry, when he noted that to write on one's own marriage was rather difficult. "After a lapse of several years," he explained, "things that one might say at the time or near the time, one does not like to express at a later period and so I will not undertake to say how happy I was as a newly married man—how long the honeymoon lasted—how pretty I thought my bride or anything of that sort."

Jane helped her young husband by giving piano lessons to the blind students. The 1860 Report of the Institution shows that when the Assistant Matron retired she was replaced by Edward's sister, Sophia Gallaudet Hunter, recently widowed, who filled this position until her sudden death in 1865. The enrollment increased rapidly. Before the end of the first year there were eighteen pupils, and the number was expected to increase to twenty-five by the next year. Conditions were already crowded, and Congress had to be approached again for funds for the erection of more suitable living quarters. But the federal treasury was low, and Kendall again aided by giving funds for the erection of a brick building which Edward planned — and brought to completion at a cost of $8,000. It was connected by a corridor with the frame house originally donated by Kendall, and before the winter of 1860 the Institution gave up the house rented from Mr. Stickney.

An action favoring the Institution was the law passed by the Maryland legislature which placed its deaf-mute children in the Columbia Institution. A larger enrollment made it possible for Edward to better classify his pupils, and also gave him an opportunity to extend his public relations. In securing this action at Annapolis Edward went over to talk with the Chairman of the Ways and Means Committee of the Maryland legislature, Mr. Robert M. Denison. He had tried for several days to arrange an interview with Denison and failed, but he was successful when he appeared in person. The personal interview was thereafter to be Edward's favorite method of approach.

During these years distressing personal problems confronted Edward. The Civil War loomed across the horizon to blot out much of life for everybody. However, while reminiscing in his *Occasionals*, on January 30, 1864, he confided: "Life's tide has ebbed and flowed, bearing out cherished hopes into the wide ocean of lost treasures, never more to return; pouring in, too, upon my soul new joys with every rising wave." He spoke of experiences one never committed to paper, or ever related except to some chosen friend or lover. These dark, mysterious happenings were the cause of his long silence—his soul having been well nigh crushed under the weight it had borne. But at this writing he saw new hope and was grateful that he had survived his dilemma. These personal conflicts took precedence over matters of world moment, and although the war years had brought stirring experiences to him—and to the Institution, his diary heard of little except Edward's reactions as events affected him.

In his *Memoirs* Edward recounted some rumors of war he had

heard through political men he drove out to his campus. On one such occasion his guest was Senator Albert G. Brown of Mississippi, former governor of the state, who was then Chairman of the Senate Committee on the District of Columbia. Brown had with him a newspaper editor from Vicksburg. The two talked "disunion" while Edward drove them in his jump-seat wagon behind his good horse Brent. In 1860 this conversation made a vivid impression on Edward for he remembered certain private utterances of William H. Seward, a man whom he knew well, and on whom he called occasionally.

During this period Edward was also having the Institution physician, Dr. Alexander Y. P. Garnett, call on him to treat a nervous condition. Garnett, a Virginian who eventually left his practice in Washington to become Surgeon General of the Confederate Army—and Jefferson Davis' personal physician, entered Edward's room one day in great excitement. Ignoring Edward's distress he launched into a vivid account of John Brown's raid at Harper's Ferry, certainly not a topic to calm Edward's already jangled nerves.

In the summer of 1861 Edward's first child was born. She was given the name Katharine Fessenden, the middle name in honor of her mother's father, Edson Fessenden. Edward had a colored woman to come and nurse Jane, a Mrs. Freeman who had been born a slave in North Carolina. She predicted that the war would not be a short one and that many lives would be sacrificed before the end, which would not come until every slave in the land was free.

It was during this first summer of war that Kendall Green and its vicinity grew to be a military camp. Regiments were located all about the Green, and a part of the school building was occupied as a hospital. More than 3,000 men secured all their water from a well on the premises. Edward lived in a state of excitement, wanting to be a part of the war as a soldier. His friends had a hard time dissuading him from leaving his work at such a critical stage. They convinced him finally that his absence, even for a short while, might cause the college never to be started. Kept among his papers, however, are passes issued to him to go within the lines and over the bridges, showing that he could not resist visiting the scene of danger. One pass is signed by Gen. Winfield Scott—"to pass the U.S. Lines, and to visit Camps on both sides the Potomac."

Meanwhile the affairs of the school prospered: buildings were erected as needed, and the enrollment reached fifty-four. The Institution had acquired a reputation throughout the country, and as Edward pulled through his period of great melancholy he was thankful for a faith that had sustained him and given him hope while all had seemed lost to him. Temptations were now behind him and he was convinced that he was more desirous of doing good in the world than of advancing his own interests; he believed God would bless his life to the advantage of others.

Someone had struck Edward a heavy blow, and he had told only three people. He did not reveal whether Jane was one of the three or not, but he was helped in pulling out of the depths of despondency by the acquisition of a new friend. This young man "lighted anew the flame of human love" and satisfied Edward that he was a person "to be respected and admired as well as loved." He was in Edward's home for four months before leaving for "a distant city," but Edward hoped for his return. This companionship at least caused Edward to pull himself together and be able to focus on the bright side again.

The war years brought two other children to the young Gallaudets. After Katharine came Grace Worden, born in December of 1862 and named for her Grandmother Fessenden. The first son was born in November of 1864 and was given the name of Edward LeBaron, for a friend to whom Edward was devoted. One is inclined to believe that this friend, Frank LeBaron, was the person responsible for pulling Edward out of his despair. They had met nearly ten years before in Hartford, and Frank LeBaron is known to have moved to Chicago.

In January 1865, before Edward sailed on a Southern cruise, his devoted sister Sophia died; in July he lost his little son. Edward and Jane had been through strenuous emotional experiences together, and Edward would always wonder how one part of his life, the school, developed so beautifully while he himself was in such turmoil of mind and spirit. Perhaps the fact that he was able to get away from the scene twice between 1861 and 1866 helped him preserve his equilibrium.

A Respite

When daughter Katharine was only seventeen days old, Edward set out on a trip to Saratoga Springs, New York, probably at Dr. Garnett's insistence. The direct object was to attend a Sunday School Convention with his brother-in-law Henry Trumbull. The indirect object was improvement of his health. While Henry would be attending meetings and listening to speeches, Edward intended "taking the waters." He kept a small Journal for Jane, inscribing it "Notes of a Journey Commenced on the 12th of July—1861. E. M. G." He

went to New York City and stopped over to see his mother who was
visiting his brother Thomas, the Episcopal minister, and saw several
other members of his family: his sister Kate and her new baby, and
brother Wallace, the financier on Pine Street.   He journeyed across
to Brooklyn to see brother William and heard Henry Ward Beecher
deliver a war sermon.

Edward then set out for Hartford, where Henry Trumbull was
awaiting him, and saw all his Hartford friends and relatives, his
mother having returned home and promised to join him later in
Saratoga.   The two men then went to Boston and to Portland, where
they visited Sabbath schools and the State Reform School.   Since
Edward was interested in buildings, he examined these structures
carefully.   On the evening of July 22 he got word of the Battle of
Bull Run and expressed anxiety for his 'dear ones' back home.   "I
thought of my dear wife," he wrote, "and of last summer when we
were journeying much in the same manner."   His letters to Jane
mentioned similar trips he and she had made and expressed a hope
for future ones.

Edward and Henry meandered back through the countryside of
Connecticut, visiting relatives and hearing more war sermons, before
continuing toward Saratoga.   In Guilford they called on the poet
Fitz Green Halleck, once private secretary to John Jacob Astor,
Halleck's patron.   "He showed the fire, of genius in his conversation
and the interview was one long to be remembered," wrote Edward.
Halleck had received an honorary degree from Columbia University
the year Edward was born.

Edward already felt better and found that his muscular strength
was returning. In Saratoga he was impressed anew with its worldliness,
and he prayed not to let his heart wander amidst all the alluring
follies!   He drank the waters, napped, wrote and read.   He recorded
that his parents had stopped in Saratoga on their honeymoon, and
had stayed in the hotel he was now in, the Union Hall.   People came
up to meet his mother who had joined him, and Edward felt that she
bore herself like a queen.   Several friends asked after Jane.   One
evening he met General John E. Wool, already 77 but destined to be
recalled to command reinforcements for Fortress Monroe and to become the Commander of the Department of Virginia.   A notable
group of people were there, even in the midst of the war.

The days passed pleasantly for Edward.   He bowled, made calls,
and admired family portraits and objects of art.   Yet through his
diary entries ran the strain of missing Jane and home, and the "wee

one." He hoped that he and Jane could return to Saratoga in another year, and while he wrote the band played numbers that reminded him of their life together. A letter from Jane made him realize how quietly and dutifully she was spending the summer at home caring for their little one while he travelled about the country pleasure-seeking. He hoped it would never occur again.

On his return to Washington he found great changes taking place. Troops were pouring into the city from several states, and on his campus a regiment from Rhode Island had been replaced by one from Pennsylvania. Out of thirty-five sick soldiers only one had died. His school building had become a hospital. He was glad his campus could offer such care to those defending the city.

During October Mr. Fessenden arrived to see his first grandchild, and helped to celebrate his daughter's twenty-fourth birthday. The Kendalls were away, having moved to Trenton for the duration of the heavy fighting around Washington. Jane wrote her friends that they had taken their furniture with them. Edward wrote his friends to "cast all fears to the winds as to the safety of Washington," that McClellan had secured everything completely and there were many thousands more troops there than people generally imagined, 2,000 men being within shooting distance of their house. Soon a wagon camp was established within five hundred yards of Kendall Green. The Potomac water was brought to this camp by a special pipe, and Edward, always alert to the needs of the Institution, succeeded in having a connection made with this pipe which brought the aqueduct water to his buildings at a cost to the Institution of about $3,200.

Branching Out

In 1862 the Capitol in Washington still looked like a shorn Buddha, rather dominating the city's architectural scheme. The Patent Office, the Treasury, the Executive Mansion, and the Smithsonian Institution were the other principal buildings. Other Government activities, such as those of the Department of the Interior, were housed within buildings not their own. The Department of the Interior was in the Patent Office, and the Library of Congress was in the Capitol. Amos Kendall had been in Washington about thirty years when Edward arrived. He knew many influential people and was quite able to advise Edward not only of the ways of politicians but also of the native Washingtonians.

Edward met and mingled with people who were an important part of the city's vigorous life. Many of them perhaps did not care for Kendall's political activities, but few could deny the man's clear perception and splendid intellect. His appearance was disarming in its simplicity, and he became the guiding spirit of Edward, who was totally inexperienced in pulling political strings.

The success of the early undertakings of the Columbia Institution was greatly due to Kendall's genius for probing a stituation, settling on a line of attack, and seeing the undertaking through with courage and ability. His generosity was revealed in a report, combined with Edward's for 1861, in which he said that Edward had shown judgment and skill in the selection of teachers, the discipline of the pupils, and general management, and that it was to these qualities the Institution was mainly indebted for the high rank it had already attained among the benevolent institutions of this and other lands.

This father-son relationship was good for Edward since it gave him a needed confidante without paternal demands, permitting him to be on his own and to build his strength. Their natures were well suited; the word "compromise" did not exist for either—a quality which might have alienated others was for them a bond. It cemented a friendship that weathered twelve years of close companionship in which their tempers clashed only once—when a technical point arose which called for compromise by one! Edward won, but on purely technical points.

Yet questions continue to nag at the back of one's mind when reading the extensive writings Edward left behind him: why did he so seldom refer to national events? Why was it that a man whose life was spent in the national political arena, in close association with many of its well-known figures, should fail to leave some impressions of those stormy days and of the men who shaped them? He dealt with names, particularly of those who helped him in his work, but did he care a great deal for what went on otherwise? His diaries are not comparable to those of men like John Adams, Philip Hone, or George Templeton Strong. Edward was not a man of leisure: he set a schedule for himself that would have worn out the average man in ten years. Instead, in that length of time he was able to look back on the accomplishment of what most men would consider the work of a lifetime. Yet, in 1867, he would be ready to take a second start.

When one remembers that, at the time of his arrival in Washington, Edward was extremely young, that his emotions were unsettled, and that he was still thinking about himself and considered his own feelings as of paramount importance, one realizes that he stepped from one life into another almost overnight. There was no gradual growing into a more mature frame of mind; what happened to him within a few months he had to accept in toto: mainly the necessity of making decisions involving other people, while simultaneously analyzing his own heart and trying to meet the exacting demands of older men. In straightening out his accumulated duties and ordering his personal life he had little time for critical analysis — on paper. As late as 1891 he asked himself why he kept a diary: "It seems almost foolish to attempt a diary. Still, it is often convenient to know just when certain things happened." The *time* when certain things happened seemed more important to him than *how* they happened. At another time, when still quite young, he wrote what later seemed to him a most conceited remark. He decided to let it stand, then added: ". . . for I don't mean to have anyone see this book while I live and when I am dead what matter whether it is called conceit or not."

But the fact remains that Edward not once recorded his opinions of Buchanan or his administration. Certainly he met Buchanan. He remarked that he took the beautiful Lizzie Hale to a levee at the

White House in 1857—but he recorded this in 1880. That was the only remote reference to Buchanan. He put down none of his views on the election of 1860, the election upon which so much depended. He did refer to John Brown's raid, mainly because it was involved with his illness, and the doctor told him about it. One wonders if he kept up with the Lincoln-Douglas debates, or the slavery question as it pertained to the Territory of New Mexico, or perhaps William L. Yancey's stand on States Rights. Secession was unthinkable to a man like Edward, and it might have been that when the Democratic National Convention met in Charleston in early April of 1860, followed by eight months of debate before the state seceeded, Edward was going through such personal torment that he wrote nothing rather than reveal his mind. Perhaps he kept up with these developments better than we know, since he had relatives in Savannah.

Abraham Lincoln was 28 when Edward was born. He could not know that his path would cross that of a young man from Hartford 23 years later, assuming Edward met the President in 1860, and that he would become the means by which that young man would found a college. In 1864, when Edward was 27, he was to face the 55-year-old Lincoln and discuss an Act of Incorporation for a college which Edward had drawn up at the request of his Board. For several years now Edward had been alluding to just such a scheme. In his 1862 Report he had insinuated the need of an institution, "like this," exerting a national influence. He expressly stated that "Until this proposed feature of our Institution is realized our labors will be incomplete."

When Amos Kendall drafted the Institution's Act of Incorporation he had provided for the admission of deaf and blind children "of teachable age" as beneficiaries of the United States, but had set no limit of time or age at which they must be dismissed, as was usual in the state schools for the deaf. Consequently, Edward felt that he had *material* for beginning a college, since he had already been authorized to keep his children as long as he could teach them anything. The matter of a college was not alluded to in his 1863 Report, although Amos Kendall did state that staff salaries were raised, Edward's to $1,500.

There was no mention made of Abraham Lincoln, or of trips to the White House, which Edward must have taken since he knew well John Nicolay and John Hay, the President's secretaries. This we learn later, but never, throughout his papers, does Edward mention having met Abraham Lincoln. However, early in 1864, Edward drew up a bill which he modeled after one giving the power to confer degrees to Columbian College, later George Washington University. Columbian College had opened in 1821 with preparatory and collegiate departments, which would now be exactly the status of the National Deaf-Mute College. Edward placed his bill in the hands of Senator James W. Grimes of Iowa, Chairman of the Committee on the District of Columbia, explaining his plans for a college for the deaf. Senator Grimes showed a friendly interest, securing favorable action on the part of his Committee without difficulty, and reported the bill to the Senate. This bill was taken up in the Senate on March 15, 1864, and soon passed the House without discussion, becoming a law by the approval of President Lincoln on April 8.

When John Hay, Secretary of State, spoke at the Presentation Day Exercises of the College in May of 1899 he told the audience: "Thirty-five years ago it was my duty as secretary to Mr. Lincoln to inform the Senate and the House of Representatives of the United States that the President had signed a bill empowering this institution to confer collegiate degress upon deaf-mutes." He continued, lauding its growth, and remarked that he was especially glad to felicitate Dr. Gallaudet, "one of the friends of my early Washington life."

THE INFLUENCE OF LINCOLN AND JOSEPH HENRY

Reference was made to the one time an argument arose between Edward Gallaudet and Amos Kendall. The argument resulted from the passage of the bill authorizing the Columbia Institution to confer collegiate degrees, which Edward had drawn up and presented without consulting Kendall or the Board.[1] Kendall was not displeased that the bill passed, but he remarked to Edward that he hoped he was not going too fast. Edward's reply to Kendall was that he was there to get up steam and move forward, and if the opinion existed that his rate of speed was too high, it was the province of the Directors to put on the brakes! Kendall called his Board together and asked that a collegiate department be inaugurated. On that occasion he told the Board he wished to have Edward inaugurated as President of the Institution *in all its departments,* including the Corporation and the Board of Directors. Twenty-seven-year-old Edward remonstrated, saying he would be satisfied to be President of the College and have Kendall remain President of the Corporation and Board. But Kendall was insistent, saying that in view of the important work about to be taken up by the Institution it would be better that the man whom the world would look to as the head of the Institution should be clothed with all possible dignity. Edward yielded, and measures were taken to so change the Constitution as to make the President of the Corporation ex officio Principal of the Institution. At the same time the number of Directors was increased from seven to eight so that Kendall could remain on the Board as a Director without displacing any of his old friends.

These changes were duly made and Edward Gallaudet was elected President of the Corporation at a meeting held June 22, 1864. A number of those who sat on Edward's Board were fifty years his senior. It seemed unfitting to him to preside over such a body, but he claims to have "accepted the situation and tried to discharge my duties in the Board with modesty." He often wondered why they did not rebel. In 1865 there came on Edward's Board one who did rebel. This was the Chief Justice of the Supreme Court, Salmon Portland Chase.

The Board was considering the purchase of a piece of property for which no provision had been made by the Government in its appropriations. In the meeting Edward suggested that the Institution might take a deed, pay what it had and give a mortagage on the land purchased to secure the balance due. Edward pointed out that the corporate rights conferred on the Institution by Congress made such a transaction possible. The Chief Justice contended that the Institution had no power to mortgage its property. When Edward expressed surprise, and asked if possession of full corporate powers did not give the right to mortgage the property of the Corporation, the Chief Justice broke out on him saying: "I do not know anything about law at all I suppose." Edward was embarrassed, and with just cause. Soon afterward he received a letter which he probably expected: Chief Justice Chase wished to resign his position as a Director. Edward later heard through Director Sunderland that Chase had told him it was not agreeable to him to continue as member of a body of which he was not the head. His resignation was accepted by the Board, but not until October 24, 1867.

Edward proceeded with his plans for the college department by developing suitable courses of study and the preliminary courses leading up to these. Richard S. Storrs, Jr., a member of the faculty worked with him, and finally the outline of the curriculum was shown to Kendall. To Edward's consternation Kendall declared a pronounced opposition to these plans. In turn he offered a scheme of regulations to the Board, the adoption of which would have made the College "the laughing-stock of all educated men" by Edward's standards. The Board allowed these regulations to lie over, and Edward was at his wit's end to secure their defeat. He tried to convince Kendall of the superiority of his own plan, which made Kendall only the more set in his way. He wrote Edward a letter, which Edward saved, in which he likened Edward to a petted child with a new doll. "No sooner," he wrote, "do you secure the coveted prize, the college, than you are preparing to pull it to pieces."

When Edward reported this news to Professor Storrs, the latter saw only one thing for them both to do: resign and give up the college! Edward assured Storrs that he had not come to Washington for any such thing, and he began at once to "pray and work for a deliverance." Edward went to Chief Justice Chase and Benjamin B. French of his Board and told each of his difficulties. Both men assured Edward of their approval of his plans, but Edward wanted further assurances. He took himself down to the Smithsonian Institution and presented his plans to Joseph Henry, Secretary, "than whom," wrote Edward, "no higher authority among educated men could be found." Henry had served on the Institution's Examining Board for Edward.

Edward told Henry of Kendall's attitude, and asked Henry to give him his views in writing. Within a few days Edward received the letter, which he held in readiness to read to the Board whenever Kendall should ask for action on his proposed regulations.

By reading Henry's letter one is made aware of how Edward planned for his course of study. This is what Henry gleaned from Edward's ideas:

"The general plan proposed by Mr. Gallaudet embraces *three* courses: the first, including the studies of the first seven years; the second, those of the two next years, and the third those of the two following years. The studies of those several courses are so arranged as to form together a graduated system from the first elements of instruction, through the immediate branches, to the subjects of a full collegiate course. These three courses or departments as here proposed, appear to me necessary in furnishing a properly graduated and a sufficiently extended course to meet the present demands of the Deaf and Dumb. It has been abundantly proved by experience that as a class they have excellent mental capacities and are susceptible of high mental and moral development.

"It will most probably be found in practice that the larger portion of the pupils will stop at the end of the second course if not at that of the first: but this should not discourage the establishment of a third course. For if but one-tenth of the pupils should be able to enjoy the advantages of the higher course the influence of these on the Deaf and Dumb, as a class, and on the public generally in their behalf, would be highly beneficial.

"The third or collegiate department should be in reality what its name imparts; that is, it should be able to afford the pupils all the facilities required for as full mental culture as their capacity will enable them to acquire. But in order to do this, the student should be well prepared to enter upon its studies and hence the necessity of the intermediate, or academic, course, in which they may receive the preliminary instruction.

"If this plan for a college course cannot be fully carried out I would advise that it be not attempted and that the name be not adopted; since a government institution, to which the eyes of the whole country are turned, should not set the example of holding out expectations which cannot be realized. The Columbia Institution should be a model for the imitation of all similar establishments, and not only do good service by the effect it produces on its own pupils but also on the Deaf and Dumb generally, in elevating the standard and improving the methods of their education.

"Not only have the general features of the proposed plan been well considered, but also all the details. The several steps of the course have been judiciously arranged and the studies well selected to insure the desired effect. I hope the plan will be adopted in full and that proper exertions will be made to obtain the means of carrying it into operation. I am sure that it would be productive of good in greatly increasing the means of enjoyment and much extending the sphere of usefulness of a class of persons who call forth, in their deprivation, our warmest sympathies and claim, in their behalf, our most strenuous efforts."

In his concluding paragraph Joseph Henry stated that the Smithsonian Institution afforded unusual facilities for the study of different branches of science and that these facilities would always be free to the pupils of the Columbia Institution.

Kendall had assumed that the Institution had a Freshman college class ready to be formed. Edward knew that only the *material* was available, and that time alone could deal with it. Kendall's scheme would have graduated a class in 1867 with B. A. degrees, when its members had completed only the equivalent of the Sophomore year. It would actually be 1869 before a class could be called Senior.

Edward put Henry's analysis, his own outline of studies, and all papers pertaining to the program together, showed them to no one except Professor Storrs after signing an official paper, and locked them in a drawer. Kendall never alluded to the subject again, and Edward's original plans were put into effect.

Abraham Lincoln, the second Patron of the Institution, did not attend the Inauguration of the College in 1864. But the presence of his spirit surely pervaded the campus that day. In the final analysis he was the instrument through which the doors were opened to higher education for the deaf. Again his mission on earth seemed to be the freeing of those in bondage. Through the admirable planning and foresight of Edward Gallaudet, and his appeal to the United States government, Lincoln took the time in his days of greatest stress to lend his ears to those who could not hear—and put his name to a document that would forever advance their cause: an Act of Congress granting the deaf a right to have a college of their own.

Enter Thaddeus Stevens

One of the most interested and helpful friends of the Institution in Congress at the time of its founding, and for several years to come, was the Honorable Thaddeus Stevens of Pennsylvania, Chairman of the Ways and Means Committee—which served as the Committee on Appropriations—and majority leader of the House. Edward had secured Mr. Stevens' interest by calling on him, self-introduced, and arranging for him to visit the Institution with one or two members of his Committee. In his state as early as 1834 Stevens had been an advocate of the Act of that year for extending the free school system of Philadelphia over the whole state. He became famous for his defense of free education and a democratic system of instruction, and labored for larger appropriations for colleges. He was known as being fiery, most aggressive, and most uncompromising. It is possible that he had known Kendall at Dartmouth, as Kendall was a Senior when Stevens entered Dartmouth as a Freshman in 1811.

Edward remembered that Stevens was quite impressed with his deaf mother, whose personality was always most attractive. Stevens observed the pupils and their silent work in the classroom with absorbed attention, and all at once exclaimed: "Great Heavens! How rapidly one could transact business in the House if half the members were like these children!" They were probably fascinated by him, too, and would remember his lame foot. It was in the summer of 1864 that Stevens had secured the passage by the House of an increased appropriation of $26,000, and also the $31,446 for dormitory accomodations for the boys. Although the Senate struck out both appropriations Mr. Stevens made a vigorous appeal in the Committee of Conference and in the House, which saved the $26,000. The following year he was instrumental in getting Congress to appropriate $29,445.87 for additions to the buildings.

By an Act of Congress passed during the summer of 1865, Edward succeeded in having his blind students transferred to the school for the blind in Maryland, thereby relieving his Institution of its dual character. As with all successful undertakings, progress meant expansion, first in physical facilities and then in pupils. Edward's Board had told him in the beginning that he would be expected to raise funds. His next step was to obtain money for scholarships.

Edward had urged in his Ninth Annual Report that Congress might "with propriety" make provision for the higher education of deaf-mutes from the states represented in the Institution. Feeling the cause urgent, he did not wait for the Government to act but went ahead and asked private individuals to give, thereby securing funds which could be converted into scholarships. Professor Storrs helped Edward with this, and together they were successful in obtaining eleven scholarships which yielded $150 each per annum. Among the donors were Amos Kendall, the Messrs. Jay Cooke and Company, Thomas Smith of Hartford, and Edson Fessenden of Hartford, who agreed to endow one perpetual scholarship with the principal sum of $2,500—provided ten similar endowments were obtained. Several men then subscribed scholarships of $150 per annum: George W. Riggs, Jr., banker; the Hon. Benjamin B. French, D. C. Commissioner; Charles Knap, and William W. Corcoran, banker and philanthropist, and founder of the Corcoran Galley of Art—both of Washington; the Hon. William Sprague, former Rhode Island Governor and later United States Senator, and George Merriam of Massachusetts. One donor preferred to remain annoymous. Young men from Vermont, Connecticut, Pennsylvania, Maine, Massachusetts, New York, Illinois, Michigan, and Wisconsin were able to enter College on the strength of this income. Over the years the Government increased the number of these scholarships until a different basis of admission was established.

With more liberal funds Edward was able to think of enlarging his faculty, bringing to it men who had fuller backgrounds in the academic field. His early staff had been composed of people he knew or knew of, from Hartford or nearby. Relatives had formed a large part of his Institution staff. They had included his mother, sister, wife, cousins, and nephews. In 1865 he added to his staff the Rev. Lewellyn

Pratt, a teacher in the Pennsylvania Institution for eleven years, who agreed to teach natural science and mathematics—and stayed for four years, until joining the faculty of Knox College; the Rev. William W. Turner, under whom Gallaudet had taught at the American School, who had thirty-two years of teaching experience and who remained to lecture on natural history for fifteen years; and the Hon. James W. Patterson, a member of Congress from New Hampshire—and a recent professor at Dartmouth, who consented to give lectures on astronomy. Patterson also served on Edward's Board from 1868 to 1873. Edward himself took the chair of Moral and Political Science. He added an Art Department to his program in 1865, securing Peter Baumgras, an accomplished Washington artist, to teach drawing and painting.

The year 1866 opened an era of further expansion. A more formal campus began to take shape under the watchful eye of Edward, through employment of the firm of Olmsted, Vaux and Company, well-known landscape architects. Their design for the grounds and the completion of buildings is to be found in Edward's 1866 Report. Frederick Law Olmsted, senior member of the firm, was a native of Hartford whom Edward knew well. He had developed the United States Capitol grounds as well as New York City's Central Park, and during the Civil War had acted as the secretary general of the United States Sanitary Commission. More people knew these facts than that he was a writer. Olmsted studied the layout and location of buildings, spending several days at Kendall Green, working with Edward's ideas of combining the already existing scheme—which Edward considered crude—with plans for a future campus of beautiful greensward, well laid walks, and chosen shrubbery. The utilitarian aspects could be sublimated and the whole picture could become one of good taste and harmony. It pleased Edward that Olmsted's firm could include the three existing buildings so that through the years one might see the interesting story of development.

In 1866 Professor Samuel Porter came to the campus to take the place of Professor Richard Storrs, who had returned to Hartford. Professor Porter, who had had more than twenty years experience in teaching the deaf in Hartford and New York, was the brother of Professor Noah Porter of Yale, later its President. Their sisters had founded Miss Porter's School for Girls in Farmington, Connecticut. Professor Porter was active in the National Deaf-Mute College for the next eighteen years, acting as Librarian after his retirement.

Another valuable addition to the Faculty in 1866 was Edward Allen Fay. This twenty-five-year-old instructor took the chair of Latin and History, staying to become vice-president of the college in 1887 and Professor of Romance Languages. A graduate of the University of Michigan, from which he received his M. A. in 1865, he had taught three years at the New York School for the Deaf. His interest stemmed from that of his father; the Rev. Barnabas Fay, who was the first Principal of the Michigan School for the Deaf. While carrying his teaching load at the College he still found time, between 1877 and 1881, to win a doctorate in romance languages at Johns Hopkins University. The two Edwards, Fay and Gallaudet, became very close over the years and their children grew up together on the Green. The University of Michigan honored Edward Fay with an honorary doctor of science degree in 1912, and Gallaudet College honored him with a Litt. D. in 1916.

James Dension, whom Edward had appointed his first teacher, took a two-year leave of absence in 1864, and Roswell Parish, Jr., left the same year, making it possible for Edward to appoint replacements. His mother also retired as Matron in 1866, feeling that at sixty-nine she deserved a rest.

Edward would soon be back hammering for more appropriations, and Thaddeus Stevens would step into the picture again; though ill and weak, he still had a contribution to make to the Columbia Institution.

The First Epoch Closes

Except for two paragraphs he wrote about Lincoln's death, of which he learned while on a cruise in Cape Hatteras waters four days after the event, Edward never referred to the Emancipator. This was the second trip Edward took during the war years; like his first, it was for his health.

Some time before April 12, 1865—perhaps before Lee's surrender on the 9th, which he mentioned enroute—Edward was at sea, headed for Charleston to watch the "raising of the flag" ceremonies at Fort Sumter. He kept an account of this trip for Jane in a dark blue leather book, inscribed in pencil. With a correction indicating he had perhaps forgotten the day he began his Journal: "80 Miles south of Cape Hatteras—in the Gulf Stream on board Steamer Oceanus, 9:35 a.m. Wednesday April 12, 1865." Professor Storrs accompanied Edward. Storrs' father, a Congregational minister, was to offer the prayer at the flag ceremonies.

Edward mentioned many people aboard, including Col. Oliver Otis Howard, whom Lincoln had selected to be Commissioner of the

newly established Bureau of Refugees, Freedmen, and Abandoned
Lands—later to be known as the Freedman's Bureau. When Howard
founded Howard University about seven years later he and Edward
would have cemented their friendship, and Edward would eventually
serve on his Board of Trustees. As they neared Charleston Edward
wrote of his feelings as he approached the "cradle of the rebellion."
Sitting in the wheelhouse near the pilot he had opportunities for
learning localities. He saw where the *Weehawken* had gone down,
floundering under her overloading; Folly Island, where troops landed
in July of 1863 when the bombardment of Charleston began; and Fort
Wagner, which guarded the portals of Charleston Harbor. (Her
resistance had caused the guns to be turned on Sumter.) Edward
was highly interested in the earthworks, and he did not wonder at the
terrible loss of life in the sad assault of Shaw and his Negroes. [2]

When he or fellow passengers shouted out news of Lee's surrender
to the crews in boats near Fort Sumter, Edward felt that it was news
to them although it was "four days old to us." He insisted on giving
the news of the surrender to the vessels at the wharves. He made
use of his voice several times and once raised a laugh, when someone shouted "Where's Jeff Davis?" by answering "Gone to Mexico!"

He gave descriptions of the landing and of the ceremonies, describing Major Robert A. Anderson [3] as "venerable," probably an apt description since Anderson was ill, but had gone to Charleston under
the President's orders to raise above Fort Sumter the very flag he had
been compelled to lower four years before when he commanded the
harbor defenses and had been fired on by Confederate forces, finally
having to surrender. When the battered flag rose under Anderson's
care Edward confessed he was "surprised into weeping." Henry
Ward Beecher read his oration from notes, which disappointed
Edward. Soon the serious part was over, and the visitors went sight-
seeing, and waited for their boats to begin the homeward journey.
Edward and Storrs were on the *Enoch Dean* and stopped at Beau-
fort where they called on Nehimiah Adams, whose pro-slavery writings
had brought much criticism. Edward also saw the Negro schools, and
expressed his horror at the living quarters of the recent slaves. "Sick-
ening," he said, "to one who believes as I do in the right pertaining
to every human being to better his condition if he has within him
the power and desire to do so." He visited Uncle James, his father's
brother, in Savannah and still rejoiced that his native New England
scenery surpassed it.

Soon he was homeward bound, and in his Journal, on the *Fulton,* he thanked Jane for inducing him to take this journey. He was back on his campus by April 27, just three months before he was to lose his son Edward.

Edward felt deep patriarchal responsibilities which many interpreted as interference in their personal lives, and his devotion to his wife and children was almost an obsession. Since he had practically been ushered into a continuation of his father's career and had felt blessed, he hoped that one of his sons would follow in his steps. His mind began to look ahead toward founding a dynasty, very much in the manner of the Adams family where a pattern of education was laid down. He had all the attributes of a man who could command a following, and as he developed into one of the country's early educational administrators he worked toward the goal of founding a college which would set a crown on his father's achievements. Because his concentration came at a time when the industrial world began to lead, Edward was caught between the literary and the scientific, and it is to his credit that he made such transitions as he did, keeping his little craft on an even keel and into a safe anchorage during his lifetime.

In spite of his participation in Congressional fights for appropriations, and other cares that demanded his time, he was able to read, visit the art galleries, and listen to fine musical artists of the period. The theatre attracted him greatly but he did not speak of "favorites," requiring only that the performance be first rate and free of vulgarity. He deplored the mind that was incapable of discrimination, and he was as quick to note a poor performance in a minister as in a circus performer. Fundamentally he liked a good show, having inherited his father's love of the drama, and enjoyed seeing men use the talents with which the Lord had endowed them. He was truly a man of inherited culture, and in this he could stand comparison with a man of the Adams family. A biographer has said of Henry Adams: "He became the man to carry the family's greatness into new areas in a new age." [4]

In 1865 when Congress failed to pass the civil appropriation bill, the Institution would have been badly off indeed had Edward not gone to the First National Bank of the city and asked for an advance of $25,200 until Congress should provide. In planning ahead for the next two years he felt it best to aggregate the separate sums asked for in the past into one sum, and have the pupils' per annum quota filed with the appropriation for incidental expenses and salaries, this to be done by relinquishing the per capita allowance and asking

Congress for the one sum. Enlarged enrollment called for more food and milk, making the next expense on the agenda a new brick barn and a cow house, for which Edward asked Congress for $51,200.

In the midst of these heavy administrative duties Edward had to face the worst of all that could happen. Jane died. She had not been well for a number of months and there are letters which show his tenderness and care, and that tell of his trip with her to the White Mountains, thinking the change would help. While Jane spent much of this time in Hartford with her parents Edward had the care of their two daughters, but finally took the children to their mother in Hartford. He had hardly returned to his school when the message came telling of her last illness, which seems to have affected her lungs. She died on November 23, 1866.

While in Hartford planning funeral arrangements he was writing letters of instruction on Institution matters. There was government property still on Kendall Green, left over from the war; and he was planning its disposal. The entry of Jane's death in his *Occasionals* was the first since baby Edward died the year before. Jane had literally gone back home to die, in the Trumbull House where she had been born and married. She never fully recovered emotionally from little Edward's death. He was five months old when her husband made the trip to the Southern waters. It is not certain if she was in Washington then or in Hartford. Edward mentioned in his Journal he kept for her that he had not heard from her in sixteen days. He prayed that he would profit by all the lessons God had taught him through her, and was grateful for the two dear children which he hoped would be spared to him and he to them.

Eight days later he was confiding to his *Occasionals* that there was an inner hidden history of his life that seemed *very* strange as he contemplated it. At times he felt a strong impulse to write about it in book form, to confide to the public, under an assumed name, the facts he could not, nor would if he could, relate to his most intimate and trusted friends. He wrote this story later, but tore it up among other papers when he retired. One may safely presume that he was astonished at the innate fire that was forever needing his control, making him grateful that the good Lord did not let it consume him, but directed it toward constructive activities so that he was at last able to bear the turbulent years through which he passed.

With Jane's death Edward felt that the first major chapter of his life was closed. He was rounding out his first ten years at the Institution, a widower with two children, approaching his thirtieth birthday. During December of 1866 he dealt with thoughts concerning his future. The National Deaf-Mute College was *un fait accompli,* as he wrote it, and the pioneer work was done. Henceforward his work should be to beautify and perfect that which had now an insured existence. Yet, at the back of his mind, there was a question that came at intervals: was he to remain there to carry on to perfection his plans for buildings, professors, students in numbers, continuing the work to which he had devoted his "adolescent manhood?" Or was he to be called to a new sphere of labor where he might again launch forth on pioneer work? He felt that no matter what he had accomplished, nor how great his work might seem, he could still take no credit for it himself. His strength and abilities were God-given, and it was upon God-reliance that he had drawn rather than self-reliance.

He felt almost in the same position he had occupied ten years before, prior to receiving Amos Kendall's letter. Perhaps he should "lie on his oars" awhile—taking time out for travel, reading and study, and then strike out on some new venture at forty. As the old year waned he wrote in his *Occasionals* on December 31, 1866:

> *"Ring out the old*
> *Ring in the new*
> *Ring out the false*
> *Ring in the true."*

"Thou has been an eventful year to me. A year of release! My heart fairly leaps within me as I think from what fetters I am loosed. Now I can *live."* He hoped he was not sinning in his feelings of joy but he nevertheless felt on the advent of the coming New Year a profound peace, a hopeful joy that he had never before experienced. "I incline to shout inwardly—to say Hurrah! to fling my cap in the air like a jolly boy—to sing—to jubilate generally—to say 1867 *How are you?* What new joys do you bring me?" It was this question he asked in his diary as he closed the year 1866 on his dead love.

Toward Greater Things

The new joys Edward wished for in 1867 were indeed to come to him. His Board minutes show that at the December 26th meeting he had asked for a trip abroad to which the Directors had agreed— "providing funds could be raised." Chief Justice Chase, at the March 1867 meeting, made the motion that Edward's salary for the quarter ending June 30, 1867, should be paid in advance "in specie, provided the same can be drawn from the United States Treasury in that currency."

Edward's motives in going were not purely personal. In the year 1867 two schools had come into being in the United States for teaching deaf children by the oral method exclusively. This, of course, was not a new idea. As early as 1772 Samuel Heinicke was teaching deaf pupils in Germany by means of speech. By 1778 he had established the first public school for the deaf in Leipzig, Germany, and although he sedulously concealed his "methods" because he wanted no others to benefit by them "for nothing," he did not deny that he used signs for the combination of ideas but stressed articulated language and writing for communicating thoughts.

The two "oral" schools in the United States were the Clarke Institute and the New York Oral School (later the Lexington School.) The first of these opened in Chelmsford, Massachusetts, where Miss Harriet B. Rogers began with a few deaf pupils. Through a benefactor who had a deaf daughter she was coaxed into taking her pupils to Northampton to a small school endowed by John Clarke, and became its headmistress. The benefactor was Gardiner Green Hubbard, whose deaf daughter Mabel was destined to become the wife of Alexander Graham Bell. Hubbard himself would become a friend of Edward Gallaudet.

The second school opened for oral teaching was on Lexington Avenue in New York. These two schools were instrumental in bringing about a re-evaluation of the state schools for the deaf throughout the country, and it was Edward Gallaudet who was ordained to be the leader of this movement. This challenge of oralism also settled Edward's troubled thoughts as to his future so soon after Jane's death, and provided the door through which he could enter the new peace which he felt the year 1867 promised him. The "possibility of still greater things" and the opposition he pined for were now at hand, giving him every opportunity for the "new hard labor which shall demand a full pressure of the *steam* which seems to be within me."

Edward called the attention of his Board to the establishment of the two oral schools, and pointed out that the Columbia Institution should not lack means that might be of help to the deaf. He proposed that someone might be sent as a delegate to Europe for the purpose of examining the oral and other schools in that part of the world. He had been much upset by the Report of the Massachusetts Legislature of 1867 on the Education of Deaf-Mutes, in which schools in the United States were criticized for not dwelling more on articulation. Only a few of the schools had oral work as part of their curriculum.

From his father Edward had absorbed the belief that the best from each system or method should be brought together to form a combined system whereby a deaf child could benefit through any method tried and found to be beneficial. The spirit of the elder Gallaudet had made the combined system so democratic in principle that the state schools, which used it, were not wedded to any one method but willing to give a fair trial to any suggestion made by an intelligent person. In the early days at the American School any child who had once possessed speech and hearing was favored with lessons in articulation so that he would not lose the faculty of speech.

In 1867 there were 28 schools for the deaf in this country; their total enrollment was about 3,000. All of the schools were elementary, and since articulation was restricted to the primary grades, Edward felt that his own primary department was being criticized for non-oral teaching. When his Board authorized him to spend six months in Europe for the purpose of examining all methods of teaching the deaf on the Continent, in Great Britain, and in Ireland, Edward formed a plan for classifying the various schools he was to visit. He felt he could classify them more naturally and effectively if he did not try to tell of his visits chronologically, but describe the schools in accordance with the system which prevailed in them. This resulted in setting up the three principal methods now in use: the Natural Method, the Artificial Method, and the Combined Method. He could then refer to the various schools as belonging under Class I, Class II,

E. M. G. with his second wife, Susy; his two daughters by his first marriage, Grace and Katharine; and Susy's nephew, Will Denison.

photograph of the Gallaudet family taken in front of their home in May, 1885.

The Gallaudet children in 1890. In front row are Denison and Edson. In back row are Marion, Katharine, Herbert, and Grace.

Some of the 34 Gallaudets who attended family reunion on the occasion of the 100th birthday of Thomas Hopkins Gallaudet in 1887. Among the children in the front row are Marion, in dark dress at left, and Herbert, second from right. Seated in second row, from left to right, are Susy, Peter Wallace Gallaudet, two unidentified persons, (perhaps Peter's daughter and wife), Kate (Mrs. Bern Lum Budd), brother Thomas, Alice (Mrs. Henry Clay Trumbull), and Mrs. Thomas Gallaudet. In third row, standing at left, are Edson and E. M. G. Woman at extreme right is Katharine.

or Class III—classes corresponding to the order of the methods.

It was to the system founded by the Abbé de l'Epée in France in 1760, and improved by his successor, the Abbé Sicard (under whom his father had studied) that Edward applied the term Natural Method. This method is based on the deaf-mute's free use of his natural language, which employs pantomimic gestures, but only "as a means to the end in view which is the induction of the mute to society by making him acquainted with the vocabulary, the grammar, and the idioms of his vernacular." This would eventually enable him to read and write the language of the country in which he lived. The extent of his learning would depend, of course, on the means and talents of the pupil. Under the Natural Method were grouped those schools in which the study of articulation formed no part of the regular course of study. All of the American schools, with the exception of the Clarke School and the Lexington School, were in this category, Class I.

The Artificial Method was founded, almost simultaneously, by Thomas Braidwood, in Scotland, and Samuel Heinicke, in Germany, in 1760. This method had for its principal aim the development by unnatural processes of the power of speech, which exists unimpaired in most deaf-mutes, and the training of the eye to take the place of the ear. The eye, from much practice, gradually learns to discern the changes in position of the vocal organs. In this category were the schools which depended on speech and lip-reading, dispensing with all natural signs as quickly as possible, thus doing away with the mute's natural language. This, Edward believed, ignored a reliable and precise vehicle for the widest range of thought. He wrote: "The extent of intellectual culture opened to mutes under this system is less within a given number of years than that afforded by the first method."

In those institutions endeavoring to combine the best qualities of the two methods described above, the term Combined Method is applied: recognizing the utility of the sign language, and at the same time giving attention to the spoken language.

Edward arranged his program of travel, so far as possible, to avoid vacations in the schools, and when he arrived abroad he extended his travels to additional countries. Besides Great Britian, France, German, Belgium, Switzerland, and Italy, he visited Russia, Finland, Sweden, Denmark, and Ireland.

He left Washington on April 3, 1867, amid great demonstrations from his teachers and pupils. He placed his daughters with their

grandparents in Hartford, and while there he visited the American
School and joined a pupil from his college, Samuel T. Greene, who
went with him to Boston for an "exhibition" before the Massachusetts
Legislature. Such an "exhibition" employed the question and answer
method, before an audience, to show a deaf person's ability to understand language, both oral and written. Evidently young Greene's
lip-reading and speech ability had been highly developed during his
schooling at the Columbia Institution. Edward was taking his fight
to the home grounds! This was his first meeting with Gardiner Greene
Hubbard, [1] who was his host while he stayed in Boston before sailing. Edward described Hubbard's home as abounding in all the
comforts and luxuries that wealth could furnish, but made no mention
of the results of the exhibition. In Boston he largely devoted his
time to visiting, and obtaining letters of credit to take abroad, as
he had done en route in New Haven and Hartford. At a dinner
Hubbard gave for him he met noted Harvard professors, Boston minis-
ters, and Mrs. Henry Lippitt, whose deaf daughter was present as
company for Mabel Hubbard. Both of these girls were the product
of strict oralism, but it was Jeanie Lippitt [2] who attracted Edward.
He stated that her power of articulation and reading from the lips
were really remarkable. She had lost her hearing between four and
five years of age and had been taught at home, her parents sparing
no pains for her education. But Edward still pondered: "How far the
generality of children becoming deaf at or after four years of age
could be made to compare with Miss L. in articulation and lip-reading
is by no means settled by the success in her case."

Edward's ship steamed out of Boston Harbor the morning of April
10th. He claimed he felt alone but not lonely. He kept a splendid account of the people he met, the food he ate, the books he read and the
sights he saw. He was liked on the boat and was asked to organize
a "sing," which he did, listing the songs on his program and commenting on the whistling of the man who rendered "The Mocking-
bird." He promenaded the decks with a lady by moonlight and made
plans with several people to see them at points on the Continent.

In the harbor at Cork he saw the first British "ironclad," *The Black
Prince*, and he noticed the architecture in the neighborhood of
Queenstown. He observed Laird's ship yards as they neared Liverpool, where the Confederate cruiser *Alabama* was built. Arriving
at Liverpool his steamer, *China*, docked, and soon Edward was
headed for the Dirkenhead Ferry. "It fell far short of the splendid

appointments of the Jersey Ferry," he commented. "This Liverpool swindle is perfectly horrible."

Edward began his travels at Chester, England, and revelled in its historic significance. He journeyed on to Oxford, presenting his letters to professors there, and enjoyed the excursions through the colleges and museums, until finally he reached London. The first thing he did on arrival was to visit a tailor. He had not enjoyed the luxury of buying good clothes for six years, so he outfitted himself at moderate price for his social life.

For the next several days Edward visited the school for the deaf at Old Kent Road. He found some of the pupils speaking well, although several assistant teachers told him that the pupils did not value articulation, and did not practice it after school. Mr. Richard Elliott, a teacher of twelve year's experience, told Edward he thought more could be done with articulation than was being done. He allowed Edward to copy his original manuscript on "A Course of Instruction in Speech for the Deaf and Dumb, together with a Pronouncing List of the Principal Words in the English Language." This consumes 24 pages of Edward's Journal.

On his next visit Edward met the Principal, the Rev. J. H. Watson, whom he described as a slow, easy-going man who apparently took little interest in the deaf and dumb. As the successor of his father and grandfather he had not tried to improve on what they did. He attributed any weaknesses to his Board of Directors and to the lack of public interest. This, of course, was no excuse to Edward. Watson confessed that few of the pupils left the institution with ability to write English idiomatically. He believed in some articulation and thought it possible to conduct lessons without a considerable use of signs, but felt very few pupils could become so skilled in lip-reading as to be able to follow and understand a public speaker. There were deaf teachers in some of the classrooms. Since the average term of a child was only five years, no great attainments could be expected.

These were examples of the comments Edward would make in each school he visited. He asked questions, examined the pupils himself, and made resumes of what the teachers, instructors, and even the pupils had to say about the method in use. He kept careful notes and nothing escaped him either in the preparation of the school's program or the physical plant.

He called at the American Legation on Charles Francis Adams and was invited to dine at his home the following Sunday. He looked up his lawyer friend Edwin W. Field and through him met interesting people: professors at Oxford, British Museum librarians, and other professional men. Henry Winter Syle, [a] a deaf man, called and brought unusual guests who were specialists in their fields of languages and educational literature. Eventually Edward would employ, in his own curriculum, the texts of Thomas Prendergast, on how to master foreign languages.

Edward went to Exeter Hall to hear the Oratorio of the *Messiah,* in which the English tenor, John Sims Reeves, was the soloist. He called on Junius Spencer Morgan who gave him a cordial greeting and invited him to dinner. He had Sunday evening at the Embassy with Adams and his family, seeing young Henry Adams who acted as his father's secretary, and Henry's sister. The quiet social evening made him think of America and especially New England where his happiest days had been spent.

Edward again visited the school for the deaf, then went for an evening to his friends, the Fields, at Squire's Mount, their home in Hampstead, a northern suburb of London. After enjoying a meal and early evening in this English home he went to the House of Commons, which he entered on a card of admission supplied by Charles Francis Adams. He described this experience as one of great interest. He heard Lord Claude Hamilton, Queen Victoria's Vice Chamberlain of Household; Charles O'Conor—commonly called the O'Conor Don; and he saw Benjamin Disraeli (spelled "D'Israeli" by Edward,) who would become Earl of Beaconsfield in 1876. Also he saw Spencer Horatio Walpole, who was Home Secretary.

As a respite Edward took French lessons from Professor James Summers in his home on Lombard Street, in the very heart of Old London. He also dined with the Morgans, meeting the family and enjoying a superb dinner served in magnificent style. Mrs. James Goodwin and her son were there from Hartford. She was Morgan's sister.

Before Edward left England for the Continent he went to water color exhibitions in Pall Mall, saw the masters' works in the National Art Gallery, and visited the Crystal Palace at Sydenham. He then paid respects to Mr. Morgan, Mr. Adams, and to Mr. Elliott at Old Kent School, before taking the cars for Dover, from which he crossed the channel to Calais. Enroute to Brussels he swapped cards with his seat-mate, Baron Edward Whetnall, Secretary of the Legation at the Belgium Embassy in London, who was taking a wedding present from Queen Victoria to the Count of Flanders, just married.

As soon as possible he called on Frére Cyrille of the boys' school for the deaf, who in turn took him to the girls' school on the Rue Rempart des Moines. There he met Monseigneur De Hearne, the 63-year-old constituent member of the convention which organized the revised government of Belgium in 1830, who was well-known for his interest in the deaf, not only in his own country but also in England and India. He received Edward with great cordiality and showed him all over the institution.

Here Edward saw 45 girls who were taught mainly by the method derived from France, although signs were not used to any extent. Articulation was taught, but not forced when there was little success. De Hearne was of the opinion that not more than one in ten born deaf-mutes attained great proficiency in articulation or lip-reading. Edward felt that the general course of instruction compared well with that pursued in American schools, and here it extended over a period of seven years. A fine esprit de corps prevailed, and the buildings were ample and airy.

Edward followed his routine of calling at the Legation. He found Secretary Curtiss, a handsome fellow about Edward's age, who was very hospitable. Henry Sheldon Sanford, the United States Minister to Belgium, was in Rome spending Holy Week. A native of Connecticut, Sanford had also been a student a Trinity College in Hartford. Edward went sight-seeing and visited cathedrals before attending De Hearne's school again. This time he heard him conduct services. The sermon was translated into signs by one of the Sisters who occupied an elevated position where all could plainly see her. During Mass the deaf-mute pupils occupied themselves by repeating prayers in signs from their prayer books. Edward was agreeably impressed.

He dined with Mr. Curtiss and went to see a fete, rather dumfounded that in Europe Sunday ended when church was out. His conscience acted up at this, yet he saw no evidences of vice. He went to Bruges on Monday and witnessed a grand Roman Catholic fete, an annual adoration of the Holy Blood. He visited the school for the deaf there and found that even less articulation was given, it being elective, and only the most successful were advised to continue this method. The Directer, the Abbé Biebuyak, thought there was great danger of injury to the lungs when articulation was taught to excess. He told Edward that some parents requested that their children not be taught to speak, they so disliked the disagreeable sounds they made.

Edward remarked in his Journal that he seemed to be living in history. He liked the Belgian people and their costumes on the holiday occasions. He liked the food but not the water. It was revolting to his taste and was bringing on diarrhea. "I have come to the conclusion," he wrote, "that when invited to dine I must accept the hospitality of my host when he sets wine before me. A refusal is often construed a rebuke. It is not understood as it is in America." He noticed that the holy fathers regaled themselves with cheroots and served Rhine wine to their guests.

The boys' school for the deaf in Brussels was visited and Frére Cyrille took him around. There were 43 boys. The Prussian System had been adopted and signs were abandoned, yet the use of natural signs were allowed when necessary. Frére Cyrille showed a decided preference for the oral method, and the pupils seemed anxious to learn to articulate. Although some born deaf could read lips and speak well, Edward still felt that as a means of easy and rapid communication between the teachers and his pupils articulation and lip-reading failed completely. Frére Cyrille was often compelled to resort to writing and sometimes to signs. Edward observed a constrained and sombre expression on the faces of the boys. Frére Cyrille told Edward that his pupils rarely talked to one another by means of their vocal organs outside the school. This was the exact point around which Edward was to evolve his whole impression of his visits to the various schools: the social life of the deaf pupils was spent as they pleased, in the manner they pleased, as far as communication with one another was concerned. Formality in the classroom, informality outside.

An invitation came to Edward to dine with the returned American Minister, Henry Sheldon Sanford. Edward was amazed by the beauty of Mrs. Sanford. "She is magnificent!" he exclaimed. There were other guests for the evening including Monseigneur De Hearne.

Edward made a return trip to Frére Cyrille's school and selected a paragraph in the elementary French reader for each pupil to read aloud. With the book before him he could see that every pupil had been enabled to form distinct sounds for the syllable uttered. Had he not had the book before him, however, he would have failed to comprehend some of the passages. Brother Cyrille was of the opinion that the power of lip-reading developed even to the highest possible degree would never suffice to enable its possessor to follow understandingly public discourses. Not more than half of his pupils would ever learn to speak with fluency or be understood by strangers, he predicted.

Soon Edward was in Paris, where the city was in a state of high excitement because of the World Exhibition. He was lucky to get rooms in the Grand Hotel, where he loved the appointments. Paris far exceeded his expectations. He visited the American Legation before finding his way from the Market Place through the Latin Quarter to the school. This was a hallowed spot to him, for here was where his father had trained to teach the deaf. His account of it reads:

"Today I entered the Institution where my honored and beloved father, more that a half century ago, gained that knowledge of the art of teaching deaf-mutes which was a germ of our great and useful work in America. My feelings were peculiar and I well nigh lost the assurance of my own identity. I felt the course of time reversed in its movements and in imagination I went back to the days when my father, at just my present age, tarried here and secured for the thousands of mutes in America then unborn, the priceless boon of education. A new sense of the grandeur of his work came over me, a new enthusiam was enkindled within me. I trust I dedicated myself anew to the work God has given me to do."

Although his visit was unannounced he found all in perfect shape. The dormitories and hospitals were particularly charming and supplied with every comfort. The shops had many trades to learn, and not any of these vocational practices escaped him. He was looking for ideas for his curriculum that would promote the health and welfare of his pupils, as well as their academic accomplishments. In Paris he recognized the method of instruction as being identical with that in America, and he encountered no difficulty in talking by signs with the pupils and teachers. He watched Professor Leon Vaisse give instruction in articulation that was most interesting and satisfactory; more so than any he had seen thus far.

For diversion he shopped, heard music in the Champs Elysées, and one evening, with three divines and a guide, visited the "demi-monde" of Paris. All of this gave rise to sad and solemn reflections. He went to church and met Senator John Sherman of Ohio and Representative John A. Kasson of Iowa, both men destined for higher posts in Washington, and the latter to become a member of Edward's Board in 1882.

Again he visited the Paris institution, seeing the gymnasium which he envied, and shaded playgrounds with space for sports and exercise.

Mr. Vaisse introduced Edward to something new in the classroom. Instead of using his organs of speech he employed written characters; each represented a certain sound, its form having a likeness to the position of the mouth when the sound is given forth. Mr. Vaisse had invented this system of written signs, and the *modus operandi* of the exercise is understood when it is explained that the sounds are first expressed phonetically and then the proper etymological order is given. Edward copied examples of this in his Journal. ' Edward was surprised that the different positions of the organs of speech, in uttering different sounds, could be so accurately presented to the mind through the medium of the eye, enabling the deaf student to imitate the sound with a good degree of accuracy.

Professor Vaisse and Edward dined together and further discussed matters concerning the deaf. Edward also dined with the United States Minister to France, John A. Dix, and attended one of the Saturday evening receptions for which the Dixes were famous. Edward barely missed his friend John Hay who had returned to the States in January upon the resignation of John Bigelow. At the reception he met Frederick A. P. Barnard, President of Columbia University, who, when just out of Yale, had taught at the American School one year and at the New York School for the Deaf several more. William Cullen Bryant, then 73, was also present. Edward went to Versailles and heard Carlotti Patti sing songs from a favorite opera, *Martha*. He made his final trip to the school on May 18th and again witnessed articulation, getting a better idea of the precise method used in its teaching.

New friends gave him letters of introduction and he travelled on to St. Hyppolite. He stopped first in the city of La Rochelle, and while the sun shed its rays over the harbor Edward was conscious of a strange presence within his soul, as he saw where his ancestors gazed for the last time when they sailed from the old land for the new. He found the American Consulate and enlisted the services of a young Frenchman who helped him look for some Gallaudet material, which he hoped some day to incorporate in a paper. Edward gave a quaint and graphic description of his equippage and of his driver, mentioning that the three-hour ride cost him only nine francs.

From LaRochelle he went to Bordeaux, saw the U.S. Consul, and finally found the deaf and dumb school—the Imperial Institution for Girls. Here he discovered the instruction to be identical with that in Paris. The building was palatial, extensively ornamented, and with a fine statue of the Abbé de l'Epee adorning its facade. He was pleased to learn how many institutions were financed by the governments. After a 346-mile trip that took him through the beautiful wine and olive growing districts of France, he arrived at St. Hyppolite, near the northern boundary of Spain. He had passed through towns musical to the ear—Montauban, Carcassonne, Toulouse, Cette, Nimes—covering the last stretch in a diligence drawn by three horses abreast, their harness loaded with jingling bells. In the quaint little town of St. Hyppolite, with its narrow streets, Edward found the school, which had only 40 pupils and followed the German method of instruction. This was the only Protestant deaf and dumb institution in France. Its Director, Mr. M. Martin, doubted if more than half the pupils could ever become expert in articulation and lip-reading. He conceded that general education was more rapid with signs.

Edward journeyed on to Marseilles and found the institution there a handsome place, with 22 boys and 20 girls. They had been dismissed for the holidays, but one of the Sisters told him she was positive that without the use of signs the deaf and dumb could not be educated. Their instruction was identical with that at Paris. Edward left for Nice via the famous Cornechi Road to Genoa, where he found everything closed, even the banks, because of a Saint's Day observance. He finally found the school and its Director, who reminded him greatly of his own father. Signor Boselli had been connected with the school since 1813, before Thomas Gallaudet had thought of teaching the deaf! The Signor felt it was absurd to try to educate the deaf-mutes without the use of signs. He assembled his boys in spite of the holiday and allowed Edward to question them.

In the school at Turin the fine old gentleman in charge considered the education of the deaf and dumb without the use of signs an absolute impossibility. One-half of his students were taught articulation, but he doubted if but a fraction of these could acquire facility in the use of spoken language. For an hour, after Edward examined the students and the building, he and Benedetto talked, by signs and in French, and the Conte manifested much interest in the condition of deaf-mute instruction in America. He was surprised and pleased to know of the college in Washington.

Edward's next stop was in Geneva, where the school was under Mr. Isaac Chomel, a former pupil of Laurent Clerc in Paris. This was the only school in Switzerland where articulation was not taught. The fact that Chomel was deaf may have influenced his choice of method.

Edward had to press on. He next visited the German schools,

home of the articulation methods. When he could not visit all schools he would gather data about those he missed. He stopped in Milan to visit the "Istituto dei sordo-muti poveri di campagna della Provincia de Milano" under the direction of Don Giulio Tarra. This was the school that was prominent later in international conferences for the deaf. In 1867 Tarra believed in combining articulation with a free use of natural signs, combined with an extensive use of pictures somewhat after the German method. In a few more years Tarra was to become a "pure oralist." Edward visited three other schools in Milan and found similar instruction, since all the teachers believed in attempting articulation.

Edward recorded the financial structure of each school and examined the buildings; he observed the teaching of trades and met the schools' Patrons; and he took pains to find out whether conditions differed between schools for the poorer class and those for the wealthy. He always used interpreters, for he did not want to misrepresent anything he saw. At Milan he learned about a training school for teachers, which impressed him immensely.

Next came Venice, and then Vienna, where Edward went out at once to find the American Ambassador. He not only met John Lothrop Motley but received his offer of services as interpreter during his visits to the schools for the deaf in that city. Motley also found for Edward a teacher who gave him lessons in German. Altogether, Edward's stay in Vienna was exceptionally satisfactory. His Journal recording of his visit to the Imperial Institution for the Deaf and Dumb, under Mr. Alexander Venus, was both stimulating and instructive. For the first time in Europe Edward saw boys and girls being taught together in the same classrooms, as in America.

At the Jewish Institution in Vienna, Edward found the ability of the children to read from the lips greater than in any school he had visited. Their ability to write from dictation and with speed on the blackboard was amazing. Edward gathered reports, pamphlets, and ideas from the Vienna school, and after some concentrated sight-seeing left for Munich, Frankfort-on-Main, Prague, Dresden, Leipzig, and finally Weissenfels, where the famous Mauritz Hill held sway. This was the German school master who, in 1867, was considered the leading mind among the instructors of the deaf in Germany.

Edward's 1867 Report gives in detail what he found in these many schools. Only the highlights have been touched in the recital of this remarkable trip. But something of the Weissenfels School should be mentioned because of Hill's outstanding reputation. Hill welcomed Edward cordially, and Edward found that the institution was run on the plan Dr. Howe had mentioned in his Report of 1865 for Massachusetts. Samuel Gridley Howe, head of the Perkins Institute for the Blind, preferred Hill's plan of distributing pupils in families, two to a household, and of assembling them only for classroom instruction. Edward found that the majority of the schools in Prussia were so organized. Hill showed Edward every phase of his work and admitted that he did not advocate the suppression or extirpation of signs in the instruction of the deaf and dumb. He felt signs were particularly necessary in the first two years. He never employed the manual alphabet. Only six years were allowed for the schooling in Prussia; not time enough to cultivate the language of signs, since speech communication was preferred.

Hill expressed interest in the National Deaf-Mute College and felt that if ever a deaf-mute college were established in Germany the professors could give lectures orally. But he was positive in his opinion that no deaf-mute could attend with profit the lectures of a university for "hearers and speakers." Edward's visit with Hill was eminently satisfactory—one of the most rewarding of his tour.

From Weissenfels he went to Berlin, where he paid a pleasant visit to the Royal Institution, founded by a son-in-law of Heinicke, founder of Germany's first school for the deaf. It was a pleasant surprise to find signs and the manual alphabet being freely used and articulation not unduly exalted; the general ability of the pupils, he noted, was equal to that in schools where signs were admitted under protest. After this visit Edward had his passport visaed for Russia.

Edward's impressions of Russia and his comments on the people and the culture were most graphic. Shortly after arriving in St. Petersburg, he called upon Cassius M. Clay, U. S. Minister to Russia. Clay welcomed him and put him in touch with the Minister of Public Instruction.

Edward found St. Petersburg a magnificent city. For four days he feasted his eyes on the wide avenues and open squares, the splendid buildings, the beautiful Neva spanned by five magnificent bridges. The cathedral bells were totally unlike any he had ever heard. He obtained a capable interpreter and recorded many facts of interest. He learned that the deaf pupils were in their summer quarters on an island about five miles from the city. Since the children came from all parts of the empire and seldom went home until the conclusion of their course of study, they were settled on the island during summer to escape the heat of the city. The director of the institution, C. Selesneff, gave Edward every opportunity to examine the pupils. Articulation was taught to all the pupils and it appalled Edward that the deaf could learn to speak the Slavonic language. He managed to converse in the sign language fairly well; its knowledge in Russia was originally derived from the Paris Institution. Signs were deemed an indispensable adjct to the instruction of the deaf. Articulation, although a part of the curriculum for almost a decade, had not been taught to the full student body until Mr. Selesneff's arrival in 1865. From the island his host took him to the school's winter quarters in St. Petersburg; he learned that the school was founded in 1806 by the Empress Maria, mother of Alexander I and Nicholas I, who gave considerable sums of money for its upkeep. There were 200 pupils and 18 teachers, and Mr. Selesneff explained the salary scale to Edward. He also told Edward what went on in the other Russian schools, in Warsaw, Moscow, and Odessa. And before Edward departed he had a swim in the Neva and a marvelous Russian dinner at Palkin's, a famous hotel on the Nevsky. He left Russia for Finland on July 13. At Abo, Finland, he found the school which he had planned to visit was closed, but learned that although they employed articulation they also used signs freely.

After obtaining information about other schools in Finland, he went on to Stockholm, where he met Joseph J. Bartlett, the American Minister. The school there, located on a beautiful island, was handsome and well appointed. En route to Denmark he rested for five days on a farm near Gnesta, Sweden, owned by a former friend of his father's, before leaving for Copenhagen to visit its three schools.

Edward completed his continental tour with quick visits to Göttingen, Lubeck, Hanover (where he acquired a mustache and an imperial) and Hamburg; and soon he was ready to return to England. There he went at once to Doncaster, where he visited the school headed by Charles Baker, then in his sixty-fourth year and well-known for his literature on the deaf. Edward discovered to his joy that Baker owned the finest library on the history of the deaf to be found anywhere. Baker sponsored the French method of instruction, and felt it impossible to teach the great mass of the deaf in artificial speech. He taught articulation only to semi-mutes.

Edward then went on to Scotland and Ireland, promising to call again at Doncaster. At Edinburgh, where the students were on vacation, he talked with members of the staff. This was the same institution in which his father had sought instruction in 1815. Edward learned that articulation was taught only to those pupils who had recently lost their hearing and that the single-handed alphabet was in use. Moving on to the Glasgow school he found through its Director, Duncan Anderson, that articulation had almost entirely been suspended, its use being devoted to those pupils who had once had hearing and speech. But it was the new buildings going up that impressed Edward; they were in the best taste of any he had seen in Europe, except for those in Bordeaux.

From Glasgow he journeyed to Belfast, where the principal rejected articulation as worse than useless. He moved on to Dublin where there were two institutions, Catholic and Protestant. Both had taught articulation but had discarded it. He then returned to Liverpool, and went from there to Manchester, where he found a nursery department he had not seen anywhere else. Pupils passed from the nursery to the upper grades, but were housed in a separate building. Virtually all of the British schools were of a mind about articulation: it was for the most part useless.

On his return trip to Doncaster he discovered the printing department, which to him was something new. He said he would endeavor to set one up in Washington as soon as possible. But again it was the library that intrigued him most. Mr. Baker let fall certain remarks that made Edward think he might be willing to see these rare books go to Washington.

Edward saw one more British school, in Birmingham, and went to London to write up his Journal. He could relax now for a week's visit with the Fields, where he found William Cullen Bryant and daughter also visiting. But there were still a few schools on the continent that he wished to see. He went to Holland and then to Paris. He saw the Rotterdam School, where articulation was lauded, and went on to Cologne, Zurich, Nancy, again to Brussels, and finally back to Paris. Through the courtesy of Minister Dix, Edward had a secretary to help him with his notes. He then began a three-week stint of confinement during which he wrote his famous 1867 Report on his European tour.

This trip, coming at the time it did, proved to be of the greatest importance in Edward's life. It gave him a new grasp of his work and so broadened his viewpoint that he was able to exert his influence over every public school for the deaf in the United States. He brought to his own campus a new vision and began to institute ideas and plan a program for his college that insured its permanence for all years to come. He reached a new maturity in 1867.

In 1872, when he mentioned this trip in his *Occasionals,* his entry was quite light-hearted. "But I did not allow my labors to stand in the way of seeing and enjoying much by the way," he wrote. "I plucked many flowers as I went along, and have made a record of my impressions." He wrote a truly magnificent record: four complete volumes, the larger dealing with his school visits, and three smaller volumes reporting his social activities and sight-seeing. Incidents overlapped, but he studiously pursued his professional life while he quite humanly did his sight-seeing and made use of his "letters of credit."

Coping with the Opposition

Edward did not enlarge upon his activities during his final three weeks in Paris. Friends he had met, Mr. and Mrs. Claghorn, were in the city at the time, and he found them pleasant company when he had leisure "to be a trifle lonely." But he became decidedly impatient to be at home, even though Professor Pratt was handling affairs admirably at the college.

His decision to stay in Paris and write the report while his experiences were fresh in mind was a wise one. His time was completely clear for his work and he was able to organize his thoughts and compose a report that filled 46 printed pages, covering the school work witnessed and his conclusions. His social activities he could talk about in his informal lectures and at meetings in which the audience wanted to hear the non-technical side of his trip. In his general conclusions he quoted teachers from all over Europe, airing the pros and cons of their similar and diverse views. The first item in his recommendations was: "That instruction in artificial speech and lip-reading be entered upon at as early a day as possible; that all pupils in our primary department be afforded opportunities of engaging in this until it plainly appears that success is unlikely to crown their efforts; that with those who evince facility in oral exercises, instruction shall be continued during their entire residence in the institution."

In order to carry out this plan without depriving the pupils of time from their other studies, he proposed that the term of study in the primary department be extended to nine years, and the age of admission be fixed at eight years instead of ten as heretofore. Of course, new teachers would have to be employed. And now Edward began introducing the ideas he had gleaned in Europe to substantiate his demands, showing that he had been alert to trends that would be vital to his own school in its growth and service to the deaf in America. He began to repeat what he had seen and where he had seen it.

He posed the question: "If we needed new teachers, and the demand began to exceed the supply—where would we get them?"

"Remember," he wrote, "that I found in Milan a normal school for the preparation of teachers of the deaf and dumb. . . . I conceive that one of the most important results of our college enterprise will be the furnishing of young men well fitted to teach the deaf and dumb. But all teachers in our institutions cannot be deaf-mutes, and I would commend to your serious consideration the desirableness of making arrangements for the reception of hearing young men and women into our institution, who may wish to fit themselves for deaf mute instruction." [1]

The reading of his Report to the Directors on October 23 occupied two hours and he noticed that some of the younger members gave occasional "signs of drowsiness" which did not surprise him since much of it was technical and dry to the unprofessional reader. He noted, however, that Amos Kendall, then in his seventy-ninth year, gave the most alert attention throughout the whole reading. He made no notes, and did not interrupt Edward with questions, but when the Report was finished Kendall sought further information on a number of points, which he brought up *seriatim*. All present observed with astonishment the evidence Amos Kendall gave of having actually taken in the Report in all its details. The Board not only acted favorably but expressed the hope that the schools of the country would be influenced to adopt a similar policy in accepting the changes Edward proposed. Edward could now start out with renewed strength to put his school and college in a new frame of reference.

During the winter plans were made to call a conference of the principals of the schools for the deaf of the country, at which "the articulation controversy" as well as "other and more important subjects" might be considered. By March of 1868 Edward officially issued a circular inviting the principals of the regular institutions of the United States to meet on Kendall Green on May 12. He wanted not only to share with his fellow teachers in this country the experiences he had had abroad but also to reach some agreement with them whereby they would begin to have speech taught in their schools if it was not already being done. Rabid oralists had criticized what they felt was this lack, but even after the circulars had gone out, plainly stating the reason for this "call to convention," it was unjustly asserted from certain quarters that the conference of principals was called with the purpose of opposing the oral teaching of the deaf, and that "with evil design" no invitations were sent to the officers of the newly started oral schools. Gallaudet made it a matter of record that there were no *principals* in these new schools when he issued the call to convention. The conference was limited to such officers, and did not include teachers or members of Board of Directors.

It was known that there were men not actively engaged in teaching, but interested in the new oral schools, who were eager, if not extreme partisans of the oral method to the exclusion of all others. And it was these men who had publicly stated that it was their purpose to do away with, if possible, "the system of instruction successfully practiced in this country for a half a century"—the Manual Method. Should any of them attend the conference and be allowed to speak, Gallaudet felt that it would prevent harmonious action. They were not and never had been teachers, and it was desired that the conference be limited not alone to the members of the profession but to the actual heads of the schools. Gallaudet frankly admitted in his *Memoirs* that there were those on the Boards of Management of the new schools whose presence at the conference he would have deeply deplored because they would have been firebrands.

Amos Kendall, following Gallaudet's address of welcome to the conference in May, announced that in accordance with Gallaudet's suggestion the Board of the Columbia Institution had decided to secure the services of an instructor in articulation, and that it was hoped it could be done at the beginning of the next term.[2] Resolutions were made and passed by the members of the conference that speedy measures would be taken to provide the funds needed for the prosecution of this work throughout the country. Several agreed to this new policy who had been in years past earnest opponents of any general teaching of speech to the deaf, and Gallaudet felt that such approval would not have been gained if there had been a partisan element introduced.

Reflecting in his *Memoirs* years later, Gallaudet remarked that he did not think that partisan promoters of the cause of speech teaching to the deaf in this country had been disposed to acknowledge the great service rendered to that cause by the action of the 1868 Washington Conference of Principals. He was confident that this action forwarded the cause of speech teaching more than any influence that had been exerted in connection with this reform.

The conference also brought about the revival of the official publication, the *American Annals of the Deaf*, and the renewal of the

Convention of American Instructors of the Deaf, both of which had been suspended on account of the Civil War. Furthermore it began the organization of the Conference of Principals of American Schools for the Deaf, a worthy group which works towards a unification of the schools and their aims in promoting the education of the deaf youth of the country.

As one example of how people went out of their way to thwart Gallaudet, the instance of Judge William Otto can be cited. Edward's 1868 Report had included the Conference proceedings,[3] with the Annual Report, to be sent to the Secretary of the Interior, the Hon. O. H. Browning. Judge Otto, the Assistant Secretary, who was not very friendly to the Institution, would not have the publication recommended. Gallaudet succeeded, however, in securing a Resolution of the Senate authorizing the publication. Upon hearing this Judge Otto addressed a letter to the Senate, while Gallaudet was out of town, alleging that the Proceedings were very voluminous and that it would cost more than $1,000 to print them. On the strength of this the Resolution to print was rescinded. When Gallaudet returned he had the pleasure of satisfying the Senate with an estimate from the Public Printer which stated that the cost of printing the Proceedings would be less than $200, and thus secured the passage of the original Resolution.

There is another story of a most remarkable opposition which belongs to the year 1868. This opposition was led in Congress by the Hon. Elihu B. Washburne[4] of Illinois against the collegiate undertaking, and had as its avowed object the complete destruction of the Institution, even to providing for the education of the deaf of the District of Columbia in some state school. Washburne's opposition actually began during 1867 while he was on the Appropriations Committee under Thaddeus Stevens. At that time he raised his voice in condemnation of what he called "the unwarranted and extravagant" action of Congress in supporting the College. Mr. Stevens, though in broken health, had been able with little difficulty to overcome Mr. Washburne's opposition on this occasion. Failing to accomplish anything against Mr. Stevens' championship during the session 1866-1867, Mr. Washburne felt more sure of himself in the spring of 1868 when he had become Acting Chairman of the Committee on Appropriations, due to Mr. Stevens' increasing feebleness: and he was determined to make a vigorous onslaught upon the Institution. In the meantime a worthy successor to Mr. Stevens as the active champion of the cause of the College in Congress had been providentially raised up in the person of Judge Rufus P. Spalding [5] of Ohio, who stood next to Mr. Washburne on the Committee.

Washburne made it his objective to hammer away on the fact that while Congress had given large sums for the purchase of grounds and the erection of buildings for the Institution, the title to all this real estate was vested in a private corporation. He also emphasized the fact that the control of the annual appropriations that Congress was asked to make was entirely in the hands of officers of a private corporation. As these criticisms could not be disputed by the friends of the Institution, and as these supporters were not only willing but anxious that the grounds for them should be removed, a bill was framed with Judge Spalding's assistance which provided that no real estate owned by the corporation should be "alienated, sold, or conveyed, except under the authority of a special act of Congress." This bill also provided for the appointment of two Members of the House and one Senator as members of the Board of Directors of the Institution. [6]

Judge Spalding secured the support of a majority of the members of the Appropriations Committee for this bill and it was reported to the House with a recommendation that it pass. Mr. Washburne, however, secured the qualified cooperation of three members of the Committee, enough to justify a minority report, and prepared for a bitter and prolonged contest. Having secured from the Treasury Department a complete statement of all the receipts and disbursements of the Institution from its foundation eleven years before, he prepared a voluminous report in which he undertook to show extravagant and unnecessary expenditures. This report he submitted to the House and had printed in advance of the discussion on the bill, [7] and caused copies to be placed on the desks of all the members on the day the discussion took place. After several postponements, the battle royal began.

Mr. Stevens, who came now only seldom to the House, was brought in by two men in a chair and placed at the clerk's desk. [8] He was not able to take part in the debate, but it was well known which side he favored. The influence of his pale, determined face, now and then lit up with a wan smile, and of the wave of his emaciated hand as he gave encouragement to his doughty lieutenant, Judge Spalding, was not to be discounted. Judge Spalding moved the previous question on the bill which gave him an hour in which to close the debate. Of this time he gave Mr. Washburne forty minutes.

The "previous question" on the bill concerned the increase of the number of pupils in the collegiate department. Mr. Stevens had introduced this bill which originally provided for 10 pupils from the several states—authorized March 2, 1867—and later asked that the number be increased to 25. Washburne had "hoped that the amendment would not be agreed to, and furthermore desired to make a statement in regard to this whole situation." Washburne in the course of his presentation now denied that the District of Columbia had the right to educate the deaf and dumb of all the states, and "to build up an immense institution here with the money of the people." He then proposed that the pupils be sent to "the best institution in any of the states." During his discussion of where and how the money was spent, he took issue over the amounts spent for an architect, travelling expenses, express hire, farming tools, kitchen utensils, carts, and even garden seed. "Every sort of thing is purchased by the superintendent out of the appropriations we make," he explained. He then proposed that no further appropriations for the Institution be made, and that the District deaf pupils be sent some other place instead of "saddling our constituents with $50,000 a year to keep up this man's establishment." He further proposed to set up a "Commission of Charities for the District of Columbia" which would have full control and direction of all the appropriations made by Congress to the charitable institutions of the District, with the stipulation that money could be drawn from the appropriations only upon the requisition of the President of the Commission. In the meantime the title of the property, real and personal, of all the institutions of the District should be transferred to the United States.

When Spalding took the floor he informed the House members that Washburne "means well in his course in this matter as he does in all his opposition to the appropriations by Congress, but he is so morbidly constituted that he cannot make any distinction between an appropriation necessary and requisite to be made and one which is improper. He does not know, he does not realize that while:

> *"The primal duties shine aloft like stars,*
> *The charities that soothe and heal and bless*
> *Are scattered at the feet of men like flowers."*

Spalding further noted that one man, Gallaudet, was not to be blamed for the appropriations Congress had made over the years, but should a finger have to be pointed, let it be pointed toward the Senate, the House of Representatives, and the various Presidents who had approved of the progressive Acts. By 1862 the Institution had been made an agency of the United States, and the Superintendent gave bond to the Secretary of the Interior. And when the Institution was allowed to grant degrees this automatically meant that pupils from all over the United States and the Territories were eligible for admittance.

Spalding then showed where Washburne, in quoting the cost figures for running the Institution, had charged over to the pupils all the expenses of the Institution. In arriving at a per capita, Washburne had taken into account all the expenses of the land, buildings, apparatus, and everything in connection with the Institution "for all the past and all time to come." He had made an over-all charge and then divided the round sum by the number of pupils the government had to take care of. During the eleven years of the Institution's existence $321,824.52 had been appropriated, and Washburne had, by dividing that sum by the total number of pupils, arrived at the per capita of $7,200. Spalding showed that this sum of $321,824.52 included the appropriation for current expenses of $164,401.50, which left the balance to be expended for grounds, buildings, furniture and fixtures. He claimed that this property "is all visible, is all tangible here. It is estimated that the property is worth at this time at least $270,000."

When answering Washburne's question as to whose property it was, Spalding explained that the very bill being introduced at the moment would dispel such questions for the Directors of the Institution had unanimously passed a resolution agreeing that Congress might, if it saw fit, provide for choosing three or more directors to be members of its Board, and have a voice in the management of all the affairs of the Institution. To round out his rebuttal of Washburne's complaints, Spalding referred to the provision of the bill concerning real estate owned by the corporation, which stated: "That no part of the real estate owned by the Institution could be alienated, sold, or conveyed except under the authority of a special act of Congress." Spalding closed his remarks by saying that the government had provided homes for the landless, colleges for farmers (the Land Grant Colleges,) and that provision had been made for the insane, with no one saying anything against the appropriations. He also pointed out that the different states had assumed the responsibility of caring for their deaf pupils, but that no state had enough deaf mutes of its own to erect a college, and that this should be done by the federal government.

Mr. Spalding's amendment finally passed, but on July 23, when the bill came before the House again (returned from the Senate with amendments,) Spalding brought it up and Washburne reported the Senate amendments. The appropriations for grounds had been reduced from $5,600 to $3,600, and the appropriation of $25,000 for expenses had been reduced to $12,500. After further debating, Washburne's amendments were agreed to, and the bill went back to the Senate. The latter refused to concur, but included in the measure Mr. Washburne's provisions for a Commission of Charities, sending the bill back to the House and asking a Committee of Conference. Those appointed were Senators Lot M. Morrill of Maine, H. P. T. Morton of Indiana, James W. Patterson of New Hampshire, and Washburne, Spalding, and Judge Samuel S. Marshall of Illinois.

In his *Memoirs* Gallaudet recalls the incidents which occurred during this stormy time. In his own words they are alive:

"As it is necessary to have the votes of two members from each House to carry a Conference Committee, our hopes were at once hung on the action of Judge Marshall. For Senators Morrill and Patterson were our friends in the Senate.

"Judge Marshall was a Democrat, somewhat of the old school, so I went to him with a letter from Amos Kendall, which carried much weight. Mr. Kendall also called on him. I did my best to make him see how much of injustice was in Mr. Washburne's criticisms of the management of the Institution, and although he was reticent with me I felt a good degree of hope that he would act with Judge Spalding on the Committee. The following day I learned from Judge Spalding that Judge Marshall had agreed to stand by a report that was, on the whole, very favorable to our side, but that Mr. Washburne was using every possible influence to lead him to change his position. Mr. Washburne had succeeded in keeping our current expense appropriation down to $12,500, but Judge Spalding had secured everything else, including Mr. Stevens' amendment, providing for an increase of our collegiate United States beneficiaries from ten to twenty-five, and keeping out of the bill Mr. Washburne's absurd 'Commission of Charities.'

"Coming into the gallery of the House the next day, Saturday, July 25, where I expected the Conference report would be handed in by Judge Spalding, I presently observed him come into the House with a document in his hand, followed by Judge Marshall and Mr. Washburne. They all went to Judge Spalding's desk, where he put his name to the document. A colloquy then followed between the three men, and I could see that Mr. Washburne was appealing most earnestly to Judge Marshall not to sign the report. Knowing that it was entirely possible he might yield to Mr. Washburne's entreaties at the last moment, it will be readily believed that my heart was in my mouth. As the consultation proceeded my constant prayer was: 'Good Lord give us Judge Marshall.' And my relief and joy can be easily imagined, when I saw Judge Marshall sit down, take a pen in hand and write his name below Judge Spalding's. The expression of Mr. Washburne's face as he rushed to his seat was one to be remembered. Shortly after, Judge Spalding presented the Conference Report to the House and it was adopted without further debate." [9]

The long agony of months was over, during which the future existence of the College hung in the balance. The strain on Gallaudet's mind and heart and nerves had been terrible, for the matter was never out of his thoughts and he had been racking his brains every day and nearly every hour thinking what he could do to advance his cause, and then doing what he had thought of. Early in the progress of the controversy he had made several efforts to induce Mr. Washburne to visit the College. He saw Mrs. Washburne and enlisted her sympathy, but she could not move her husband. Dr. Sunderland of the Institution's Board saw Washburne and urged him to visit the College, but he was told by Washburne that that was just what he did not wish to do, for he knew if he came within the influence of the College and its work he would be converted.

The day before the session of Congress was to close something compelled Gallaudet to go to the Capitol and look after the enrollment of the bill. He went to the enrollment room, and upon inquiring was informed by the Chief Clerk that he had just detracted and caused to be corrected a radical mistake in the enrollment of the bill. The *Report of the Conference Committee* had been revised, the important sections for the advantage of the Institution had been omitted, and Mr. Washburne's provisions for the Commission of Charities had been inserted. Had this not been discovered the destruction of the College might have come about.

VI

Alone and Lonely

In anticipation of Gallaudet's moving from his apartment in the Institution into the new President's Home, a family Supervisor had been appointed who would take over certain duties which Gallaudet had previously assumed. In March of 1868 his brother, William Lewis Gallaudet, was appointed to this place.

With his responsibilities lightened, Edward began to think of a release from institutional cares and felt the need of more intimate companionship. His diary refers to trips north during the winter of 1867-1868 when he visited New Jersey, calling on the former "little girl of a dozen summers" who had so intrigued him back in 1856. Her image had beckoned him all these years. That such an impression could have stayed with him so long, when he lived in the nation's capital where he saw dozens of attractive women, is rather odd, except for one fact: Edward lived in the romantic past. He had referred to her scarcely a month after Jane's death, wondering how she had developed over the last ten years. "If the promise of her childhood has been fulfilled she must now be a magnificent woman," he remarked.

He found her "a well appearing, rather handsome woman, but falling far short of being the one that was to command my heart," he confided. He wondered if he would ever marry again. "The woman that wins my heart in time to come will have my *manhood's* first love," he exclaimed. He was convinced that if he knew himself at all his power to love exceeded all his other powers. He wished for "the earnest, pure, fervant, tempered warmth of matured youth" and wondered if he would be permitted to have this experience.

Having been disappointed in his New Jersey visit he began to think about another "impression" made upon him while he was still married to Jane. It had actually been stronger than the first, but when he was free again she was promised to another. While visiting in Royalton, Vermont, the summer of 1864, previous to the birth of his son, he had met a young girl of seventeen, "possessing more than an ordinary share of beauty, both in form and feature." She had attracted him strongly. Susan Denison was the sister of his Primary School Principal, James Denison. He had heard her sing Gottschalk's Cradle Song and was profoundly stirred, in spite of his wedded state.

Four years had elapsed since this episode, and in the spring of 1868 he learned that "this fair mountain girl" was free from her so-called engagement. He soon hied himself to the Green Mountains of Vermont with a curiously expectant heart. There he passed several restful, happy weeks, during which time his surrender to Susan was quick and complete. "She who was to make or mar my future as the queen of my affections came within the orbit of my life," he wrote. They became engaged the night of August 26, 1868, "on the green bank of the Connecticut where it babbles by Chesterfield mountain near Brattleboro, Vermont." He claimed that no giddy youth of one and twenty was ever more hopelessly, perhaps even foolishly, in love than he, "a staid experienced man of the world of thirty-one winters."

Edward returned for Susan four months later and they were married in Royalton December 22, 1868. They stopped off in Hartford en route to Washington, where parties were given them, and Susy, as he ever afterwards called her, met many of Edward's old friends. They honeymooned in New York City, visiting in the St. Denis Hotel before speeding on to Washington to the new home waiting for them.

Susy was ten years younger than Edward, and aside from her youth she had an abundance of auburn hair and large dark eyes. Her father was a doctor and she had grown up among her brothers and sisters with a sprinkling of relatives always nearby. A cousin was Chief Justice Chase, another the Hon. Horace Maynard. The Hon. Dudley Chase Denison, United States Senator from Vermont, was her granduncle. These men had long been in public life, but Susy was to have her first taste of such living, with its round of social activities and obligations, when she became the first lady of Kendall Green and assumed her role of a college president's wife.

The cards announcing their marriage indicated three days when the young couple would be "at home" to their friends during January of 1869. On the first day Edward remembered his wife awaiting the coming of her new friends, standing in the parlor while he reassured her. The front door bell rang, and presently Amos Kendall entered, his face beaming with cordial smiles. He was the first to welcome the bride to her circle of Washington friends, and his fatherly, affectionate manner put Susy at once at ease. The fact that he was their first caller was a precious memory to the Gallaudets for many years.

Susy is remembered as being hospitable and gracious, meeting her husband's friends with dignity. Her heart was touched by Edward's children. With her own nieces and nephews the home was never empty, for the Denisons and the Gallaudets were fond of their relatives and had many visitors. Gallaudet, in his *Occasionals,* eventually spoke of Susy's childish traits. She was not heartless by any means, but inclined to be self-centered. This, more than likely, was due to Edward's own devotion. Adoration can make one self-centered and self-willed, and she had been elevated to a position of importance in comparison to her quiet Vermont existence. Her ambitions were high and noble: one resident of Kendall Green wrote that Mrs. Gallaudet's desire to give pleasure to others was a part of her religion. The Kendall Greeners found her kind, friendly and neighborly, and they knew she was always there in time of sickness and sorrow. She entertained the college students, the younger pupils, and the children of the professors. Soon her own would mingle with them. It is sure that her adaptability grew with the years, although Edward felt at times that Susy did not easily adapt herself to circumstances and situations "differing from those in which she had grown up."

Perhaps he was unsure of her affection for him. He expressed his fears by stating that there was a conventional falling in love on her part, and maybe she *thought* she loved him, but he wondered whether she could love him in any real sense of the word! He probably neglected to take into account her youth and inexperience. Nevertheless, Susy held Edward Gallaudet's love the rest of her life, and he grew out of his first few years of disappointment in not attaining a purely artificial, idealized situation he had set up in his own mind. Susy was a success in Washington, and deaf graduates still remember her as a most regal and elegant woman.

It seems to have been a trait of Edward Gallaudet's to seek another outlet when one proved too stubborn to conquer. He retained the trait attributed to General Sickles: when one of the strings of his bow broke he replaced it with another. During the first year of trying to become re-adjusted to matrimony and feeling rebuffed, he sought companionship among his friends on the Green. The September following the August engagement to Susy a young student had entered college who was about eight years Edward's junior. They were the same height, and the youth had a slim figure and a bright handsome face. In November of 1869, during an excursion of the students to the Great Falls of the Potomac, Edward was attracted to this youth and felt he had acquired a real friend, such as one he had known years back while married to Jane. His nature needed a close friendship, for when he felt appreciated and understood his whole life took on new meaning. His friendship with young Amos G. Draper proved to be a source of strength and encouragement to him, and tided him over his "hurt" with Susy.

Amos Draper was born in Shaftsbury, Vermont, becoming deaf at the age of nine. When fourteen he had entered the American School, two years after Edward had left for Washington. He stayed there two years before moving to Illinois where he continued his interest in printing, acquired at the American School. At sixteen he became a compositor in the newspaper office at Danville, Illinois, and when he moved to Aurora he worked on the *Beacon*. In 1866 he heard of the National Deaf-Mute College, through Henry W. Syle and John B. Hotchkiss. He entered the College in the fall of 1868, and stayed the remainder of his life. In his senior year he acted as private secretary to President Gallaudet, and the fall after his graduation in 1872 he became an Instructor in Mathematics and Latin. By 1878 he was an Assistant Professor and in 1891 a full Professor. He filled many positions of trust while on the campus and acted as treasurer for important funds, finally representing the College at the 1889 International Convention in Paris. [1]

Amos Draper's friendship continued to sustain Edward over the years. He seemed to find a warmth in this man's nature that was lacking in other members of his Faculty—unless it was the deep friendship of his brother-in-law, James Denison. Susy seemed to accept such friendships in good spirit, always referring to Edward as "my dear husband," or "dear Ned." To him she was "my dear Susy" or "my darling girl."

VII

A Growing College

During the short session of the 1868-1869 Congress, Rep. Elihu B. Washburne resumed his opposition to the college but he took a more cautious course. He was able to secure the concurrence of the Committee on Appropriations to a paragraph which appropriated $15,000 for the care of the deaf and dumb of the District of Columbia in some state institution, under the direction of the Secretary of the Interior. No appropriations whatever were made in the Sundry Civil Appropriation Bill, or in any other bill reported to the House for the Columbia Institution for the Deaf and Dumb. Gallaudet interpreted this to mean that Washburne's intention and hope was to actually break down the Columbia Institution by this legislation.

Judge Spalding, who had been appointed a Director of the Institution under the Act of July 27, 1868, secured in the House a modification of Mr. Washburne's paragraph, so that the Secretary of the Interior, if he saw fit, might expend the $15,000 allowed for the deaf and dumb of the District for their care and education *in* the Columbia Institution. Spalding felt that it was not best to resume an open controversy in the House over the Columbia Institution, for Senator Patterson of New Hampshire had also been appointed a Director and was thus in a position, Spalding thought, to secure without difficulty all needed amendments to the Senate measure in the Conference Committe, of which he was sure to be a member.

The Senate Committee was very late in its consideration of the Sundry Civil Bill, and as the end of the session was near it was rushed through rapidly. Senator Patterson had agreed to secure the substitution for Washburne's paragraph, which would make up the deficiency in last year's appropriation and also appropriate $30,000 for the year ending June 30, 1870. But in the rush of business Patterson forgot to ask the Committee to make the desired changes in behalf of the Institution. This would not have been discovered had Gallaudet not gone down to inquire on the evening of March 3. He found that

Washburne's paragraph remained in the Sundry Civil Bill, that the measure was already under consideration in the Senate at a night session, and that its passage was expected in a few hours.

Patterson was chagrined and mortified, but assured Gallaudet that Senator Morrill of Maine could easily have the matter put right in the Senate. He advised Gallaudet to see Morrill at once, promising to do everything to aid him. Gallaudet immediately followed this advice. He had known Morrill for several years and considered him a friend of the college. When Morrill came out of his office to meet Gallaudet he was looking haggard and nervous from the strain under which men in his position are always placed during the closing hours of a session of Congress. After Gallaudet explained the situation, without mentioning Patterson's name, Morrill stated that it was too late to do anything, that the Senate rules would not permit what Gallaudet proposed. When Gallaudet in desperation urged him as Chairman of the Appropriations Committee to use his power, Morrill became extremely angry, bursting out that he knew the rules of the Senate "as well as any one" and that it was too late to do any more.

In his *Memoirs* Gallaudet wrote that his feelings were wrought up to such an extent that he went away with tears in his eyes and sought a corner of the corridor in which he might collect himself. Instead of feeling hopeless he plunged in with renewed vigor, going swiftly into the room of the Secretary of the Senate and asking for a sheet of paper. On this he wrote a note to Senator Morrill, expressing regret if he had shown too great persistence, but stating that in view of the serious misfortune impending over the Institution he had hoped that Morrill would take advantage of any possible suspension of Senate rules to secure the replacement of Mr. Washburne's paragraph by those needed for the proper support of the Institution. Gallaudet then told Patterson and Spalding what he had done, but they offered little hope of success. Having done all he could, he went into the Senate Gallery at ten o'clock that night to await results.

At half past eleven he saw Spalding enter the Senate Chamber and hold a short conversation with Senator Patterson, then retire to one of the sofas. It was almost midnight when the clerk completed the reading of the Sundry Civil Bill. It was about to be put on its passage when Senator Morrill arose. Half the Senators were asleep, and he addressed the Chair in a voice Gallaudet could scarcely hear. Morrill then presented the amendment of the deficiency of $17,500, ending with an expression of hope that he had the consent of the Senate to offer it. This amendment was agreed to. Morrill then offered the amendment for the current expenses of $30,000. He stated that this was the first time the Government had failed to appropriate a sum for the Columbia Institution's maintenance since he had been in the Senate, and that the proposed appropriation should have been on the legislative and executive appropriation bill, but was neglected. It had been referred to the Committee on Appropriations informally, but was not passed upon by the Committee. This amendment also was agreed to.

Gallaudet saw Spalding get to his feet and become a wide awake listener as soon as Morrill began to speak. Because of the general atmosphere of sleepiness, Gallaudet was surprised to hear a loud "aye" when Morrill put the question, and soon realized that it was Judge Spalding who in his intensity had forgotten he was not in the House but in the Senate.[1] The amendments for the Columbia Institution were the last added to the Sundry Civil Appropriations bill. A few moments after they were agreed to, the bill was passed by the Senate. This was after midnight of March 3, 1869. This important bill then went at once to the Conference Committee, whose members had to be up all the rest of the night so that the bill could be reported to both Houses by 11 o'clock the following morning, in order to get the signature of the President before the final adjournment of Congress at noon on March 4.

It so happened that amid all the rush of sending this bill through no one, not even Mr. Washburne, thought of the $15,000 which had been the original sum which Washburne specified the school should get, if it got anything. So the $15,000 appropriation stayed in the Sundry Bill too, and was enacted into the law. Instead of the $30,000 for current expenses there was $45,000 to the Institution's credit at the Department of the Interior.

After five years of "raising up" a class of college men from raw material, the time had come for a first graduation. This would be the first public event celebrating the College since its inauguration in 1864. These exercises were held in the First Congregational Church at the corner of Tenth and G Streets, on June 23, 1869. Among those occupying the platform with the faculty and graduates were Amos Kendall, the Rev. Dr. George W. Samson, President of Columbian College (later to become George Washington University,) William W. Corcoran, Judge John Sherman, and General Oliver O. Howard, founder and President of Howard University.

In his *Memoirs* Gallaudet stated that the most interested and in-

teresting personage present was Kendall, then venerable and somewhat enfeebled by age, but full of life and vivacity. He regarded the
event as one of the great occasions of his life. His address to the
graduating class was eloquent and pathetic. At these exercises an
honorary master of arts degree was bestowed upon James Dension,
and similar degrees upon J. Scott Hutton of the Nova Scotia Institution and Richard Elliott of the London institution, whom Gallaudet
had visited in 1867. Following commencement the first alumni dinner
was held at the Kirkwood House in Washington. During dinner
Gallaudet heard William W. Corcoran, the banker and philanthropist,
say that he would rather have the satisfaction Mr. Kendall could
justly take at the development of the Columbia Institution than to be
the hero of Waterloo. Among the guests was Professor Joseph Henry
of the Smithsonian who had sustained Gallaudet five years before in
his plans for the organization of the College, in opposition to the
scheme advanced by Amos Kendall, and who had urged the propriety
of the federal government's full support of the College.

After the strenuous legislative season and the first commencement,
Gallaudet and his bride of six months were finally able to get away
for a belated wedding journey abroad. Gallaudet was grateful for
this means of regaining his strength of nerve and body, which, as the
sequel will show, was much needed for the work of the three years
that were to follow. Among the places they visited were Baden and
Doncaster. In later *Memoirs* Gallaudet recounted again seeing
Charles Baker in 1869, and it was on this trip that Baker really promised Gallaudet his rare books on the deaf should go to the library of
the college in Washington at his death. Mrs. Baker promised to let
Gallaudet know, and one year later Gallaudet got the message. [2]

Gallaudet opened the school year of 1869-1870 encouraged by the
increased enrollment, and the progress of the building program. By
October, however, he realized his old and true friend, Amos Kendall,
was ailing. Kendall had missed both Board meetings in the fall, his
last meeting having been on June 21, at which time the degrees had
been voted the first graduates. His last official act was in voting the
honorary degrees conferred at commencement. Gallaudet marked
that Kendall's mind was clear, and his spirits showed no depression
at the prospect of being soon called to leave the earth. He called
on Kendall for the last time in early November. "I shall never forget,"
he wrote, "the saintly, almost angelic appearance he presented as he
lay, white haired and with a face like marble, propped up by pillows.
His clear blue eyes shone with the lustre of young manhood and his

smile as he greeted me was full of sweetness." They chatted on a variety of subjects. Kendall expressed the greatest satisfaction that he had been permitted to live to see the establishment of the college assured, and spoke of the struggles all had gone through in attaining the goal. He said that he felt the future of the Institution was safe so long as Gallaudet headed it. He then bade an affectionate good-bye and Gallaudet left his presence heavy hearted, feeling that he had heard for the last time on earth "the voice of one who had been as a father" to him. Amos Kendall died on November 12, 1869.

"My memory of Amos Kendall is one of peculiar tenderness," Gallaudet wrote. "That he should give me the confidence he did when I came to Washington a youth of twenty was a great surprise. The internal management of the institution could not have been committed more absolutely to me than it was. I was invited to be present at every meeting of the Board, was always made Secretary pro-tem when Mr. Stickney was absent, and was treated in all respects as though I were a member of the Board, until at Mr. Kendall's suggestion I was elected to the Presidency in 1864." Differences of opinion had been settled most amicably, even the one about the diplomas, when Gallaudet had proposed they be filled in in Latin and Kendall had called a special meeting to argue the point in favor of English. In the meantime Gallaudet had looked into the matter and learned that a number of colleges did use the English; hence he had no further opposition to Kendall's proposal, which the Board adopted.

Gallaudet continued with his duties, and upon the retirement of Elihu B. Washburne as Chairman of the Committee on Appropriations two events occurred which were of the greatest importance and advantage to the College. Mr. Henry L. Dawes [3] of Massachusetts was appointed Chairman of the Committee on Appropriations and at the same time named by Speaker James G. Blaine as one of the members of Gallaudet's Board of Directors. Gallaudet was told by Dawes that Washburne, now Ambassador to France, had written him a long letter full of suggestions as to the business of the Appropriations Committee, and among them made a strong appeal to Dawes to "wipe the Deaf Mute College out of existence." Dawes was too level-headed to accept this narrow and prejudiced policy, and became a warm friend and earnest supporter of the College in Congress. At the first session of Congress after becoming Chairman of the Appropriations Committee, Dawes secured an appropriation of more than $100,000, over and above current expenses, for the completion of the Main Central Building which had been started in 1867 and was still unfinished.

A picture of E. M. G. at his desk in March 1900.   Photo was taken by a student.

Dr. Thomas Gallaudet, brother of E.M.G., with his wife Elizabeth in an **1895 photo**. He founded St. Ann's Church for the Deaf in New York City.   Note "bowler" on right.

It housed the world's first—and only—institution of higher education for the deaf.

An 1870 photo showing the buildings of Gallaudet College, chapel, and the primary sch

The winter wore on into the early part of 1870, when the executors of the Kendall estate offered for sale in small parcels the 81 acres of ground adjoining the premises of the Institution on the North and East. Gallaudet's immediate reaction was to recommend the purchase of the entire tract by the Institution with a double purpose in mind: to secure grounds of ample size for all time, and to protect the existing domain of about 19 acres from occupation by undesirable neighbors. Several viewed this scheme as bold since there was no sum of money in the treasury and the demands on Congress for buildings had been heavy. Gallaudet talked it over with President Samson of Columbian University who was strongly in favor of the purchase. Jacob D. Cox, then the Secretary of the Interior, ' gave similar advice. After Gallaudet had brought him to Kendall Green, to a point at the edge of the woods from which he had a commanding view of nearly the whole estate, Cox became enthusiastic at once for the purchase, saying he would not hesitate, but would trust to Providence for the means to pay for the property.

With this backing Gallaudet brought the matter before his Board. The Directors immediately adopted a liberal policy. With only $5,000 in hand they voted to buy Kendall Green for $85,000. Negotiations were concluded by March of 1870, with the agreement that the property should be transferred on April 1, on which date Gallaudet would have to sign as President of the Institution notes for $80,000, with a mortgage to secure the loan. The birth of Susy's first child, Denison, on April 1 postponed the signing, and so the signatures for the transferrence of property were signed April 2.

Gallaudet's original contract with the Columbia Institution stipulated that he would have to raise funds for his school. Although he had done this for 13 years the real push was yet to come. During the winter of 1870-1871 he determined to secure about $20,000 from Congress to help pay for Kendall Green. He succeeded in getting the amount put in the Sundry Civil Bill in the Senate, and obtained the approval of the Committee of Conference. Feeling reasonably safe from resistance he was greatly surprised that Mr. Dawes, Chairman of the Appropriations Committee and a member of his Board of Directors, had the Bill recalled from the Senate and the item stricken out. This filled Gallaudet with consternation since he had consulted Dawes in regard to the purchase of Kendall Green, and had understood him to be favorable. Bitterly disappointed, Gallaudet turned to private subscription, enlisting President Grant's interest and obtaining a letter from him commending the college to his friends.

With this letter Gallaudet visited Philadelphia [5] and was able to secure several $250 subscriptions. Among the subscribers were the Hon. A. E. Bone and A. J. Drexel. James L. Claghorn, whom he had met abroad in 1867, gave a dinner for him at the Union League Club at which Joseph Harrison and other prominent men were present. [6]

Gallaudet called on Clement Biddle, who received him rather coldly, although Gallaudet stated his cause as well as he could. Mr. Biddle turned to his check book with a pretty severe look on his face. "How much did you say you wanted?" he called to Gallaudet over his shoulder, to which Gallaudet replied, mustering up courage, "I am trying to get ten subscriptions of $250 each, but of course I cannot dictate the amount." Biddle's only reply was a "H'm," but he continued to scratch away in his check book. He handed Gallaudet a check for $250 with a grim smile on a very old, wrinkled face. He admonished Gallaudet to "keep on, not to become discouraged with refusals they won't all say no."

From Philadelphia Gallaudet travelled to Hartford, then to Boston, actually begging for his school, and was rewarded by the receipt of nearly $10,000 from the three cities—enough to pay the maturing obligations [7] on the Kendall Green purchase.

It was during the winter of 1870-1871 that Gallaudet had occasion to confer with James G. Blaine, then the Speaker of the House, in regard to the appointment of the two Directors from the House. The first such appointment of Directors had been made in 1868 by Speaker Schuyler Colfax, who named two Republicans: Hon. Henry L. Dawes of Massachusetts and Hon. N. Boyden of North Carolina. Following this precedent Mr. Blaine's first appointments in 1869 had been Mr. Dawes and the Hon. William H. Kelsey of New York, the latter being of the same party as Mr. Dawes. During this period, however, the number of Democratic members of the House was very small. This seemed to Gallaudet an undesirable situation. He believed his House Directors should be appointed from both parties. He brought this out in his talk with Speaker Blaine, suggesting that as Mr. Kelsey was to be no longer in the House his place should be filled by a Democrat.

This appealed to Blaine. He winked at Gallaudet, seeming quite amused. "You are looking ahead, aren't you?" he asked. Within a few days he had reappointed Mr. Dawes and named the Hon. James Brooks of New York as the Director. This manner of appointing Directors from the House was followed by all succeeding Speakers.

By autumn of 1871 Gallaudet submitted with his ordinary estimates to Congress one of $70,000 to pay off the obligations from the purchase of Kendall Green. He did not feel encouraged about raising this balance by private means. At this time a good friend of the College, General James A. Garfield,° was Chairman of the Committee on Appropriations. Where Dawes had opposed asking Congress to pay for Kendall Green, Garfield was friendly to the measure, being disposed, however, to having Gallaudet ask for the appropriation in the Senate, promising to do what he could to save it in Conference Committee.

Senator Edmunds of Vermont,° who was on the Appropriations Committee, had become warmly interested in the College, partly through Mrs. Edmund's friendship for Mrs. Gallaudet, both being Vermonters, and partly because one of Senator Edmund's childhood playmates was a deaf son of the late Senator Phelps of Vermont, with whom he had learned to communicate by means of the manual alphabet. Senator Edmunds promised Gallaudet to do his best to get his committee to put the $70,000 in the Sundry Civil Bill. The winter dragged on and Gallaudet was not feeling well physically, yet went ahead with his work.

Relying greatly on Senator Edmund's promise to get the $70,000 through the Senate Gallaudet was disturbed on the morning the appropriation bill was to come up when he received a note from Mrs. Edmunds saying that her husband was ill in bed. She advised him to go to the Committee room and do the best he could, with the assurance of Edmund's continued interest in the measure. Gallaudet's heart sank within him but he lost no time in reaching the Senate Committee room. He was fortunate in knowing quite well Senator Cole of California, Chairman of the Committee, and Senators Roscoe Conkling, William Windom, and William Sprague, prominent members of the Committee. He had a friend also in Mr. Pickard, the Clerk of the Committee—a quiet but clear-headed man from Maine who had been Clerk for many years.

When Gallaudet reached the Committee room he found Mr. Pickard there alone, and was disheartened to learn from him that there would be no formal meeting of the Committee that day; that the bill was practically completed and would be reported to the Senate in the afternoon. Gallaudet quickly informed Pickard how interested Senate Edmunds was in the measure, showing him Edmund's note and adding that General Garfield had promised his support if the Senate put the amount in the bill. Pickard promised to put the item on, but Gallaudet left the Committee room with very little hope of success.

Later in the forenoon he saw Senator Cole who was disposed to let the item stay, but the session was so near the close that Gallaudet was unable to see Conkling, Windom, and Sprague. However, in the afternoon when Gallaudet knew the bill had been reported to the Senate he went to Mr. Pickard for news, learning that the item had stayed in. It seems that Conkling had looked over the bill and when he learned that it was for Gallaudet, and that Edmunds wanted it too, he had endorsed it, and Windom and Sprague had done the same. Luckily Senator Edmunds recovered in time to give his countenance and support to the measure and it passed the Senate without opposition. [10]

TIME OUT FOR HEALTH

Gallaudet had passed through a hectic and trying time. There had been months of Congressional activity, the negotiations for Kendall Green, the planning and superintending of the erection of buildings, and the heavy executive duties and teaching. It was during this period that Gallaudet's second son, Edson Fessenden, was born, April 21, 1871. By the early part of 1872 Gallaudet's health began to give way in an alarming manner. The pressure of the long fight with Washburne had also been a factor, proving too much for the physical and nervous endurance of a young man of 35. A great sense of fatigue was upon him. He would awaken every morning at about 3 o'clock, his brain actively at work on his duties. He sought the advice of his physician, Dr. Nathan Lincoln, who recommended a prolonged rest after June, preferably a whole year, since continued activity might mean death. Edward was given a prescription of phosphorous and other strong tonics. Some days he hardly knew what he did. The Board of Directors with their usual consideration voted him a year's leave of absence with salary, and a gift of $1,500 to help meet the expenses of his family for a year's stay in Europe, where his doctor had advised him to go. It was in this condition of nervous prostration that Gallaudet had made an almost dying effort to secure the means of saving Kendall Green from reverting to its heirs.

Gallaudet thought his bill in Congress was safe, since it had the promise of Gen. Garfield's favor in the House. He was therefore staggered by Garfield's declaration that in order to win the Committee's backing for the $70,000 he must have the clear and definite approval of the Directors from the House, Messrs. Dawes and Brooks.

Knowing that Dawes was against this appropriation Gallaudet again went through mental strain, finally deciding to write Dawes a letter in which he would state how it was within Dawes' power to secure the $70,000 for the Institution or to prevent it. He placed this letter in the hands of Dawes' daughter, Miss Anna, a very good friend of both the Gallaudets, who was known to exert a great influence with her father. Gallaudet confided that he was depending on her to bring her father around from his position of opposition. She did not fail Gallaudet. He soon learned from Gen. Garfield that Messrs. Dawes and Brooks had given their approval to the measure and that the Committee had agreed to it.

The Sundry Civil bill, with the $70,000 in, passed the House, and Gallaudet's anxiety was ended. He closed up the business of the term with a thankful heart, drew the $70,000 from the treasury, paid off the mortgage on Kendall Green, put all his private affairs in such shape as would make a settlement of his estate easy if he never returned, and sailed for Europe in July of 1872. He was accompanied by his wife, daughters Katharine and Grace, sons Dension and Edson (one 27 months and the other 15 months old), the faithful nurse Mary Keely, Susy's nephew Will Denison and his cousin Gertrude Denison, who would study abroad; and his niece, 21-year-old Virginia Gallaudet, his brother Thomas' daughter, who would act as Susy's companion, and whose expenses he paid. Amos G. Draper, just graduated from the College, went for the summer at his own expense.

They travelled on the Cunard Steamer *Abyssinia* to Liverpool. After short stops in Chester and London they journeyed to Switzerland via Brussels, Cologne, the Rhine, Heidelberg, Basle, and Berne, locating in the Pension Picaud. While the family remained there, Draper and Gallaudet made a tour of a few weeks in Switzerland, Italy, and Germany. When they reached Paris, Gallaudet was summoned back to Geneva because of the severe illness of Edson. After he had sufficiently recovered, Gallaudet moved his family to Belle Rive, the charming home, turned pension, of the DuRoveray family, which was destined to become a "second home" to them. Gallaudet's health did not improve perceptibly during the summer, but he was able to travel and enjoy a good deal. This sizeable menage was more than he should have undertaken at such a time, and Susy apparently did not help matters by her attitude. Yet she certainly had her problems too. Four children were not easy for a 25-year-old mother to handle in strange surroundings, especially when two were not her own and were of an age to ask questions. However, matters settled themselves before long.

In his *Memoirs* as well as in his *Occasionals* Gallaudet recalled vividly when he began to feel his health coming back. About the 20th of November he was walking out from Geneva to Belle Rive when he became suddenly conscious of a change in his system—so great as to induce him to say aloud, "From this moment I am well!" He ran, jumped, and shouted as he continued his way to Belle Rive, and from that day he declared he felt 10 to 15 years younger.

During the autumn he wrote a monograph on "The Ethics of Friendship" and translated a large part of Calvo's *Le Droit International*. For the four years after his return home he would work on this, seeking advice from experts in the field of international law until he evolved a manual. His interest in the subject was paramount to his other fields of thinking. While at Belle Rive he received an appointment from Hamilton Fish, Secretary of State, to be an Honorary Commissioner of the United States for the Vienna Exposition of 1873. This Commission carried a special passport. Gallaudet's Report of the Exposition was published by the United States Government Printing Office in 1875, and with its publication he had taken his first step toward becoming an acknowledged educational ambassador.

In January of 1873 Susy and Virginia, with the boys and their nurse, accompanied Gallaudet to Leipsig where they stayed three months. Kitty, Grace, and Gertrude Denison stayed at Belle Rive, and Will Denison was at a boarding school near Geneva. They heard fine music and mingled in the society of professors in the university. They returned to Belle Rive in April, and in May Gallaudet took Susy and Virginia to Vienna to see "Welt Ausstellung." From there they travelled to the Villa d'Este, on Lake Como. It was here that Edward and Susy seemed to iron out their difficulties. It was truly a time of joy for them both.

By September of 1873 they sailed home, greatly benefitted by their year abroad. Gallaudet's health seemed completely restored and he resumed his duties at Washington with zest and enthusiasm. Although he had visited schools for the deaf while abroad he had found nothing he deemed worthy of reporting; no facts came to his notice which served to change the conclusions set forth in his 1867 Report. During his absence Professor Fay had assumed the duties of Acting President, and affairs had progressed successfully.

Although the country was on the eve of a money panic, and banks had begun to fail in New York City by the latter part of September,

Gallaudet made no allusion to it in his *Memoirs* even though his 1873 Report showed a deficit of $10,697.46. He did not feel that it was proper or wise to borrow again a portion of the annual appropriation for the support of the Institution, which the Board had previously advised. And since the real estate of the Institution was vested in the United States, he ventured in his 1873 Report to direct the attention of Congress to this indebtedness, and to ask that an appropriation be made. He also published a full list of the donors to the purchase of Kendall Green.

In 1874 Gallaudet made the purchase of the Baker Library, already referred to, and he published in his Report an estimate of funds he thought would be needed to complete his building program. Including the deficit of $10,697, the figures showed that between 1864-1874 Congress would have contributed $115,697. This, he felt, compared favorably with the cost of such government establishments as the Military and Naval Academies, the Insane Hospital of the District, and many of the recently constructed state institutions.

It was also in 1874 that a change was made in the old College custom of having annual public exercises at the end of the academic year, when the weather is almost certain to be hot. Gallaudet conceived the idea of having the anniversary exercises in May and of calling the occasions Presentation Day, a term formerly used at Yale University. The Seniors were presented as candidates for degrees rather than as recipients of degrees, which would come after their final examinations. Such a large gathering often included ambassadors, Government officials, and other dignitaries. Often the President of the United States presided in his role of Patron of the Institution, as when President Grant dedicated the Main Building upon its completion during the winter of 1871, at exercises held January 29 in the hall of the new building. At the proper moment Grant arose and in his usual cryptic manner uttered the words: "Ladies and Gentlemen: I hereby pronounce to be complete the dedication of this institution to the humane purposes to which it has been assigned by the various acts of Congress making appropriations for its erection and support." From President Grant through President Theodore Roosevelt, the only President who failed to visit the College since it had observed public anniversaries was McKinley. Taft promised to appear, but at the last moment was detained by official business.

It was during the winter of 1873-74 that Gallaudet presented his final plans for the completion of the College Building. This was discussed by his Board in the room of the Senate Committee on the

Judiciary, of which Senator George F. Edmunds of Vermont was Chairman. Edmunds had succeeded Senator Patterson as a member of Gallaudet's Board. The present argument involved the matter of the ornamental stone work of the exterior design. Edmunds, while friendly to the College, was nonetheless economical, and Gallaudet feared he might object to the ornamentations. Immediately after Gallaudet explained the plan Edmunds put his finger on the stone ornamentation design and asked how much it would cost to finish the building without it. Bravely Gallaudet answered, "About $10,000." At that moment there was a rap on the door and Edmunds was called out. As he left he addressed the whole Board, asking to be excused and saying he would stand by any decision they reached. William E. Niblack, a Board member and judge from Indiana, noted for his liberality to educational and scientific enterprises, moved that the plans be adopted, and soon they were. Niblack later told Gallaudet that he saw no use in losing time for Edmunds might have appeared at any minute!

ACADEMIC NEEDS

Gallaudet had not neglected the basic reason for the Institution's existence, which was the Course of Study. [11] Beginning in his 1872 Report he ran outlines of the studies, with the names of textbooks for each year. Among the textbooks listed is found the *Prendergast Mastery Method of Learning German,* the author being Thomas Prendergast whom he had met in London April of 1867, and under whose tutelage he had picked up the German language so quickly.

Other names noted are James Dwight Dana, the scientist, and Theodore S. Woolsey, authority on international law. In his 1875 Report Gallaudet paid particular attention to the listing of the Course of Study for the Lower and Higher Preparatory years, and to the Undergraduate studies. He made a point of showing the integration of all the studies, revealing his ideas for electives early in his planning. For instance, Greek was optional while Latin was not, and prominence was given to French and German and a critical study of English, including the History of the English language and of English Literature, with frequent exercises in original composition required of all students.

Gallaudet's friend, Joseph Henry of the Smithsonian Institution, addressed the graduates on April 26, 1876. During the course of his speech he told his audience that "Institutions for the education of the deaf and dumb illustrate in a striking manner civilization of the present age in contrast with those of the past . . . . The scientific examination papers of last year were submitted to me for report as to their character; while they involved the solution of questions in mathematics, physics, chemistry, geology, etc., requiring accurate knowledge and profound thought, *the answers were such* as to do honor to the undergraduates of any college in this country." He also told his listeners—including Daniel Coit Gilman, President of the newly formed Johns Hopkins University; the Hon. Zachariah Chandler, Secretary of the Interior; and the Rev. I. L. Townsend, Chaplain of the House of Representatives—that in 1864 Gallaudet had submitted to him for examination a plan of a graduated course, terminating in a collegiate curriculum. He now expressed his happiness over the outcome of the experiment, and paid high tribute to the attainments of the deaf scholars.

Following Henry's talk, President Gilman, whose academic career had been phenomenal, addressed the audience which included several of his associates of the Johns Hopkins Foundation. He told of the pleasure it gave him to witness the attainments of the young men before him, and referred to his trip over on the train that morning when he had read telegrams from Paris describing "the brilliant assemblage which was held but yesterday, April 25, in the capital of France to commemorate and perpetuate the ties of friendship between the Americans and the French." [12] He related this directly to the good will France had shown to an American in 1815, when Thomas Hopkins Gallaudet had studied with the Abbé Sicard in Paris, bringing back to America the art and knowledge of teaching the deaf and dumb. He spoke of the "Catholic and the Huguenot, the teacher and the scholar, by whose joint labors, once united and then far apart, this College has been made possible." He spoke of knowing something of the difficulties encountered by skillful teachers in training the minds of those who have the use of all their senses, and wondered at the success of those who teach only by appeals to the eye, while the portal of the ear, on which so many ordinary teachers exclusively rely, remains closed to their instructions. As a rule Gallaudet interpreted such addresses himself in the sign language, for the benefit of the deaf in his audience.

In June of this same year the Emperor of Brazil paid a visit to Kendall Green. Dom Pedro d'Alcantara, who was to be the last Emperor before Brazil became a Republic, was touring the United States and on his visit to Kendall Green was accompanied by le Vicomte de Bom Retiro, Chamberlain to his Majesty, and Senor

A. P. de Carvalho Borges, Brazilian Minister. Receiving with Gallaudet was General John Eaton, the United States Commissioner of Education, by whom the officers of the Institution were presented to the distinguished visitors. Dom Pedro showed the greatest interest in the work of the College, and sat down by one of the students in a classroom and put his arm around him, questioning him on his studies. As his visit came to an end, the Emperor planted an ivy vine at an angle in the Terrace Wall, receiving it from the hand of Gallaudet's mother. Professor Amos G. Draper, who later wrote a sketch of Mrs. Gallaudet's life, referred to this occasion: "Each of them advanced in years, each still retained much of the precious dew of youth. Each seemed to enter at once with kindred spirit into the emotions of the other. They were both of imposing but kindly presence and most courteous manners. It was like a meeting between sovereigns." Dom Pedro had been to the Centennial Exhibition at Philadelphia where he met Alexander Graham Bell, who was exhibiting his "telephone" there, and when Bell's speil caught the ear of the Emperor he and his entourage stopped to gawk and attracted quite a crowd.

On June 28 Gallaudet took his student body on an excursion to Philadelphia to see the Exhibition, and in all probability met Bell too, although he never referred to the incident. Bell was in Washington showing his telephones to the Philosophical Society in 1877, and as a member Gallaudet might have heard him. Bell and Gallaudet were destined to become friendly enemies in the ensuing years.

It was in June of 1874 that a daughter was born to the Gallaudets whom they named in honor of Susy's mother, Eliza (Skinner) Denison. Called by the pet name of Ellie, she grew up to be a child "beautiful in spirit and in person." In 1875 the family spent the summer in Vermont to escape the Washington heat. No sooner had they settled than all of the children caught whooping cough from a neighbor's child. Baby Ellie was seized with dysentery before recovering from the cough and for ten days was dangerously ill. The village physician was unable to cope with the situation and on August 28 Ellie died. Her death was a life long sorrow to the devoted parents.

In the summer of 1876 son Denison suffered a severe fever which the family thought was caused by exposure to the sun. The result was a paralysis of his right ankle from the effects of which he never fully recovered, even though Gallaudet sought the finest medical care. He took Dennie to Philadelphia to the famous neurologist (and novelist) Dr. S. Weir Mitchell, who predicted that Dennie would overcome the limp somewhat as he grew older. However,

"Dennie's affliction" was a great trial to his parents, and Gallaudet continued to seek aid, having special shoes made for him and keeping in touch with the latest medical advice.

In September of 1876 another child was born, on the 12th, named Herbert Draper, his middle name given in honor of Gallaudet's cherished friend Amos Draper. In the years to come Gallaudet was to see fulfilled in this child one of his own cherished dreams of earlier years, that of being a minister.

The year of 1876-1877 was marked for one of quiet prosperity in the Institution generally. In his Annual Report of 1876 Gallaudet made an appeal to the governments of the respective states of the Union to make provision for the support of beneficiary students in the College. This move was brought about by the recurrent arguments of Board members as to the constitutional duties of the federal government to provide the free education of students from the states. Judge William E. Niblack was urgent in his opinion on the point, and later J. Randolph Tucker of Virginia would be just as insistent when he became a Board member. [13] The Hon. Frank Hiscock of New York, when Chairman of the Committee on Appropriations, took this ground but finally said after a visit to the Institution: 'If this were before me as a new measure I should feel bound, on principle, to oppose it; but since the Institution has the sanction of many enactments of Congress I suppose there is nothing left for me to do but to vote for the means to run it."

After Niblack started the discussion in 1876 Gallaudet prepared the communications and sent them to the Governors of the States, and made it a matter of record that not over two or three acknowledgments ever came back to him. His own position was clear: he held that it was entirely equitable for the United States government to provide for the higher education of the deaf of the States since they were barred by their infirmity from participating in the benefits of the great Agricultural College Grants which Congress had made to all the States. He used this argument many times to members of Congress and never found an able answer to it. However, Gallaudet's main labor during this year was the superintendence of the erection of the College Building, the ornamentation of which has already been mentioned.

In May of 1877, while visiting with her son on Kendall Green, Mrs. Thomas Hopkins Gallaudet was stricken with apoplexy. That same day Gallaudet had taken his mother to the city to change her glasses. She had enjoyed the ride very much and had seemed unusually bright. That evening Gallaudet and Susy went to make a social visit to Dr. Nathan Lincoln, the school physician, and when they returned they found Mrs. Gallaudet in her attitude of prayer, but insensible. She lingered only a few hours. Funeral services were held in the Chapel, exactly 20 years from the day on which Amos Kendall had written the young Edward a letter asking him to become the Head of the little school Kendall had founded. Mrs. Gallaudet's body was taken to Hartford for burial. The services were held in the Old Center Church, with all living children present and many of her grandchildren. Pupils of the American School, which her husband had founded, put flowers on the coffin, and the body was laid beside that of her husband who had been separated from her by death 26 years before.

The summer of 1877 was spent visiting relatives in Durham and Guilford, Connecticut, and Grandfather Fessenden in Hartford, where Katharine celebrated her sixteenth birthday. Gallaudet attended the Commencement ceremonies at Trinity College and again walked with his brother Thomas in the procession and heard him give an oration. He attended the festival of Trinity's Beta Beta Chapter of Psi Upsilon before taking his family to the seashore, at Indian Neck near Branford. Periodically he would leave them a few days to make hurried trips to Washington to his work while his children developed friendships with the children of his old friends in Connecticut.

During this summer of 1877 Gallaudet read a paper at Saratoga before the Social Science Association, taking Mr. Draper with him for short trips en route, including a visit to Washington Irving's home.

The years passed quickly as the Institution assumed its final form, and the internal management expanded to keep pace with the building program. Gallaudet's brother who had acted as Family Supervisor since 1868 lost his health in 1871, and the domestic affairs were then handled by the Matron and her Assistant. Melville Ballard or another male Instructor often helped, for it was difficult to find suitable men for the position. Much of the arrangement and labor devolved upon Gallaudet, from which he was anxious to be relieved. In the autumn of 1877 he selected John B. Wight, a native Washingtonian who had been in the hardware business and had served as the Superintendent of the Sunday School. He soon became Gallaudet's right hand man. He was quick at understanding the methods of management and possessed a cheerful disposition. He also acted as office clerk when James C. Balis, class of '75, resigned to accept an instructor's position in the Maryland School. [14]

In 1878 the Anniversary of the Incorporation of the Institution was observed. In writing any list of names in his diaries or journals Gallaudet always referred to women by their husband's titles—and to men by their titles. His list for the above occasion named among those present the "President of the United States and Mrs. Hayes; Vice President William A. Wheeler, who was for two years a Director of the Institution; Mrs. Speaker Samuel J. Randall (the Speaker of the House of Representatives being unavoidably absent); Senators Edmunds and Dawes, and Governor Claflin of Massachusetts; Congressional Directors of the Institution and their ladies; the Corporate Directors and their families; Frederick Withers of New York, architect of the new buildings; Members of the House; Mr. and Mrs. Robert Fox and Mr. and Mrs. E. C. Cutter, the ladies being daughters of the late Amos Kendall; and the Hon. Dudley Chase Denison, Mrs. Gallaudet's grand-uncle." [15]

Gallaudet recorded some interesting sidelights of this occasion. President Hayes kissed baby Herbert, 17 months old, and Mrs. Hayes performed a gracious act while inspecting the rooms of the building. As the party came to Mr. Draper's apartment, where a fire was laid, he asked her to apply a match to the first fire the chimney was to receive. With a gracious smile she stooped down and presently the firelight of the new hearth was illuminating the room. It was also on this occasion, Gallaudet recalled, that Mr. Dawes made public acknowledgment of the change of heart he had experienced in 1872 as to the purchase of Kendall Green; but he failed to give his daughter Anna the credit that was due her for bringing this about.

At the Presentation Day exercises on May 1 General Garfield made an earnest and eloquent speech, declaring his continued interest in the College and his gratification that he had been able to help forward its interests in Congress. Gallaudet later found that the *Journal de Bruxelles* of August 13, 1878, contained an appreciative article about the College from the pen of Monseigneur de Haerne, referring to the degree of master of arts which the College had conferred upon O. F. Kruse, the German deaf-mute who had distinguished himself as a teacher and writer. The article said that this was a powerful encouragement to deaf-mutes in general, in as much as this honor conferred upon one of their number tended to raise them all in the social scale by removing the barrier which in the eyes of the world separated them in their instruction from the rest of society. [16]

The outstanding event of 1879, according to Gallaudet, was the splendid address made by President Noah Porter of Yale at the

Presentation Day Exercises.   He spoke on "Modern Teaching: Its Opportunities and Its Perils."   In this address his theme was "Modern Education in three aspects of Research, Exposition, and Examination —or the Modern Instructor as a Student, as Teacher, and as Examiner of the work of his pupils."   In introducing President Porter, Gallaudet called attention to the fact that Yale University had furnished an unusually large number of teachers of the deaf from among her graduates, beginning in 1805 with his own father.[17]

In writing his 1879 Report Gallaudet introduced for the first time his plans for a gymnasium.   How well he remembered the beautiful pools in the Scandinavian countries, and in Russia!   What a wonderful addition they were to the health and happiness of the school children.   He submitted an estimate for a gymnasium in this year. Another important event of this year was the birth of a daughter, Marion Wallace, who would be their last child.

Taking Stock of Resources

In bringing to a close the first 22 years of the Institution's existence Gallaudet could show for his work a primary department complete in its appointments; the inauguration of a college program which had already demonstrated its success; and the broad domain of Kendall Green, with its buildings complete, and its resources, assured by the legislation of Congress, sufficient for the work it had to do. From now on the Institution would enter upon a new existence, having successfully weathered its formative and experimental stages. Henceforth its work would be in the line of direct, untrammelled, feasible educational effort, with teacher preparation a definite aim for promoting the philosophy of the Institution.

The earliest graduate, Melville Ballard, was an instructor in the Primary Department of the Institution,[1] From the class of 1869 came the Principal of the Western Pennsylvania Institution for Deaf-Mutes in Pittsburgh, the principal examiner of the U.S. Patent Office, and a professor of the National Deaf-Mute College. The class of 1870 supplied the principal teacher of the young deaf-mute institution of Oregon, and instructors in the deaf-mute schools of Connecticut, Ohio, Tennessee, and Ontario, Canada. The class of 1872 contributed a professor of the National Deaf-Mute College, the editor and publisher of a newspaper in Massachusetts, the head of a school for deaf-mutes in Cincinnati, and teachers in the schools of Nebraska and Mississippi. From the later classes teachers were furnished to the states of Minnesota, Iowa, West Virginia, Maryland, Indiana, Ohio, New York, and Pennsylvania; one became an accomplished draftsman in the office of a New York architect, and another was taken into a lawyer's office in Columbus, Ohio. It was estimated that the graduates of the Columbia Institution were training upward of 400 children and youth in the deaf-mute institutions of this country and Canada.

The course of study had been examined and carefully outlined in

Gallaudet's 1878 address on Presentation Day, and his whole program, between 1870 and 1880, showed evidence of remarkable achievement in coordinating sections of an educational institution into a cohesive whole. From one small wooden structure the Columbia Institution had developed into a fine group of well-equipped brick buildings, and the many ideas gleaned abroad by Gallaudet in 1867 had been incorporated into working realities for promotion of the intellectual growth and physical well-being of its students. Such achievement for his Institution took constant thought and effort, for Gallaudet acted as his own public relations officer. Paris had recognized his ability with a diploma and medal from its Exposition of 1878, awarded to the College for its advanced work in educating the deaf. But regardless of the Institution's fame abroad there were those in Congress who still wanted to cripple its work, or at least keep its officers in a state of agitation.

As 1880 neared the debate took place in Congress on the long-hackneyed argument of proposing to charge one-half of the expenses of the Institution to the District of Columbia Treasury. Although the effort of these men failed, Gallaudet felt deeply chagrined that, in spite of all his labors and the fact that the Institution had many friends in Congress, there still remained on Capitol Hill those who made bold to legislate on matters to which they had given little study. In his *Memoirs* Gallaudet wrote out this full debate on the Sundry Civil Appropriations, showing how the writer of the bill managed to get the whole scheme tangled up with Gallaudet's request for an appropriation for a gymnasium. This is how it stood: "For erection and fitting up of a gymnasium for the use of students and pupils $5,000, and for the improvement and enclosure of the grounds of the institution $2,500; in all $7,500: Provided, that hereafter one-half of the expenses of the institution shall be paid out of the revenues of the District of Columbia."

Those taking part in the debate in the House were Eppa Hunton of Virginia, James Henderson Blount of Georgia, Joseph Roswell Hawley of Connecticut, [2] William Drew Washburn of Minnesota, and Henry Sanford Neal of Ohio. Gallaudet stated that General Hawley's friendliness to the Institution and his ability in debate were conspicuous. When the question was taken up following the motion of Mr. Hunton to strike out the proviso, the division lay ayes 77—noes 48; and so it was stricken from the measure.

Earlier in the story there was reference to Thaddeus Stevens and his work for the Institution. An incident had aroused his ire. A constituent from Pennsylvania had wanted to enter a son in the college and had found through Gallaudet that there were not enough free scholarships in the college. No law allowed Gallaudet to enter or accept the young man. "There should be such a law," Stevens had announced. It followed that the proviso was added authorizing the free admission of 10 deaf-mutes from any of the states and territories of the United States. One of these scholarships went to Stevens' constituent and he made a creditable record.

The number of free scholarships was increased from 10 to 25 in 1868. In 1871 Congress increased the number of free scholarships to 40, and in that year 23 states and the District of Columbia were represented in the college. The number was increased again in 1889, to 60, and in 1900 Congress upped the number of scholarships to 100, through Speaker David B. Henderson's effort.

The enlargement of the college dormitory was completed in 1877; the gymnasium in 1881, and a building for the primary department in 1885. The latter was named "The Kendall School." In 1886 Congress would make an appropriation for a new laboratory, to which an addition would be made in 1895. Still in the offing was co-education, a normal department, a dormitory for the younger boys, and plans for a technical department. Many struggles were bound up in the execution of these plans, but the men interested in seeing the schemes developed would not stop fighting for the college and school.

Constant vigilance was necessary, for oftentimes plans that seemed settled had the strangest ways of going awry. Three times the Interior Department insisted that it should control the disbursements of the Institution. [3] The first time this was proposed the matter was settled in favor of the Institution by a decision of Assistant Attorney General McCammon of the Interior Department, and in the second instance by an opinion in the Institution's favor by Acting Attorney General Holmes Conrad.

The third time the matter came up, in 1897, the prime mover was a man named Acker, then the head of the Miscellaneous Division of the Interior Department. He sought Attorney General McKenna's opinion without alerting the Institution. It so happened that Rep. Sereno E. Payne of New York, the leader of the House, was on Gallaudet's Board and a personal friend of Secretary of Interior Cornelius N. Bliss, also of New York. Senator Hawley of Connecticut accompanied Gallaudet to the Attorney General's office and they saw Mr. McKenna and Soliciter General Richards who had written the "opinion." Both were quite set in their views and neither

Hawley nor Gallaudet could budge them. The following day Gallaudet went alone and talked to Assistant Secretary Thomas Ryan, who had been a member of the Institution's Board when he was in the House of Representatives. Judge Ryan told Gallaudet that Secretary Bliss, who was in New York, cared nothing about controlling the Institution, and suggested that it would be easy to get legislation from Congress to override the Attorney General's opinion.

Two of Gallaudet's Board members advised him to seek counsel of some eminent lawyer. Gallaudet chose a leading Washington lawyer, R. Ross Perry, who thought the matter could be put into good shape without difficulty if Secretary of the Interior Bliss would acquiesce in the course proposed. Mr. Ackers added another disagreeable note: he wrote a letter claiming the Institution was paying unreasonably high prices for many articles. Gallaudet had to take time to prove this charge was without foundation. He made an appointment with Secretary Bliss and took General John W. Foster and Sereno E. Payne with him. Bliss assured them he would interpose no objection to their securing legislation from Congress to settle matters as Gallaudet's Board wished. The Board agreed to the course Gallaudet suggested, of seeking legal advice.

When Congress first enacted legislation governing appointment to the Institution's Board it had limited the Director's services to the term of a single Congress, thus leaving the Board without Directors from March 4 to the first Monday in December, in alternate years. Gallaudet now drew up new legislation which he referred to Mr. Perry, who let it stand as written. This new legislation provided that Directors appointed under the provisions of section 4863 of the Revised Statutes of the United States should remain in office until the appointment and acceptance of office of their successors: and the Directors of the Institution should have control of the disbursement of all moneys appropriated by Congress for the benefit of the Institution, accounts for which should be settled and adjusted at the Treasury Department as required by the provisions of section 236 of the Revised Statutes.

This was secured after much labor. Gallaudet believed that Acker exerted himself a good deal in opposition to the measure. Interviews with Representatives Joseph D. Sayers and Joseph G. Cannon[4] satisfied Gallaudet that they had been "labored with" by the opposition. Mr. Sayers was a member of the Institution's Board at the time, and a hostile attitude on his part would have been damaging to the Institution's cause. This matter dragged on into the next year at which time the Conference Committee finally agreed to the Institution's proviso. Always after such a fight and victory Gallaudet felt ten years younger.

It was in 1888 that Gallaudet contended with Samuel J. Randall in Congress. Randall, when a Member of Congress in 1880-1881, had spoken at the College on Presentation Day. Now, as Chairman of the House Committee on Appropriations, he was making an effort to cut down the Institution's appropriations for current expenses. Without calling Gallaudet before the Committee he had cut the annual support fund $5,000, and had the Sundry Civil Bill reported to the House. Gallaudet's Directors advised him to try and get the cut restored. He called on Randall and told him that such a cut would seriously cripple the Institution if Congress sustained it. Randall was unmoved. Gallaudet then told him he would try to get the Senate to restore it; this so infuriated Randall that he shouted. "If you try that I will make you sorry for it."

Undaunted, Gallaudet put the matter up to his friends in the Senate and they did restore the $5,000, but Randall fought this in Conference and succeeded in cutting out $2,500. Gallaudet had to wait until the following session to get the amount put into the deficiency bill.

When the winter session of 1888 opened and Gallaudet showed up to renew his fight for appropriations, Randall seemed rather jovial and asked him if he had come for his "post mortem." Randall was actually ill, but that did not deter him from trying to restrict the current expense appropriation and limit the salaries and wages of the Institution to the absolute sum of $25,000. He also attempted to do away with free admissions to the College. Burnes of Missouri, who worked in support of Randall, was invited by Gallaudet to visit the College. He accepted but did not show up. Between the 13th and the 24th of the month Burnes died, but Randall carried on, using his power as Chairman of the Committee on Appropriations and holding to his measure. However, the proviso forbidding the poor students in the College free board was amended so as to make the law much more favorable than it had been. "The debate," wrote Gallaudet, "was long and animated and developed a feeling of marked friendliness to the Institution in the House." Two of his Directors, Robert R. Hitt and John J. Hemphill, worked nobly for the Institution. In this struggle against Randall, Senators William B. Allison, Eugene Hale, and Arthur F. Gorman were helpful and friendly. The battle ended with the close of Congress, Gallaudet getting a handsome increase in the appropriations for salaries as well as an increase in the number of beneficiaries.

A young man from Randall's state had asked him for an appointment and Randall had refused it. The boy's father turned to Gallaudet, who went to Randall, who still refused it. Gallaudet then asked permission to write the boy's father. Randall, who was ill in bed, rose on his elbow and told Gallaudet he would conduct his own correspondence with his constituents. The boy missed a year of college because of this, but when Randall's successor was appointed after his death the boy was recommended. It was not until 1890 that Congress approved the passage of a bill repealing the legislation which forbade giving free board to students of the College. Gallaudet secured the friendly cooperation of Joseph G. Cannon, then Chairman of the House Committee on Appropriations, who prepared a paragraph which gave the Institution the right to receive and care for its free students.

IX

Marking Time Constructively

In 1880 Gallaudet moved into a fresh arena of social activity. His 1880 diary, which marked the beginning of his year-by-year, day-by-day diary keeping, told of his having dinner with Alexander Graham Bell. It was quite an occasion, with Mrs. Bell's newly engaged sister, her fiancè, and a dinner served "in French style."

Gallaudet's daily writing gave a better picture of the family man he had become. There were shopping sprees for his children; the baptism of baby Marion, "radiant with her little canton flannel rabbit;" friends calling, and receptions in the homes of friends. He helped Susy receive calls, and took her to a lovely reception in the home of Mrs. Spencer Baird, wife of the Naturalist who had worked with Audubon and Agassiz. Life was full and there was more time to give to civic matters and pleasurable activities, with the Institution running smoothly under a competent staff. The only problem now was Susy's headaches. She suffered horribly with them and often could not be with her husband. The small children also kept her close to home. Katharine and Grace were in school at Hartford, living with their Grandfather Fessenden.

The Gallaudets numbered their friends among several groups that Washington afforded: the literary, the scientific, the journalistic, the medical, and the Congressional. They also had many friends within their church. In the year 1880 they were accustomed to call on the widow of Benjamin B. French, or on Mrs. Hayes in the White House; they stopped by to visit with Alexander H. Stephens, Congressman from Georgia, or attended a party at William Claflin's. Gallaudet, particularly, was loyal to the Literary Society, and in this year he read a paper on "The Poetry of the Deaf" before the Society at the home of James A. Garfield, who was president of the group. Another time they met at the home of Frances Hodgson Burnett, later to become famous for her book *Little Lord Fauntleroy*.

On Susy's day to receive, Mrs. Kate Sprague was a frequent caller.

She was the beautiful daughter of Salmon Portland Chase and wife of William Sprague, the Senator from Rhode Island. Another guest was Mrs. William Henry Hunt, wife of the jurist of the United States Court of Claims. And Gallaudet's own faculty members would call. The campus inhabitants were like a large family, and Gallaudet enjoyed being the nominal head. He often roamed about the campus making calls when duties were not pressing. He also sought sympathy at brother Jim's or Professor Fay's when his home was lonesome with family gone.

1880 was also the year the gymnasium was built, and Gallaudet made a trip to Boston to talk with the expert, Dudley Allen Sargent, head of the Hemenway Gymnasium at Harvard, who served as advisor on the new building at the Institution. At 43 Gallaudet was a busy man, and must rush back from Boston in time to attend the President's Levee or a meeting of the Literary Society at the home of John Nicolay, former secretary to Abraham Lincoln. He took Susy to a party at the Pomeroy's home where they met Professor and Mrs. Edwin Augustus Grosvenor of Robert College in Constantinople. Returning to his campus, Edward might attend the lecture by Professor Fay on the origin of the French language.

It was a pleasure to Edward to hear such an erudite performance on his own campus. While working on his doctorate at Johns Hopkins University, Professor Fay had become so engrossed in the study of Romance languages that he had made himself proficient in Italian, enough so to become a member of the Dante Society of Cambridge. He had made a Concordance of the *Divine Commedia* which was backed financially by the Dante Society. He had even had letters from James Russell Lowell and from the Queen of Italy.

Gallaudet's Board had given him leave to attend the International Congress of Instructors of the Deaf, to be held in Milan the coming summer, voting him $500 toward the trip. Inspired by Fay's erudition he began French lessons in preparation for his trip. Whom should he meet on arrival at his French teacher's but Vicomte Ferdinand de Lesseps, the French diplomat and promoter of the Suez Canal. On one occasion Col. Garrick Mallery, head of the Bureau of Ethnology of the Smithsonian, brought a party of the Ute Indians to the campus. Gallaudet sprinkled his diary pages with witty entries about horseback rides, ice skating, and long rambling walks. His favorite trip on horseback was through the Soldiers Home Grounds and back by Rock Creek Park. Once after a four-mile walk with Mr. Draper he went out to a dinner party at Senate James G.

Blaine's. Another time he dined with the Hills of Colorado, sitting down with President and Mrs. Angell of the University of Michigan, and Senator Baldwin of Michigan.

Gallaudet also knew many eminent men through his affiliation with various organizations such as the Cosmos Club, of which he was a charter member; the Archaeological Society; the Washington Monument Society; and the Literary, Philosophical, and Science groups. His life beyond Kendall Green had so broadened his horizons that his activities encompassed the social and political life of Washington. Founding and operating a philanthropic institution is not always conducive to personal friendships: many men working under similar conditions could be absorbed by the tediousness of their responsibilities, never fully realizing the potential elements of such a background. However, whether Gallaudet talked to a deaf student or an ambassador he maintained the tenor of his ways. He seldom quoted or told anecdotes which would contribute to history from the point of view of being "new" or adding to posterity's knowledge.

Anyone reading his journals would know that Gallaudet was not an outstanding diarist. What his writing reveals is about himself, and herein lies the greatest value of his writings—they are all we have of him, and he did not fear revealing what he thought about Edward Miner Gallaudet. He had the ability to analyze himself, a trait most people shy away from. But Gallaudet was the soul of honesty and without being brutally frank he told all it was humanly possible to tell, whether directly, by implication, or deduction. He felt security in his friendships and in the progress of his Institution. He established public relations with the White House by calling on W. K. Rogers, President Hayes' secretary, and having his name put on the invitation list. When he needed advice he sought it, never hesitating to go to an expert on the matter. He deplored his lack of scientific knowledge yet became a member of several scientific societies. He developed the habit of concentrating upon the subject within his grasp and in this way became an authority on international law. He planned ahead, as for the Presentation Day programs, and went out and got his speaker personally. In 1880 he invited J. Randolph Tucker to speak and received his acceptance. After these exercises Gallaudet presented honorary degrees, one to a deaf editor, Edmund Booth, who had graduated from the American School, and another to Alexander Graham Bell "in recognition of his important services in the cause of deaf-mute education, and his well-deserved renown as a scientific discoverer." This was Bell's first collegiate degree. Several days later he made a call at Graham Bell's laboratory, meeting Bell's father, Melville Bell, and dining with the family that evening. But he continued to work on Congressional matters, for the time was drawing near for his European trip, on which he would be accompanied by his brother-in-law, James Denison.

"Articulates in Full Force"

Gallaudet and James Denison sailed on the steamer *Algeria* on June 14, 1880, and docked at Birkenhead, England, on the 24th. They planned to go their separate ways, meeting at intervals before leaving London for the Continent. Gallaudet made calls on the Fields and on Junius Spencer Morgan during his several days in London. He suffered a stiff neck while there and had to stay in his hotel, "trying a flat iron as well as a flax-seed poultice" to cure the pain.

With Denison he crossed from Dover to Ostend, then proceeded to Ghent and Brussels. Again Gallaudet saw Monsigneur de Haerne, and the Sanfords entertained them at dinner. Among the guests were United States Minister James Osborne Putnam and Count Liederkerke, a prominent member of the Belgian Parliament. Sanford, who had been Minister in 1867, was now making his home in Brussels, having done work for the Belgium government since 1876 under King Leopold II.

While in Berne Gallaudet attended a meeting of the International Law Association and enjoyed an interview with Sir Travers Twiss who had been for many years Professor at Oxford and a writer on international law. After several days at the Villa d'Este, Gallaudet and Denison arrived in Milan where they were welcomed at the Hotel Pozzo by Signor Tarra of the Milan Institution. They arranged to visit the Institution and to see an exhibition of the pupils. While there Gallaudet saw his old friend Kierkegaarde-Ekborhn from Bollnäs, Sweden. A year later Gallaudet was to give him an honorary degree from the College.

The Congress opened "with all the formality, with the 'articulates' in full force." Gallaudet recorded that his speech on the Combined Method covered seven pages of foolscap and took him 15 minutes to deliver. He felt that it was well received, yet he knew that while many agreed with him they would "vote on the other side." He sat by St. John Ackers, who had a deaf child, and was one of the most rabid oralists. This particular Congress was to cause terrific repercussions throughout England and pave the way for the schools to introduce oral teaching if they liked. Even as Gallaudet sat by

Ackers he felt him an opponent, and at dinner they had several lively discussions.

Gallaudet visited Tarra's institution again and secured Tarra's promise to give him time for a paper on the National Deaf-Mute College. One evening the pupils of the Royal Institution gave a play—all in speech—which was very well done. Beer and lemonade were passed through the audience during the play. The following day Gallaudet was asked to read his paper on the "Higher Education of the Deaf."

When the Congress ended he and Denison left in separate directions, Denison for Paris and Gallaudet for Belle Rive, where, as he said, "I cleaned myself from the dust of the Milan Congress, and felt like myself again." Meeting later in Paris they did bank errands, shopped, saw Isaac Lewis Peet of the New York School and paid a number of visits. Gallaudet called on the U.S. Consul and on several friends, including Frederic Rene Coudert, a New York lawyer. He visited the Paris Institution and saw Mr. Vaisse before leaving Paris.

In London again he visited Susannah Hull's [1] articulating school. From there he went to Ealing to see the Normal College and Model School under Arthur Kinsey, one of the English teachers who had trained in the oral method in Germany, under the sponsorship of St. John Ackers. Kinsey taught in the school founded and financed by Mr. Ackers, under the Society for Training Teachers of the Deaf and the Diffusion of the German System. After observing the work Gallaudet thought the results good, but no better than he had seen at Northampton, in the Clarke School in Massachusetts.

Both travellers bought clothes before leaving London, and they were invited to visit Mr. Ackers at his country seat, Prinknach Park. While there they met Ackers' 11-year-old deaf daughter who read from the lips readily. After a pleasant overnight stay they were back in London where Gallaudet wrote a letter to the *London Times* about the Milan Convention. They then sailed for home on the *Gallia*. After an uneventful voyage they were glad to land on October 5, and find Grace waiting for them.

Susy was in New York for a doctor's appointment and she stayed on while Gallaudet returned to Washington. He could see from the train something of the grand illumination the students had arranged for him. He was met by a body of students near the corner of Seventh and K Streets, bearing torches and lanterns, who escorted him to the College gate over which was the word "Welcome," in gas jets. There were fireworks, too, and the buildings were illuminated with Chinese lanterns. At the gate they took the horses from the carriage and pulled it themselves to Gallaudet's door.

Susy returned, improved in health, and took the first walk of any length she had taken in Washington for a long time. Soon Edward received two copies of the *London Times* containing his letter about Milan. He entered into the campus life again and was on hand when the Lawn Tennis Club was organized by the young people of the Green. During the summer Katharine had become engaged to John H. Denison, a cousin of Susy's, although the engagement was called off months later.

Gallaudet completed his Annual Report and took it to Secretary of Interior Carl Schurz, the Prussian - born politician who was also a distinguished journalist and a soldier. On the day of the Presidential election Gallaudet and Professor Chickering spent two hours on Pennsylvania Avenue and in the Cosmos Club learning about the results. Gallaudet's only comment was that "The news was highly favorable to the Republican cause." The next day, November 3, Garfield's election was officially reported.

Gallaudet concentrated upon writing an article about the Milan Convention, reporting that this Convention had been composed of 164 members, of which number 87 were from Italy, 56 from France, 8 from England, 5 from the United States, 3 from Scandinavia, 3 from Germany, 1 from Belgium, and 1 from Switzerland. The Convention had primarily dealt with the instruction of the deaf in articulation. The two Milan institutions had been laboring for the development of speech and lipreading for several years. Because of ample means they were able to assign a teacher to every eight pupils; the proportionate number of teachers being thus double that provided in the majority of American institutions. In his report Gallaudet stated that the Italian language lent itself to easy acquirement by deaf pupils, and the Milan school had succeeded in imparting speech and lipreading to a much larger proportion of their pupils than had heretofore been considered possible in articulating schools for the deaf. The results had been brought prominently to the attention of the convention in a variety of ways, exerting so great an influence that it was not difficult for those who were interested in the pure oral method to secure the adoption of such resolutions as they desired to have passed.

Instructors of long experience in England, France, Belgium, Sweden, and the United States urged the claims of the *combined system*, in which articulation is accorded due prominence, but in which the language of signs and the manual alphabet are made use of as adjuncts too valuable to be dispensed with. Their views, however, did not prevail, and the convention by a large majority adopted resolutions proclaiming the oral method preferred. Gallaudet elaborated on how such resolutions were inadequate for a greater part of the deaf and dumb since a large proportion of them could not be taught to read from the lips *well*. It was therefore a waste of time and money trying to impart speech to those incapable of achieving more than a partial success. The Milan resolutions were open to the very serious criticism of disingenuousness, for they recommended an entire abandonment of signs in the instruction of the deaf. In the debate which preceded its adoption many supporters of the "pure oral method" freely acknowledged that they used signs to a certain extent, but voted down a resolution which recognized this fact. "What is objected to most strenuously," wrote Gallaudet, "is that a procrustean method should be insisted on, the general adoption of which would not fail to bring disappointment and serious loss to many who under a system adapted to their needs might reach satisfactory results."

Gallaudet stated to his readers that among the papers discussed at the Convention was that of the collegiate education of the deaf and dumb. No high schools or colleges for deaf-mutes had been established in Europe, and the Convention had listened with great interest to a paper presented by the president of a college for the deaf, which gave an account of the practical solution of the question of higher education, in the successful operation of such a department which was then 16 years old and supported by the United States government.

It would take time for the many reports of the several nations to be published, and comparisons made, but records show that the British delegates returned from Milan "in a fervor approaching that of the anti-slave traders of the previous generation." [2] A meeting was called in England of most of the governing bodies of schools to consider the resolutions of what St. John Ackers called "the deaf child's Magna Carta." They decided to lay the whole matter before the government. [3] Nothing was done immediately on a wholesale plan, but no effort was made to keep each school from proceeding as it thought best. Some headmasters began oral work with the new students entering, but it would be a while before complete changes were made in all the schools.

The Milan Convention brought to a climax the growing enthusiasm for teaching speech started at the first international conference of teachers of the deaf which was held in Paris in 1878. The Abba Tarra had so inspired the delegates with his eloquence that the whole audience rose as a body and shouted "Long live speech." It was voted to have another international conference at Brussels in 1883. Gallaudet's work, already of national importance, had just begun on an international scale. The year 1880 opened his eyes to the real power of publicity and public relations, and he determined to renew his concentration on furthering the kind of education needed by the deaf in order to insure them a secure life after finishing school.

Gallaudet spent much of his time in the 1880's and 1890's in giving more publicity to the Columbia Institution. Susy did her part by mingling with the ladies in Washington and entertaining when her health permitted. One of the most elaborate and satisfying luncheons she ever gave was in honor of Mrs. James A. Garfield in 1891. Her guests at this luncheon included Mrs. William Henry Harrison, the wife of the President; Mrs. James G. Blaine, Mrs. John W. Noble, Mrs. A. P. Carter, wife of the Hawaiian Minister to the United States; Mrs. Henry L. Dawes and daughter Anna, Mrs. Zachariah Chandler, Mrs. William D. Washburn, Mrs. Frederick W. Lander, Mrs. John Hay, Mrs. Anthony Pollok, and Mrs. Samuel Clarke Pomeroy—all wives of eminent men in the political life of the day.

Gallaudet took his son Denison abroad with him when he attended the Congress of Deaf Mutes of Great Britain and Ireland, held in Glasgow, where he delivered a paper. In 1892 he represented the Institution at a Conference of Principals in Colorado Springs, taking son Herbert. In 1897 he made one of his most unusual trips, when he carried a "Message" from his Board of Directors to the educational authorities of a number of European nations.[4] The purpose of the trip was twofold: to carry the "Message" and to meet educated, adult deaf-mutes in a number of cities in Europe, to learn their opinions as to the relative value of teaching methods. He felt that the trip was successful, and hoped he had been able to "sow the seed in various countries for the Combined System, and in England for the establishment of a college."

By 1889 the Columbia Institution had received three awards from foreign nations: a Gold Medal Award from the Paris Exposition Universelle of 1889; one from Chile as early as 1875, and one from France in 1878.

A Home Has a Name

One of the first things Gallaudet would do when he built his home in Hartford in 1887 would be to name it. In its formative stage he and Susy lovingly termed it "O.F.H."—for Old Folks Home—but upon completion it acquired the name "Quiescas," a word taken from the Gallaudet motto, "Ut Quiescas Labora," on the coat-of-arms brought by the family from France. Gallaudet planned his name in a design of carved wood over the front entrance to the home. Although he did not occupy it continuously until after his retirement in 1911, he spent the first two years in it after it was bulit, then rented it to friends for the next 24 years, occupying it at intervals during its vacancies.

He developed the habit of building homes when he bought some property at Indian Neck, near Branford, Connecticut, in 1882, and when men were digging the cellar they unearthed an Indian skeleton. To commemorate the Indian burying-ground Gallaudet named this cottage "Quinipi." It was long to be the summer home and playground for family vacations. Later, when the family separated for other trips, "Quinipi Lodge" was rented. Renting it, however, did not deter Gallaudet from calling on the occupants, and out of season he would make a swing by Branford, walking from the station to the shore just to be near this lovely spot.

At the time he bought the Indian Neck property he also bought an island a quarter of a mile from shore on which he planned to build a "storm house"—a kind of shack to which he could row, to read or rest in quiet. He dreamed of building something permanent and small, to which rooms could be added, just as he intended doing with "Quinipi." At first he put up a piano box hut, really a "sun shade," and he called it "Quietus." Many a paper for Conventions or the Literary Society took form in his mind on Green Island. He wrote a poem to it, called "My Garden—far Out at Sea." He would row out and take a swim in the nude far off its side, and he trained each of his children to love the place, giving each a responsibility in clearing it off: to weed, to move a hedge, to pick the berries. Each learned to handle a boat, of which there were several—with names like Petrel and Sharpie—and of which Edward spoke as though they were personalities. They had to be bailed out, captured when loose from their moorings, and kept in good shape. His whole school year was woven around the thoughts of freedom, sea air, sunshine and rest. While Edson and Herbert were at Yale he would take a train up from Washington during the winter, meet one or the other son in New Haven on the week-end, and take him to "Quinipi Lodge" for two days. They would build a fire and cook their meals while they talked and read. This outing would "refuel" Gallaudet for the next grind coming up in his busy Washington life, besides affording him the companionship of a son. How he missed his children when they left him! The first four had spent their high school years in Hartford, then the sons in college. Grace had spent one year at Smith and finally he lost Marion to Miss Porter's School in Farmington.

Gallaudet basked in his two older daughters' companionship and attention, just as he had done in his sisters' when a young boy. Susy was his love, but she was often ill. He would read to her, see that she was comfortable, as he did with his children, and then seek other company.

On his return to Washington from the seashore Gallaudet felt increasingly the need for a quiet spot. In April of 1885 he began to evolve a plan for a wooded retreat on the back acres of Kendall Green. His walks there always brought solace and rest from his worries, and so he conceived of his house in the woods. Quietly he went about his plans, and the little place was built. He called this place the "Hermitage." He had hoped it would be his Washington retreat, but soon his family discovered it, and Susy loved to use it for her painting sprees. She studied water colors at the art schools and she became a familiar sight going up to the "Hermitage" with her palette and brushes. The children liked the place too, and there were picnics with games and sings. There were times, of course, when Gallaudet had it to himself and he made the most of these occasions. Two hammocks were strung from the trees, and the "Hermitage" was strongly built, with a fireplace; he could be inside or out, according to the weather. Papers and lectures were written there, and it stood as another instance of Gallaudet's desire for peace and quiet.

A stone house went up on Green Island in 1890, and with the additions to the Lodge it was possible for the whole family to enjoy the Indian Neck property in comfort, and to have visitors. They took turns in staying in the Lodge and on the Island. It almost broke Gallaudet's heart when he saw his family losing interest in this haven. With Marion grown and wanting to go elsewhere, Gallaudet gave up his Lodge and his "Garden in the Sea" one summer to let his family have a fling in Norfolk. Susy and Marion thought it was "smarter." It is significant that they changed their minds—decidedly. "Quinipi Lodge" looked mighty good the following summer. When Gallaudet did agree to sell the Lodge in 1899 he received $6,300 for a place that had cost him about $2,500. He kept the Island much longer.

In exploring theories as to why Gallaudet liked to name his dwelling places, one might remember that he saw the Czar's Hermitage while in Russia, and he loved Venice, "the city in the sea." His Washington home was Kendall Green, and the Patterson property adjoining it was Brentwood. Salmon Portland Chase's home out from the city was called Edgewood, and in Hartford he had known the Colt mansion as Armsmere. The English country seats fascinated Gallaudet. His visit to Tatton Hall, near Manchester, during his 1886 trip to England revealed the epitome of elegance to him, and Belle Rive, in Geneva, like Villa d'Este, was a jewel. Gallaudet's horses, dogs, and cats all had delightful names: Twilight, Diane, Chloe, and Shandon are examples. When the Gallaudets migrated to the shore in the summer they left Washintgon in relays, the older being responsible for the younger, with the rear brought up by the servants and the pets. Once a kitten, Topaz, had a fit en route to Jersey City and died in her basket. Gallaudet was along, and he moaned having to let it down to its watery grave while they all looked on sad-eyed.

His energy and imagination created a happy background for his growing family. No chore was too hard or too menial for Gallaudet to perform for his "dear children," and what is more he gave them himself, wholeheartedly, while he played and provided for his Susy and the six apples of his eye. Kendall Green, Quiescas, Quinipi, Quietus, and the Hermitage were stamped with his thoughts and his aspirations for their welfare.

The Ladies Come to Stay

The question of admitting young ladies to the college was first mentioned at a faculty meeting on January 11, 1881. Gallaudet recorded the fact under that date, then made a statement which he seemed to do with relish: "The Faculty showed no disposition to change the policy of the College which declines to admit ladies." Silence reigned on the subject for the next three years and then Gallaudet made a long-deferred trip, visiting the schools of the South and West, his idea being to explain to the students the standard of study and preparation required for admission to the Columbia Institution. When he reached the Council Bluffs, Iowa, School he had an evening with the pupils and teachers, answering their questions and enjoying a social hour. Someone suddenly introduced the subject of co-education. "I opposed co-education," he announced briefly.

But co-education for the National Deaf-Mute College was in the air. When the Convention met in California the summer of 1886 a paper was presented in which a very bright deaf young lady urged that the doors of the College be opened to those of her sex. In his Annual Report for that year Gallaudet mentioned that a communication had been received by him from the Western Association of Collegiate Alumnae which had met that May, urging that women be permitted to share the advantages that the young men had.

Sometime between 1881 and 1886 Gallaudet's faculty softened toward the admission of ladies. They were considering accepting them "as an experiment," and planned to call the attention of Congress to the matter. In September of 1886 the faculty discussed the subject again, and recommended this important step to the Board.

During these growing pains of co-education Gallaudet himself was planning an important step. He had already asked his Board's permission to have John B. Wight, the Institution's Supervisor, become responsible for disbursement of the Government funds, relieving him of this responsibility. In October of 1885 he spoke of this change as

Gallaudet College students of 1885 posing in front of chapel.

Students of 1886 esconced on the stairs leading to the chapel.

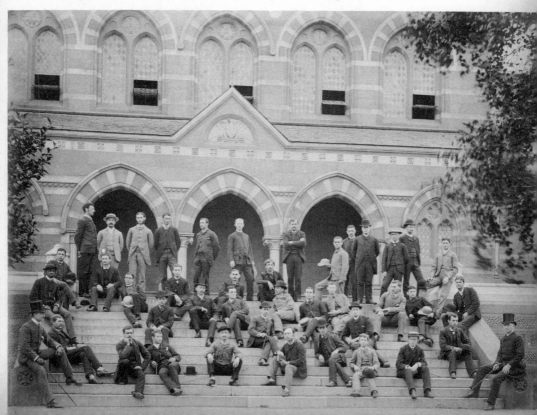

Gallaudet's Barons of the Bat in 1893.

The college's baseball team of 1886.

College students and professors cycling in the 1890's. Prof. Amos Draper is second from left in lead. E.M.G. is the bareheaded gentleman seated on a tricycle at the right.

Gallaudet students practicing gymnasium exercises in 1891.

A photo of members of the faculty and of the Normal Department's class of 1891, the college's first class for graduate study. Prof. Porter and Miss Mary T. G. Gordon stand to the upper left. Prof. Joseph Gordon is in center holding derby; Charles Ely is seated on his left. Ely later became a professor and vice president of the college.

Gallaudet College ablaze as Washingtonians look on in February 1910.

his first step toward retirement; a gradual cessation of his many duties. He was then 48 years old, and had been remarking since 1881 that he had a strong feeling he ought to rid himself of the responsibilities of the Institution before he was much older: he had feared a breakdown in March of 1881.

During the year 1884 he came to the decision that he would like to retire to his old home town, Hartford, when the time came. His summer home at Indian Neck had convinced him. In June of 1885 he was looking at lots in Hartford and although he discovered a choice one on Forest Street it was too expensive. He finally found one "at my price" on Woodland Street. By September of 1885 affairs had shaped up pretty much to his liking and he asked Professor Fay to become Vice President of the College. This, too, would diminish his duties, so that he could afford intermittent absences from the College and could build his Hartford home. He then asked the Board again to admit young women, a few at first; and then he conceived the idea of lodging them in the President's Home on the campus.

When the Board met in January of 1887 a resolution was read which said that "beginning with September of that year young women would be admitted to the College on the same terms as the men; that an additional Matron would be hired to take charge of the young women in the President's Home, the President absenting himself while the experiment was being tried, visiting his family when such absences could be arranged." This was not voted by the Board until February, but in March Gallaudet had the plans for his Hartford home in the hands of the builder. Since all arrangements were made the work went along quickly. By June he began closing his home of 19 years in Washington, and moving his possessions to Hartford. His family spent the summer at Indian Neck, and remained there until they could take full possession of the new home, on October 20, 1887. [1]

Where he had once opposed co-education it was now the means by which he was able to carry out his personal plans which at the time he honestly believed would be the stepping stone to permanent retirement. He could not reckon with the many factors which the next three years would bring, personal as well as professional. But the "experiment" did give co-education its chance to take a firm hold. It was eventually found that the situation of numbers could be handled in one of the existing buildings for a while, and the girls finally landed in a dormitory and made their campus home.

Gallaudet recruited his co-eds by sending out circulars to the

Superintendents and Principals of the schools for the deaf over the country. Miss Mary Gordon, who had been acting as Matron at the Institution, was transferred to the residence. This removed the prejudices Gallaudet had entertained against co-education: he had feared that college education of the sexes together might lead to unsatisfactory results. With the young ladies in his own home, he no longer felt concerned.

The experience of the first year, though not perfectly satisfactory, was so much more so than he had expected that he continued the experiment—and during the years his apprehensions were never realized. In fact, he felt the young women had a favorable influence. On Presentation Day of 1893 the first woman received a degree in course from the College. She was Agnes Tiegal of Pennsylvania. Other states represented in this first class of six co-eds were Illinois, Maryland, Nebraska, and Indiana.

In the autumn of 1888 eight young women appeared, and their number for several years did not rise to the point that made housing difficult. However, in 1899 Gallaudet's Report included in his estimates for the year a small paragraph to the effect that the dormitories for both sexes were filled to their limit, and though no estimate for new buildings was submitted he did want to call the attention of Congress to this necessity. This hint was dropped again in the 1900 Report, and in 1902 a note of desperation was sounded when the crowding threatened the pupils' health and comfort. Efforts to obtain money for enlargement of living accommodations continued, but not until 1911, when Gallaudet became President Emeritus, were the funds requested outright, to the amount of $75,000. The building in use had served the campus since 1859 and was neither fireproof nor sanitary. This dormitory was called the most urgent need of the Institution. This new dormitory for women hung on the books until 1916 before Congress passed an Act, and by this time the request had risen to $90,000. Additional amounts had to be requested for the next two years, but finally the women got their building and the dream started in 1886 came true: the women at Gallaudet College were there to stay. They named their building the Sophia Fowler Hall, in honor of the wife of Thomas Hopkins Gallaudet.

Mark Twain Enters

In Gallaudet's diaries there are a number of entries about Mark Twain. There is no record of when they first met, but Gallaudet may have met Mark Twain following the Civil War, when Twain lived in Washington for a while. Twain first went to Hartford in January of 1868 and again in June of 1869, when he and his fiancee attended a friend's wedding, and Twain took advantage of the opportunity of convincing his future bride of the possibilities Hartford held as a place to settle. After living under the shadow of his wife's people for two years in Elmira, New York, he finally made the move to Hartford in 1871, living for three years in the John Hooker home on Hawthorne Street—a street that crossed Forest Street almost at its South end, the other end of Forest stopping short on the north at Farmington Avenue. Mark Twain soon began to think of building his own home, selecting a lot which ran south from Farmington, into the forest, and eventually constructed a home that became famous for its Mississippi River Boat design and its beautiful interior with Tiffany motifs. He moved into this in April of 1874.

While Gallaudet lived in Hartford during the years 1887-1889 he renewed his friendships with many people. Hartford had long been a city of culture. The "Hartford Wits" of the early days had been replaced by the Nook Farm Circle of the 1880's, a group of families who built their homes on acres once belonging to the William H. Imlay estate. Gallaudet built on Woodland Street which ran perpendicular to Farmington Avenue, making a dead-end almost in Mark Twain's back yard—Twain's front yard, of course, being to the rear of his home, as it was situated on Farmington Avenue. As many as could of the group had built with their home-fronts facing the interior of the Farm, or estate, which was first settled by John and Isabella Beecher Hooker who had purchased the estate with Francis Gillette—finally subdividing the land among congenial friends who could well afford the high prices. Charles Dudley Warner, editor

of the Hartford *Courant,* first lived in a small cottage near the Hookers
until he could purchase the Thomas C. Perkins' place; deep in the
trees with the Park River winding behind the house and along the
side of Twain's home.   Joseph R. Hawley's home was near by,
Gallaudet's good friend who had been governor of Connecticut and
a United States Senator—later sitting for many years on Gallaudet's
Board of Directors.   Harriet Beecher Stowe returned to Hartford
after her husband retired from the faculty at Amherst, and in 1864,
after building a mansion too large to handle, she finally settled in a
home on Forest Street where her back yard spread out into the yards
of her neighbors.   From this group had come William Gillette, the
actor, who had make his debut on the New York stage in 1874 in a
small part, in Mark Twain's *The Gilded Age,* and was to play in
Hartford in 1875 and bring out the clergy to the theater for the first
time.

The Reverend Joseph Hopkins Twichell of the Asylum Hill Congregational Church was a bosom friend of Mark Twain and lived
across the street from Gallaudet.   All in all the neighborhood was an
ideal one for a person of Gallaudet's temperament.   The Twichells
and the Gallaudets saw one another often: they swapped visits and
dined together.   Twichell eventually made a Presentation Day
Address at the College for Gallaudet.   Often Mark Twain would drop
in on one or the other while they were visiting each other, or invite
them to his home.   Twichell's friendship with Mark Twain actually
brought him more attention than his career as a minister, although his
vocation was the piece de resistance between the two friends.   Mark
Twain never was a church-goer.

During his commutings between Washington and Hartford,
Gallaudet was drawn into a plan that greatly appealed to him.   He
learned in March of 1888 that Mr. Twichell's parishioners wanted to
buy him a home.   This struck a responsive cord in his heart because
it brought back the memory of his father's Buckingham Street home
made possible by his former Board of Directors.   Gallaudet invited
Mrs. Twichell to call, as she was in on the plan and had managed to
keep it from her husband.   She gave Gallaudet the names of several
who had expressed an interest in subscribing to the project, and
Gallaudet immediately set about making calls, reviving interest in
this gift.   In two days he had collected $1,500.   The man who owned
the property he had wanted to buy on Forest Street at first refused
to donate, and Gallaudet went to bed that evening despondent.
Early the next morning, however, C. B. Smith arrived at Gallaudet's

home with $1,000, inspiring Gallaudet to renewed efforts. Late that afternoon he made a call on Mark Twain. "He was favorable to the plan," wrote Gallaudet, "but did not want to put his name down."

Never one to give up easily, Gallaudet tried a different approach the next morning by sending his son Edson over to the Clemens' home with a note—and stood by to see what happened. His wait was not long for Edson soon appeared bringing with him Mark Twain's subscription of $1,000. Newton Case, Theodore Lyman, J. M. Allen, Atwood Collins, Kitty and Grace, and Gallaudet himself boosted the subscription sum to $5,000. The women's donations began to come in: Mrs. J. F. Morris and Mrs. Charles Dudley Warner made pledges. Gallaudet had to make a quick trip to Washington and on South, attending the Convention of Principals in Jackson, Mississippi, taking daughter Grace with him. After seeing his College through Presentation Day he hastened back to Hartford and learned that several men were in favor of proceeding to buy the house for their pastor.

He went to work again. Mrs. Frisbie and Mrs. Cassius Welles each gave $500, and Seth Talcott made a pledge. The responsiveness of the congregation so excited Gallaudet that he took a drive out West Hartford way to look at the scenery. "There is more beauty in one New England village than in the whole South," he exclaimed. Mrs. Twichell and daughter Susy called, and were jubilant over the prospect of owning a house. So far Mr. Twichell knew nothing, but neither did his congregation know that he was in New York City being interviewed by men who wanted him down there! The fund had reached $10,000.

On May 27 Mr. Twichell gave his yearly birthday sermon, and the possibility of his leaving Hartford seemed passed. That evening the long expected presentation of the home took place: Susy Gallaudet served coffee and received much attention. Gallaudet called Twichell the most grateful man he had ever seen. No mention was made of whether Mark Twain was present, but it is doubtful. He probably felt that his $1,000 had represented him adequately.

In Pursuit of Memorials

When Gallaudet began his job as official fund raiser for his institution the desire to succeed at this gained momentum. When any need was brought to his attention he went into action. He never minded doing the leg-work if he considered the project a bonafide one. A workman hurt on his grounds or, unfortunately, killed—as happened when the gymnasium was being built—started him collecting a purse for the family, which he delivered himself. If he heard of a former pupil who was ill, or an elderly parent of one who was hard up, he went to pay his respects and incidentally to leave a sum of money.

Gallaudet's first step in bringing original art work to the Institution was taken in 1878 when his Board authorized a portrait of Amos Kendall for the Chapel. He desired a copy of the Huntington portrait of Kendall, and with the $300 the Board stipulated for the commission he commissioned Monsieur Louis Mathiew Didier Guillaume, French born, but an American after 1855. He came to New York City in 1855 and settled in Richmond, Virginia, in 1857. Sometime between 1872 and 1880 he moved to Washington, and Gallaudet referred to him as "the Washington artist." Later, when Gallaudet wanted a companion piece, the Board voted the same amount for a portrait of Thomas Hopkins Gallaudet. This was done in 1880 by E. F. Andrews, of the Literary Society of Washington. He asked for $50 additional, and this was also voted by the Board.

Following Garfield's death in 1881 the desire grew to commemorate his memory because of his services to the Institution. The deaf over the country subscribed to this, collecting the sum of $1,461.52. Daniel Chester French[1] was chosen to execute a bust of Garfield which was unveiled in the Chapel in 1883. Edwin A. Hodgson,[2] the distinguished deaf editor, made the principal address.

Gallaudet had an uncanny way of getting behind an idea and seeing it executed. His next idea was to honor his father by having a memorial window installed in the old Center Church in Hartford where the Gallaudet family had worshipped. He went to New York, called at Lamb's, church decorators, and found that they would furnish a window of the finest quality and original artistic design, installed, for $500. Since this was a family affair he went to see his broker brother, Peter Wallace Gallaudet, in his New York offices; before he left his brother had promised to finance the window.

For a number of years the deaf of the country had wanted to honor Thomas Hopkins Gallaudet by having a life-size statue placed on the campus of the College. During the course of their second convention, held in New York City in 1883, this plan was adopted and a campaign for funds was launched. At the same time the question arose as to who would be the sculptor. Daniel Chester French had been successful with the Garfield bust and his name was proposed for the Gallaudet Statue. He was the son of Judge Henry Flagg

French who was half-brother to Benjamin B. French. Both of the older men were close to the Washington Gallaudets. The great majority of the deaf favored French, although a deaf sculptor approached Gallaudet for the commission, even after the decision was made to have French do it. Mr. S. Ballin called on Gallaudet as late as June 2, 1887, asking him to use his influence to reopen the matter so that he might have a chance to prepare a life-size model. Gallaudet finally convinced him that his opportunity had passed.

French visited the Campus on November 18, 1885, making a study of the best position for the statue,[3] looking at portraits of the elder Gallaudet, and dining with the family. On December 10 of 1885 the Gallaudet Club of New York gathered to celebrate the elder Gallaudet's 98th birthday anniversary. Edward attended with French, who exhibited a model of the contemplated statue, with which the deaf were pleased. Gallaudet kept in touch with Theodore Froelick, the chairman of the statue committee; he had also been to Concord, New Hampshire, where French had his studio; and he made a second trip in November of 1887, seeing the beautiful model of his father as a man of thirty, seated and teaching the deaf Alice Cogswell the manual letter "A".

The statue was unveiled on June 26, 1889. French had placed it during a downpour of rain the day before, but the weather was fine when Herbert and Marion Gallaudet performed the unveiling. This was the high-light of the meeting of the National Association of the Deaf, followed by a luncheon for over 300 people, all pleased with how the $13,000 had been spent. The sum represented every state and territory of the United States, and was more than enough to pay all expenses. A $500 balance was put aside to be invested for a permanent fund to be called the Gallaudet Memorial Art Fund, the income to be devoted to the purchase of other works of art. The time and effort Gallaudet had devoted to this over a period of six years would be hard to gauge.

Following his retirement as President the Gallaudet College Alumni Association presented to the College a portrait of Edward which was executed by Grace's husband, William B. Closson. Gallaudet posed for this during August of 1906, in Magnolia, Massachusetts. There is also a Medallion profile of him in the College Chapel, which was done by a student, Roy C. Carpenter of Michigan, when he was a senior in 1902. But Gallaudet would be profoundly moved if he could see the beautiful new Edward Miner Gallaudet Memorial Library which now graces the campus in his memory.

XIII

Fathers and Sons

In temperament there could have been no two men more opposite than Alexander Graham Bell and Edward Miner Gallaudet. Graham Bell, as he was known to his friends, was the son and grandson of men who had spent their lives either being vocal themselves or coaxing others to be so. The grandfather, Alexander Bell (1790-1865), of London, England, was an elocutionist and a corrector of defective speech: the object, to correct defects brought about by the incorrect position of the vocal organs. He had also been a minor actor.

Two sons, David Charles Bell of Dublin, and Alexander Melville Bell (1819-1905) of Edinburgh, followed their father's profession. Melville Bell branched off as a kind of inventor, calling what he invented Universal Alphabetics, or Visible Speech. His son Graham, born in Edinburgh in 1847, took up his father's work, introducing it into Miss Susannah Hull's school in Kensington, outside London. During his teaching he began the study of the nature of vibrations, the phenomenon that occurs while speech is being uttered. He determined to capture these speech vibrations in some manner so that his pupils could see forms of vibrations characteristic of the various elements of speech. He had the viewpoint of a scientist, with the idea of making deductions. In this early conception was the seed of the telephone. One might say that Graham Bell's dedication to teaching the deaf to speak was scientific and medical. He propounded a theory, proceeded to work it out by experimenting with the deaf, and endeavored to create a commodity that would help. He adapted Visible Speech and its teaching to the work for the deaf, adding to it a system of notation that improved it for use with the deaf.

Graham Bell had his grandfather until he was 18 years old, his father until he was a man of 58. Melville Bell was with his son Graham many years, watching over his work and lending advice. He knew many men of science, and young Graham grew up meeting such men as Alexander J. Ellis, the translator of Helmholtz's work; Henry

Sweet, the phonetician; and the editor of the Oxford dictionary, Sir James Murray. The latter had made Melville Bell's classification of speech sounds the basis of his method of noting pronounciation in his dictionary. Ellis had explained Helmholtz's work with the tuning forks and electricity to Graham Bell, causing his first interest in electricity. With these tuning forks Graham began his study of sound vibrations. He made a number of electrical inventions based upon the utilization of musical notes as telegraphic signals, which led gradually to the invention of the telephone itself.

What better laboratory than a deaf person, whose imperfect mechanisms of hearing and speaking presented a direct challenge to a sound investigator? From early times the deaf had been looked upon as a resource for experimentation. It was only hoped that through resulting inventions the deaf might possibly benefit.

When Bell settled in Washington the winter of 1878 he established a school while continuing his experiments. By 1880, with his invention of the telephone patented, he won the Volta Prize from France. He then began to branch out in his organization for promoting the teaching of speech to the deaf, using his prize money.

An entry in Gallaudet's diary in January of 1880, which mentioned his having dinner with Bell, was the first reference to their friendship. Bell's father-in-law, Gardiner Greene Hubbard, had probably brought these two together, since Gallaudet had known Hubbard for 13 years. In April of 1880 Gallaudet dined with Bell again, and on May 5 Bell attended the Presentation Day exercises at the Institution and received an honorary Ph. D. degree, his first collegiate degree and the first of many honorary degrees that would come his way. Although Bell had won the Volta Prize Gallaudet did not mention it in his diary.

In contrast to Bell, Gallaudet had lost his grandfather when he was a boy of six. There is no record that he ever saw him He lost his father when he was 14 years old, and so greatly missed him that he began a diary to fill the void. And when he was 75 he would still be wishing he could be like him. On his own since 14 and tackling his Washington job only six years later, it is little wonder that he sought older and more experienced men, and leaned toward men of accomplishment. He was 10 years older than Graham Bell, and evidently admired the younger man wholeheartedly. He enjoyed his company and was eager to join forces with him in a combined effort to do everything possible for the deaf, whom he had accepted in their natural state, just as his father had before him. His aim was to educate them and open up to them a full life of arts and science, enlarging their knowledge as a means of coping with the outside world. He did not believe the object of a deaf person's education was to acquire speech. On the other hand, to make speech work a part of the curriculum, an added study, was an object to be achieved. As a main objective, however, the emphasis was misplaced.

Bell, on the other hand, demanded speech from the deaf. He based his belief in the ability of a deaf person's learning to speak upon the theory that the vocal organs were in perfect condition and therefore usable. He remained skeptical for a while as to their lipreading ability. This was what led him to devise apparatus that rendered speech "visible," finally resulting in the telephone. When he travelled he took his work with him. He did not care to read for the sake of reading, and showed no pronounced taste for literature per se, nor did he care for "Art." Gallaudet cared for both, and won his relaxation in reading and pursuing philosophical phenomena, liking both novels and what would now be termed "science fiction." Art galleries drew him, and he liked to experiment with words: in his reading, in his writing, and in encouraging his pupils to express themselves in good language.

Through all Gallaudet's relationship with Graham Bell he admired him greatly and wished from him nothing more than a friendship based upon mutual respect for each other's work and achievements. His nature craved intimate friendships, which Bell's did not seem to require. Yet in certain respects the two were remarkably alike. Neither had a desire to write the story of his own life. Bell gathered family records for preservation, which is about all Gallaudet did. Just as one of Bell's biographers claims Bell's work is so interwoven with his desire to help the deaf that his own life could not be written without revealing both, so it was with Gallaudet's: his contribution to the deaf was his life, and the work he accomplished at Washington could not be told without giving the story of his life. Both men also were closely associated with deafness in their families. Thomas Gallaudet gave Edward a deaf mother, and Graham Bell, whose mother had acquired deafness, chose a deaf girl to become the mother of his children. Each man, however, was motivated not only by sympathy for the deaf but by love—both filial and marital. It would seem that in their lives both Graham and Edward were primarily inspired and influenced by their fathers.

In Gallaudet's desire to be close to Bell he reached out to share what he had, but Bell always withdrew because he felt that what he already had was better. This Gallaudet could never understand.

He honestly thought there existed something to be gained by an alliance that would be more beneficial to the deaf than a division. He hoped that Bell would eventually understand that he, too, wanted the deaf to be given the privilege of learning to speak, so that they could enjoy all the advantages that oral study could give them. But he also hoped Bell would come to see that the great mass of the deaf would never be financially able to secure enough individual attention to attain adequate speech, and that in any event, their individual differences would thwart such attainment. What, then, would become of those who preferred to live as deaf people—which they were —if they had their natural language of signs and spelling taken from them? Whose right was it to take away a man's natural manner of communication? There was a more liberal way to follow, and this way could also lead to a beautiful and full life, and a social adjustment far beyond the circumscribed manner of learning that Bell prescribed.

The great aim in promoting the Combined System of teaching the deaf, advocated by Gallaudet and his adherents, was to teach language. "Signs and spelling" per se were used as tools for this accomplishment. Articulation was another tool. The slightest gesture to a deaf person could open up an entire sentence and provide the missing word that blocked the way. To spend a whole class period in communicating the one word "orally" when a "sign" allowed the lesson to proceed seemed ridiculous. When Bell said, "Give every deaf child the opportunity to use language, instead of signs, to the avowed end that 'dumbness among the deaf, like illiteracy among the hearing, will be considered as a mark of defective education,' he was stating the case in too strong terms. He believed in language before comprehension. Signs have never been used instead of language, but have stood as a symbol of the word, and the word was taught also. One has only to read the essays written by the early pupils of the American School, samples of which were published in the Annual Reports, to see that the *language* of the pupils was excellent. In the early days all words and language were taught to the pupils in America by means of the sign with the written word. "See this hat?" And the hat was shown, and the word was written on the blackboard, the "sign" for hat being demonstrated at the same time. The pupil saw how the word looked; he wrote it on his slate; he spelled it in the air on his fingers by means of the manual alphabet; and he made the sign. He had three approaches to learning the word and impressing it on his mind. An institution in which signs were used could not turn out a product different from the product which entered it, except that the product was bound to know more than when he entered in a state of complete blankness. Bell openly stated that such an institution, using signs, would turn out deaf-mutes. Well—it certainly could not turn out hearing-mutes.

As articulation took hold in all the schools, owing to Gallaudet's brilliant 1867 Report and the fact that he called the Principal's Convention in 1868, the term "dumb" was dropped from the vocabulary by educators of the deaf and only "mute" used when it became evident that a pupil's vocal cords were impaired or that he simply could not give back speech.

It was to the adult deaf that Gallaudet looked—to discover what their education had really given them. The little ones in school learned by the method imposed on them, but they did not stay little forever—a point that many teachers overlooked in their eagerness to develop good speech-givers. These children grew up and escaped the control of those who made them live in an artificial world. It was different, of course, with Mabel Hubbard and Jeanie Lippitt, coming from homes with every advantage. Neither ever had to face the world and earn a living. In their nurtured and cultured way of life they were outsanding in their accomplishment, which was reading the lips and giving back speech. But the effort needed to become proficient in that art precluded much competition in the world of affairs.

Gallaudet experimented with the minds of the deaf educationally; Bell experimented with them scientifically through his technical knowledge of anatomy. It was here that the two men deviated, for certainly each had the greatest desire to help the deaf and each truly devoted his life toward the end of helping humanity. Bell's was much the broader field because of his inventions, but who can say that to the great number of the deaf the name "Gallaudet" does not mean more?

REVIEWING A FRIENDSHIP

Bell added to his Volta Prize of 50,000 francs the sum of $100,000 and he founded the Volta Bureau in Washington in order to establish a permanent place for information on the deaf. Later more funds were added to found the Volta-Bell Fund to promote oral teaching, and from this grew the "American Association to Promote the Teaching of Speech to the Deaf"—long to be referred to over the country as the "A.A.P.T.S.D."

Gallaudet's money came from the United States government, and was tagged for specific purposes before he could use it, and was often "cut" below the original amount he had requested—frequently making it hard for him to meet the bills of the Institution. His resourcefulness showed itself in making $3,000 stretch over what he had estimated would take $5,000 to cover adequately. There was no other source of money for him except government funds.

In 1881, after seeing Bell a number of times through the many clubs and societies each belonged to, Gallaudet made preparations to go to Saratoga where he was to speak at the Social Science Convention. After writing his paper, which he named "The Best Method of Educating the Deaf," he took it over for Bell to read and then asked Bell to be at the meeting in Saratoga to sustain his views, which Bell agreed to do.

Susy accompanied her husband and they had a beautiful trip to Saratoga. The day after they arrived Gallaudet read his paper. Graham Bell did not arrive until a day later and stopped at another hotel. As soon as Gallaudet heard he had come he cut a meeting short to go out and greet him. He then looked up Franklin B. Sanborn, an officer in the Association, and asked that Bell be given time to speak.

Two days after Bell arrived he delivered an address on methods of teaching deaf-mutes. "He agreed with me on some points," Gallaudet recorded, "but differed on others, very much as I expected." After Bell's address Gallaudet asked for three or four minutes in which to reply but Mr. Sanborn refused him—"and was rude in his refusal," Gallaudet added. However, the paper Gallaudet had read was published in the *International Review* the following December.

In September of 1881 Gallaudet lost his good friend, President Garfield, who had shown interest in the Institution for many years. Gallaudet's diary of that year made no further reference to Bell. During the following year there was no mention of him except for casual meetings, until November when Gallaudet went to a friend's home for a call and found Bell there. They spent a pleasant evening having a "sparring match" over deaf-mute matters. In December Bell called on Gallaudet prior to a Literary Society meeting, held at the home of Judge Charles Daniel Drake, where Bell read a paper on early English pronunciation. Gallaudet thought the occasion was brilliant.

Several months later, into 1883, Gallaudet and his wife dined at the Hubbards and met interesting guests, including, as Gallaudet enumerated them, "a grand company of Bells: father, mother, uncle, aunt, cousin, and brother-in-law Bells." The following month Bell

gave a party in honor of the Academy of Sciences and Gallaudet took
daughter Katharine and James Denison. For months Gallaudet pursued his own interests, reading another paper at Saratoga on "International Ethics" and attending to school matters, before he again
encountered Bell in Bell's own laboratory, where he was whisked
off to see Bell's new schoolrooms.   Later Bell gave Gallaudet an outline of the paper he was to deliver the following night before the
Philosophical Society.   Bell and Gallaudet spoke for 45 minutes
each on the topic of "Fallacies Concerning the Deaf." About a week
later, in its October 31 issue, the Washington *Star* gave a glowing
account of Bell's new school for the deaf, into which was woven much
of the address Bell had given before the Philosophical Society.
Gallaudet then wrote a letter to the *Star* commenting on Bell's views
on deaf-mute instruction, as published in that paper. He let Professors Fay and Gordon read it before he took it down to Mr. Kauffmann
at the *Star* office. Kauffmann preferred to have this redone as an
interview, and the next morning sent Wilhelmus. H. Bryan out to
Kendall Green for that purpose. Gallaudet took him to a class in
articulation so that he would get an idea of the work. Before the
afternoon was over Gallaudet went down to the *Star* office to read
proofs of the interview. The reason for the thoroughness was that
Gallaudet wanted to print Bell's address in the *American Annals of
the Deaf.* He took a copy of it to John Eaton in the Department of
Education for discussion.

In July of 1884 there was a Conference of Principals in Faribault,
Minnesota, to which 26 heads of institutions went. There were 53
other persons present, mostly teachers of the deaf, directors, and
other school officers, invited to sit as honorary members. Among
these was Bell. The question of speech was greatly discussed, and
Gallaudet felt that this conference would exert a great influence on
the work. He made a speech to which Bell responded with considerable feeling. The group moved on to Madison for further discussion
and Bell spoke there. Gallaudet visited him later at his hotel, and no
mention was made of conflict.

There seems to have been a series of meetings, and a Committee
was formed to discuss future conventions and their committees. An
all-day meeting took place at Kendall Green with Mr. Crouter of
Philadelphia, Superintendent of the Mt. Airy School for the Deaf.
Bell, Professor Fay, and Gallaudet had the teachers in for the evening,
and the next day Bell took the group to his home to dinner, after
which Crouter lectured.

In December of 1884 Gallaudet took his brother Thomas to call on Bell. The last time Gallaudet saw Bell that year was when Bell brought out an imposter, a man posing as a deaf-mute, whom they turned over to the police. With the exception of a fine dinner for many scientific men of note, at Bell's home, Gallaudet recorded seeing Bell only twice in the following year, 1885. They had a habit of sharing their guests with each other and when the noted Dr. Francis J. Campbell[1] of London visited the Green in January of 1886 Gallaudet took him to call on Bell. Dr. Campbell was born in the United States but lost his sight and after study eventually taught music at Perkins Institute, later going to England where he established a Normal School for the Blind. He had brought some of his musicians with him from England and Bell and Gallaudet arranged a concert for them.

To Gallaudet's horror he forgot a dinner invitation at Graham Bell's in February of 1886, having relied on daughter Grace to remind him. He telephoned Bell as soon as possible, then hurried over and sat down for dessert between William Walter Phelps, former Minister to Austria-Hungary and a Congressman at the time, and Governor John Davis Long of Massachusetts. Gallaudet missed the horse-cars home and had to walk. The two men kept in close touch with each other and did not stand on formalities with one another.

In June of 1886 Gallaudet attended the Convention of Instructors of the Deaf in Berkeley, California. There, on July 19, he introduced a set of resolutions that committed the convention to the Combined System, "intending to use them [the resolutions] with the Commission in England." An invitation to appear before the Royal Commission had come to him on June 1 while he was preparing to go to California, setting a date in July, but Gallaudet had to postpone an acceptance until fall. After his return from the West he resumed his correspondence with the Commission and went to the Capitol for an interview with the Secretary of State, Thomas F. Bayard—a man who had served on Gallaudet's Board from 1879 to 1885. Bayard took him in to interview the British Minister, Sir Lionel Sackville-West. With all matters concerning his trip settled, he left October 6, to give evidence in behalf of the Combined System before the Royal Commission in England. He took with him a letter from President Cleveland, telling of his pleasure at Gallaudet's being chosen to go, and he also took along a complete bound set of the *American Annals of the Deaf* for the Commission.

The Commission was of international interest. It was an outgrowth of the 1880 Conference in Milan, at which time oral work was beginning to take such a hold over Europe.[2] One of the members of the Commission was St. John Ackers, whom Gallaudet had met in Italy. Another was the Rev. William B. Sleight. Gallaudet made short visits to nearby schools to get ideas about the Commission. He learned that to many Mr. Ackers was a "bear." He called at the Embassy on Minister Edward John Phelps who had succeeded James Russell Lowell, and by request he visited with Charles Edward Drummond Black, the Secretary of the Royal Commission. He then "boned down hard to work" with his books spread out around him, and completed his preparations for appearing before the Commission. Feeling satisfied that he was ready, he made a quick trip to the Continent and visited schools before returning to London for a dinner in his honor. He was royally entertained at Delmonico's by the Headmaster of Ealing and other heads of schools for the deaf.

Finally, he went to the Commission rooms. Lord Egerton of Tatton was very affable as were all the others "except Mr. Ackers," he wrote. Gallaudet spoke nearly five hours, with a half an hour for lunch, going through his ten subjects. He rested for an hour and was given a dinner by another group of headmasters. The cross-examination by the several members of the Commission began two days after his testimony. Mr. Ackers asked no questions in his turn but towards the close had something to say as to the "breadth of the invitation to the Milan Congress." Then Gallaudet had a chance to "sit down on him and did."

Gallaudet made many more interesting calls and was invited to Tatton Hall by Lord Egerton, who was chairman of the Manchester School for the Deaf. He spent a memorable two days there, meeting Lady Manners, Lady Cochran, Sir John Rou, Sir James Ferguson, and of course Lady Egerton. He was able to get the stenographic notes on his evidence in London, and he corrected the proof.[3] The return voyage gave him time to relive his experiences, look at the testimonial so handsomely engraved on parchment which a group of headmasters had given him, and remember the toastmaster who alluded to his father, being grateful that they could extend, even belatedly, hospitality to the son. It was an experience ever to be remembered.

THE HATCHET

The profession of teaching the deaf was in particular need of young men and women college graduates who wished to do post-graduate work in its special field, yet there was no national training center offering this work. Some of the state schools had what is now called "in-service" training, but a college degree was not required for entry. Since Gallaudet had first seen Abba Tarra's normal department in his school in Milan he had dreamed of establishing such a department in his own college. On his return home from his 1867 trip abroad his Board had voted to put such a plan into the minutes, and had passed resolutions to that effect. One resolution was to hire an articulation teacher; a second asked that articulation and lipreading be introduced the next academic year; a third asked that the period of study in the primary be extended to nine years, and the age of admittance be eight instead of ten, as heretofore; a fourth asked that the President be allowed to admit as students *speaking* persons of suitable age and attainments who might fit themselves to teach the deaf and dumb. There were several reasons for the delay: Kendall's death and the purchase of Kendall Green; the building program; Gallaudet's illness and year abroad; the urgencies of the gymnasium, and co-education. But now the time was ripe for teacher training. By 1890 the demand far exceeded the supply.

Private citizens were becoming interested. L. S. Fechheimer of Cincinnati, who had helped establish an oral school there and whose deaf son was in the Clarke School at Northampton, wrote his Congressional Representative, who happened to be the Hon. Benjamin Butterworth, a friend of Gallaudet's. Fechheimer wrote Butterworth a letter in which he suggested that he lay before Congress the matter of establishing a normal school and mentioned the National Deaf-Mute College as being the logical place. He stated that the Congress of the United States had been great-minded and generous in maintaining the College at Washington under the able and wise supervision of Edward Miner Gallaudet, and with a small additional appropriation a normal school could be easily and quickly established: that everything for the purpose was right there, and with it "each and every State in the Union can send their candidates as teachers to receive a careful and scientific training in both the normal and oral methods . . . and the teaching of the deaf would become uniform and based on scientific principles."

Early in 1890 Mr. Butterworth laid Mr. Fechheimer's letter before the Appropriations Committee of the House, which deferred action until the next session of Congress. Fechheimer visited Gallaudet personally on February 27 and 28 of 1890, looking over the school and college and discussing the situation of a normal school from every angle. It all seemed settled to Gallaudet and he proceeded to include estimates for the Normal Department in his 1890 Report, asking for an additional $5,000 for this purpose. In speaking of this plan to Graham Bell some months later—as a sure thing—he invited Bell to be a lecturer when the plans materialized. Bell seemed pleased to accept, acting as though he approved of the idea of a Normal Department.

Gallaudet considered the whole scheme a providential interposition to show the Appropriations Committee the importance of the Columbia Institution. He was confident it would help his efforts. Fechheimer had brought a warm letter to Gallaudet from Butterworth and told Gallaudet that Butterworth had received his proposals very cordially. In fact, laying this bill before the Appropriations Committee of the House was Butterworth's last official act prior to retirement in 1890.[4]

It is conceivable that Gallaudet should bask in the security of his belief that all would go well. He entertained Gen. William Cogswell of Massachusetts who was a member in Congress of the Sub-Committee on Appropriations, and later in the month he attended a dinner at Graham Bell's in honor of S. Weir Mitchell, the doctor-novelist from Philadelphia. In May he read Bell's evidence given before the Royal Commission two years before, now in book form.

The first happening that seemed out of line was at the Convention of Instructors in New York that August. When Gallaudet as chairman of a special committee gave its report, a motion was made to postpone election of a committee since a plan was on foot to reorganize the Convention. Graham Bell was acting as temporary chairman of the Convention. The Committee, however, was not dissolved but added to, and Gallaudet was made chairman. When he reported the following day he advised postponement of reorganization until the next Convention in 1893. This created a "breeze" and Z. F. Westervelt of the Rochester School proposed resolutions to elect Gilbert O. Fay, formerly a Superintendent of the Ohio Institution but then teaching at the American School, as president of the next Convention—to be arranged for at Chicago. Finally all these plans fell through and the original report of Gallaudet's committee stood. Gallaudet later learned that Gilbert Fay had instigated the whole plot: it had been under way since the California Convention, and Fay had been in correspondence with A. L. E. Crouter of the Philadelphia Institution.

Gallaudet had been keeping in touch with his Congressional Directors. In January of 1891 he called on Joseph G. Cannon and Sereno Payne of New York, and he left them feeling that Cannon would give support to the proposed Normal School. While at President Harrison's reception on January 24 he learned through General Cogswell that Graham Bell had asked for a hearing before the Appropriations Committee to oppose the Normal School.[5] He talked with Professor Fay the next day and Fay offered to go and speak to Bell about taking this unfriendly attitude without any consultation with Gallaudet. But Gallaudet preferred to go himself. He found Bell stirred at the prospect of a Normal School at the College succeeding. Nothing Gallaudet said seemed to have any effect upon him. "He sees plainly," wrote Gallaudet, "that with both College and the National Normal School here, it would be hard work to make headway against such a citadel of the Combined System." When Gallaudet left Bell he went to the Capitol and saw Dawes, Hawley, Cannon, Cogswell, and Courts, the clerk, finding that he and Bell would appear before the Appropriations Committee the next day.

When last with Bell, Gallaudet had inferred from his attitude that Bell was claiming to have understood from the talk of several months back that the normal school was to train deaf people to teach the deaf, and it was for this reason that Bell contended he felt compelled to oppose what Gallaudet was trying to do. Gallaudet told him he was entirely mistaken; that no deaf persons would be admitted to the Normal Class, and that all its members would be trained in the oral method of teaching the deaf.

On the appointed day both met at the Appropriations Committee Room and Bell spoke for 45 minutes. He flatly asserted that the purpose of the Normal Department was to train deaf teachers of the deaf —and he opposed the plan mainly on that ground.[6] Gallaudet's reply consumed 13 minutes, "laying bare Professor Bell's disingenuousness." Gallaudet felt that he had triumphed before the Committee. He and Bell had kept their good natures during this bout, and parted in a friendly way, but Gallaudet could not refrain from feeling a good deal aggrieved. He learned later that the Committee had sustained the Institution fully against Bell's attack. General Cogswell told Gallaudet that the Committee was not disposed to do anything for Bell. Quiet reigned for a while. Bell met with Gallaudet and Professor Fay concerning the census of the deaf, but was still warlike as to the Normal School.

Gallaudet went to the Capitol and learned that the full Appropriations Committee had given the Institution everything requested for the Normal School but had omitted $3,000 for the improvement of grounds! Several days later Gallaudet checked at the Capitol with his Congressional friends Hemphill, Cogswell, and McComas, finding all favorable for the Institution, and left thinking Graham Bell would "come home shorn" from his little wool-gathering picnic. He took Susy to a doctor in Philadelphia and made a call on Crouter, telling him about Bell's actions. Crouter appeared to think Bell's opposition a piece of impertinence. Journeying on to New York he called on a prospective oral teacher there. Returning home he visited his Senate friends and learned that so far Bell had made no move. But something warned him that more was coming. "It is a pitiful spectacle—considering Bell," he mused, "to see a man of naturally generous impulses given over to partisan spite." He had just learned that Bell had sent a letter to Senator Allison "full of garbled statements and misrepresentations." Bell had been in correspondence with a number of oral schools from which he had secured petitions against the Normal School measure, still holding it was being formed to train the deaf to teach the deaf.

On February 17th Gallaudet met Bell before the Senate Committee when Allison gave them each two minutes. Dr. Phillip Gillett of the Illinois School arrived in Washington and tried to reconcile Bell but was unsuccessful.

The Senate Committee's action was unfavorable. They struck out the $5,000 given the Institution by the House for the Normal Department. A telegram came from Fechheimer saying he had gone over to Bell's side. Then Gallaudet began to hear from his friends. From all parts of the country he received telegrams. He called on Cogswell, Cannon, Washburn—all of whom promised aid. Then to his surprise came a letter from Bell saying he had called on Dawes and found him prepared to offer an amendment for $3,000 for Oral Teaching in the College—and that he, Bell, had seen Allison and urged him to favor the amendment. "Bell," said Gallaudet "has heard from the 'back districts'. " Gallaudet told Dawes to push the measure in the Senate.

Toward the end of the month, on February 25th, Gallaudet was informed that Allison had accepted the $3,000 amendment and would offer it in the Senate. Two days later Gallaudet learned that Allison had not tacked on the $3,000 amendment in the Senate, so he had to scurry for aid. When Cogswell went out to see Gallaudet, Bell's secretary met him with a note from Bell asking an interview. Gallaudet heard Cogswell say, "Tell Professor Bell I have no sympathy with his cause and no time to hear about it." Gallaudet could not keep back an inward chuckle. He felt that his work for the session was over, deciding to leave the result to Providence and his friends on the Conference Committee.

After Bell succeeded in getting the appropriation cut he had wired some of his friends that "the Normal Department was defeated." But it did not turn out that way. With the $3,000 Congress gave, plus a small fund made available to him by the Directors, Gallaudet was able to go ahead with his project and organize the Department exactly as he had planned, and the Fellowship program was effected. The young man Gallaudet had tried to recruit in New York did not accept, and Gallaudet then turned to Professor Joseph C. Gordon of the College, and Miss Kate H. Fish who had trained at the Clarke School in Northampton; and these two, with Miss Mary T. G. Gordon of the Primary Department, set up the articulation schedule. Gallaudet later recounted the ordeal through which he had passed to President James C. Welling of Columbian University. Welling described the circumstances as resulting from "the development of the millionaire spirit."

Gallaudet went to Baltimore to talk over his plans with Daniel Coit Gilman of Johns Hopkins, who had been most successful with his Fellowships program. Gilman was struck favorably with the "new departure" program of the Columbia Institution, and promised Gallaudet a letter to lay before his Board. Just as Joseph Henry had done, Gilman reviewed Gallaudet's Normal Fellows program and sent a résumé of it to Gallaudet to read before his Board. The plan was scheduled to go into effect the following fall: six Fellowships of $500 each, with instruction in both manual and oral methods.

Soon everyone in the profession of teaching the deaf knew both sides of the situation. Many tried to get matters patched up between Bell and Gallaudet. Gallaudet himself considered the Bell opposition "dead beyond recovery." He composed a statement of the "Genesis of the Normal Department," which he asked Professor Fay to submit to Bell in hope he might write something to go properly with it in the *Annals*. Fay carried out the mission but his report to Gallaudet was not favorable. Gallaudet decided Bell was "in a bad hob" out of which it was not easy to crawl. He wrote a personal letter to Bell in regard to their differences and Bell's answer tried to justify his course in opposing the Normal Department. Gallaudet then went to see President Welling of Columbian University taking a packet of his own and Bell's letters and asked for advice. Welling counselled him to accept Bell's assurance that he had not intentionally misrepresented Gallaudet's views, and Gallaudet wrote Bell to that effect. In the

meantime Bell's letter refusing to meet Gallaudet came, but after
he had read Gallaudet's most recent note Bell wrote another, most
cordial, saying Gallaudet's last letter had "removed a load of sorrow
from my heart." Things looked well for a reconciliation. Gallaudet
answered and insisted on a personal interview, at Gallaudet's office.
Bell showed up in indifferent spirit, still inclined to justify his course
and not willing to concede that he had treated Gallaudet unjustly.
Gallaudet pressed him on several points, and finally one good was
gained: they could meet thereafter on a friendly basis, at least
outwardly so. "The hatchet is buried," said Gallaudet, "but I know
where it is."

Room Enough for Two

The belief sprang up that Graham Bell and Gallaudet had "tiffed"
and had never got over it. It would not be fair to either's memory
to let this assumption stand. They did disagree over methods of
teaching the deaf, and their arguments were in the open between
1890 and 1900 because of the Normal Department and another matter
which came to a head in 1893. This was a proposed plan originating
with Gallaudet to merge the Convention of American Instructors of
the Deaf with the American Association to Promote the Teaching of
Speech to the Deaf, doing away with the necessity of organizing the
Convention into an Association. Bell agreeable to this, but as later
events proved he preferred to keep his own Association separate.

The Chicago Convention took place in July when the Executive
Committee of the Convention adopted Gallaudet's idea for merger
of the two organizations. Bell was holding his Association meeting
at the same time at the University of Chicago. When the Executive
Committee's report was adopted Bell announced on the same day
that the A.A.P.T.S.D.'s new President would be Phillip G. Gillett, the
Illinois principal who had been trying to smooth matters between
Bell and Gallaudet. This new move to put Gillett in to head Bell's
organization hoodwinked Gallaudet into feeling sure the merging
of the two organizations would follow.

In November Gallaudet sent an overture to the oral association from
the Executive Committee of the Convention. For the next few weeks
he wrote letters to Bell, Crouter, and others about the "Union," and
he talked with his own professors. In December Gillett and Crouter
were his guests and they discussed union in such a manner that he
was convinced both men favored it. When Bell called he seemed
to feel much as did the others. He claimed he saw no good reason

why the two organizations should not join, but did fear that oral teaching might be relegated to a secondary or subordinate place. Early 1894 found matters the same, Gallaudet sending out copies of the overture to all interested groups, and waiting for replies. He learned that Bell was following him up to know what schools voted against the Committee's report on classification of methods. "This looks as if he was determined to prosecute his warfare," commented Gallaudet. Soon Gallaudet had a letter from Gillett informing him that the A.A.P.T.S.D. had decided to postpone the consideration of the Convention's overture. Gallaudet considered this "a bootlicking surrender by Dr. Gillett of his independence to Bell." It made him feel that Bell was like an octopus trying to get its tentacles around the whole profession of instructors of the deaf.

In May Gallaudet made plans to go to Chatauqua in July, where he would give an address in behalf of union. He was becoming wearied of "the long grind of deaf-mute matters." But duty called him to continue as a standard bearer a while longer. An invitation came for him to meet at Bell's with Crouter and Gillett to talk things over. Mr. Hubbard was there, giving Gallaudet a surprise by proposing to consider the matter of union favorably in the near future, "say after another year," if Gallaudet would not press the matter against their wishes that summer. Bell and Hubbard agreed to give Gallaudet all the time he needed at Chataugua during the Association meeting, provided he did not press for a vote.

Since Gillett now headed the A.A.P.T.S.D., Gallaudet thought it best he retire from the Executive Committee of the Convention; he wrote him and told him so. Gillett's reply was that the Standing Executive Committee had no legal existence! Gallaudet, because of Hubbard's and Bell's friendliness, stood convinced that the two, with Crouter, were on his side and that it was Gillett who was holding out against union. Hubbard had assured Gallaudet that he would be at Chatauqua and sustain him. While Gallaudet was resting at Quinipi before going to Chatauqua a letter arrived from Hubbard saying he could not be at Chatauqua for the opening; that Crouter and Bell would be there to stand by him. But when speeches were made by the Association members none favored union at all, and it was revealed that the Directors of the Association had voted to "appoint a committee to meet a committee" from the other side to work further on the matter of union. A joint committee finally met in Hubbard's room, when Bell rather disappointed Gallaudet by speaking of the importance of having members of the Association who were not teachers, but who would "pay well." At a business meeting that night Gallaudet and Bell had a tilt in which Hubbard supported Gallaudet. The meeting at Chatauqua settled nothing.

This situation remained the same into 1895 when Hubbard called on Gallaudet to give him his "plan of union." To Gallaudet it was a perfectly absurd and cumbersome scheme providing for three distinct organizations instead of his own proposed one. Gallaudet was now convinced of Hubbard's utter disingenuousness for the past eight months. It was after this visit that Gallaudet began his article on "The Tongue of the Dumb Shall Sing." He returned Hubbard's ridiculous plan for the federation of the Association and Convention.

In May Gallaudet and Fay began to work on plans for the Convention in Flint, Michigan. When beginning his own paper Gallaudet said, "It seems a great undertaking to 'do up' Professor Bell, but I think it must be done. The material is abundant—and needs only to be used." He asked for wisdom to do it right. When he finished his paper and read it to Professor Fay it seemed to scare Fay a little, but Gallaudet figured that Fay was naturally a noncombatant. He read his paper on "The Tongue of the Dumb Shall Sing" before the Anthropological Society, put the finishing touches on his Flint paper, then went to New Haven to receive an honorary doctor of laws degree from Yale University.

Gallaudet and Fay met and journeyed to Flint. On the opening day of the Convention Gallaudet reported the new constitution and proposals which the Standing Executive Committee had adopted.' Bell then rose and in his speech declared that the A.A.P.T.S.D. did not decline the scheme for union, but proposed a plan for union which the Joint Committee had declined. Gallaudet admitted he then went for Bell in rather strong language, and as one said, "drew the first blood."

The day arrived for presentation of Gallaudet's paper. Its reading created a tremendous stir. Bell was not present, much to Gallaudet's regret, but he met Bell later and was asked by him for permission to see a copy of his "tirade." Gallaudet referred him to the secretary for a copy. On July 5 Bell was given time for a rejoiner. He did not attempt any reply to Gallaudet's attack, and Gallaudet felt it was because Bell could not dispute his statements. Instead, Bell told his audience how very sorry he was that Gallaudet should so misunderstand him. "It was all lame and impotent," declared Gallaudet.

Gallaudet was elected President of the Convention at Flint and he

held the office until the day of his death. Bell tried to become an
active member of the Convention but, as Gallaudet put it, "his money
was refused." Bell did not try to see Gallaudet again until December
of 1899, when Gallaudet was invited to a meeting of the Census Committee of the A.A.P.T.S.D., but the message came too late for
Gallaudet to accept. However, on January 4, 1900, a special message
was delivered to Gallaudet from Bell, asking him to come to him
after dinner and go with him to see Senator Eugene Hale on the
census matter. They met at the Capitol on the 12th. "We stood
together and I hope our speeches did good," Gallaudet wrote. On
the evening of the 13th Gallaudet went with the Fays to Bell's home,
to a meeting of the Literary Society. This was the first time he had
been in Bell's home in four years. "I hope the hatchet is finally
buried now," was Gallaudet's only remark. And it was; each was
convinced that there was room for the other.

XIV

A Man About Town

One of the most amusing tales Edward Gallaudet ever told on himself was about the time, soon after his arrival in Washington, when he was authorized to purchase a horse and carriage or light wagon for the use of the Institution. He bought a handsome creature, quite speedy, which he thought was about 10 years old. Happy in his purchase he was driving along Pennsylvania Avenue one day when a gentleman stopped him to say a kind word for the horse. This man had owned the same horse several years before; the history of the animal disclosed he had been on the Louisiana race track and that he was 20 years old. Gallaudet thought the horse would soon be of no value, but he lived another 13 years and was turned out to grass at the age of 33. He then died gracefully and was buried in the forest on Kendall Green.

One has a good picture now of how the young Superintendent looked driving down Pennsylvania Avenue in a jump-seat wagon behind a horse named Brent, speedy despite his years. With this outfit he made calls on friends like William H. Seward, Secretary of State under Lincoln. It was probably through his connection with the Sewards that Gallaudet was invited to join the Literary Society of Washington, which had first been suggested by Miss Olive Seward, the Secretary's adopted daughter. John Nicolay had drawn up its constitution with Dr. Samuel Tyler. Gallaudet became a member in 1878, and in the group met a man who became his friend: Carl Schurz, the Prussian-born politician who became the United States Minister to Spain before joining the Union Army. Some of his earliest friends in the city were members of the Literary Society. They included Ainsworth Rand Spofford, the Librarian of Congress, and John Nicolay who was Lincoln's secretary. The daughters of these men became his daughters' friends. He met the early mayors of the city, and the men who set up the early territorial government: Alexander Robey Shepherd, the half-brothers Henry D. and Jay

Cooke. Shepherd was head of Public Works while Henry Cooke was the first Governor of the District. Henry D. Cooke also served on Gallaudet's Board from 1868 to 1881. Many fine improvements took place in Washington while Shepherd headed the Public Works and in all probability Gallaudet's own campus profited by these improvements: gas lamps, sewer system, water system, and sidewalks. Although Congress investigated Shepherd's record he was later fêted as a public benefactor.

Diplomatic life expanded between 1880 and 1890, and White House etiquette was revised. Great Britain, France, Italy and Germany raised their envoys from the rank of Minister to Ambassador. By 1892 the U. S. had equality of power with these older nations. Sir Julian Pauncefote became the first Ambassador in Washington and first dean of the Diplomatic Corps. He and his Lady were guests at Kendall Green several times, and in 1896 when a Normal student from India, Jamini Nath Banerji of the University of Calcutta, spoke to the audience about the work he hoped to do in India, Sir Julian who was present was moved to break his rule and speak to the audience also.

Gallaudet attired himself correctly for every occasion, and he believed in being loyal to his tailor. He had discovered while shopping in New York that a deaf-mute by the name of Abraham Lincoln Thomas clerked at Rogers Peet and Company, and he tried to do as much of his shopping there as possible. A dress suit, a Prince Albert coat with vest to match, a grey serge, a dark blue cheviot suit were mentioned among other items. He went to diplomatic receptions and exclusive dinners, dined with the President and Mrs. Hayes at former Governor Claflin's, and attended brilliant parties at Vice President Hobart's. He went to the coming-out party of Secretary of State Hay's daughter and attended innumerable receptions in the large homes of the city.

There were musicals at the embassies, stag dinners, scientific society meetings, and always his visits to the Cosmos Club, of which he was a charter member. Once he lunched with Professor Samuel Pierpont Langley on the yacht *River Queen* when there were about 50 guests, mostly scientists, and among them Sir William Osler, the famous physician and teacher. Gallaudet was at the British Embassy in 1893 to attend Queen Victoria's Birthday Ball at which the Spanish Infanta and the Princess Eulalie were presented. He remembered Eulalie as pretty and engaging, but Antoine was a "stick." Another evening Gallaudet and Susy attended dinner at the Swiss Minister's, and after a wonderful evening continued on to a ball at the German Embassy. When they could they gave parties and dinners, not only to guests from town but to their Kendall Green friends and staff members.

It was toward the end of the 1890's that social events began to pall and Gallaudet started to refer to the great rush, and to the "coming-out," as the Social Racket. He once remarked that the social racket did not improve his daughter Marion's disposition. Another time he jotted down that "Susy and Marion are hard at work on the social racket these days, I go in moderately." Marion finally made her own debut after graduating from Miss Porter's School for Girls, and went up to New York to be in Rosemary Grant's wedding when she became Mrs. Sartoris. Son Herbert received a special delivery note from Mrs. Theodore Roosevelt inviting him to daughter Alice's coming-out ball at the White House in January of 1902. Son Dennie married Alice Wemple, the daughter of Edward W. Wemple, former New York Representative, and Edson was married to one of the beautiful daughters of Senator Francis M. Cockrell, a Missourian. Herbert married the gracious Elizabeth Young of Pine Orchard and Marion, the youngest, married John W. Edgerton, of the Yale Law School.

It was in 1896 that daughter Katharine presented her father with a bicycle. They were in Indian Neck at the time and he waited until his return to Washington to learn to ride it. His experiences with his wheel are highly entertaining and he made no bones about how hard it was for him to learn to ride. At first he got his exercise on the wheel, but soon he began to speak of exercising the wheel! He took many falls, and one time was too frightened to take his hands off the handlebars to tip his hat when Mrs. Grover Cleveland rode past although he managed to "bow low." Professor Hall helped him in the early stages of learning, but he was like a bird leaving its nest for the first time when he ventured forth alone into the city. Soon he became a familiar sight wheeling along the Avenue.

When the Potomac froze in the winter Gallaudet could often be found skating. He also enjoyed sledding and other winter sports. He did not mind admitting that he took a "belly-buster" when going down a steep hill on his sled. Following Mr. Fessenden's death in Hartford Gallaudet took his sleigh to Washington, driving the horses to it, with the tinkling bells.

Gallaudet developed into a needed civic-minded person. As early as 1883 he helped organize a Trinity College Alumni Association in

Baltimore which combined with Washington in its early years, with
Gallaudet as President. When Washington organized separately in
1894 Gallaudet acted as chairman and was elected Vice President.
He also attended his Psi Upsilon alumni meetings, and once at a
reception for the Bureau of American Republics President Taft greeted him with the Psi Upsilon grip!

Gallaudet found a real outlet for his talents and abilities in these
civic activities. He spent months and years working toward persuading the Baltimore and Ohio Railroad to remove its tracks from the
school entrance. The trains were a constant menace to the deaf and
the tracks an eyesore. He called on Senators, Commissioners, obtained signed petitions from the neighborhood, went over to Baltimore
to the main office and talked with officials, visited newspaper offices
for publicity on the project, and finally, after weary days, brought
about the definite surrender of the Baltimore and Ohio Railroad to
the wishes of the Institution. He was in accord with the new Great
Falls Railroad company's plan for a cross-town railroad. He worked
on public health, the asphalting of the streets, later the paving, and
an Industrial School for Negroes, a Market House on H Street, and
the Newsboys Aid. He first heard Theodore Roosevelt speak at a
meeting in behalf of the newsboys.

Gallaudet served on the Boards of both Columbian University[1] and
Howard University and during the years was asked by each to serve
as acting president—which he could not manage to do. He helped
the former a great deal in ideas about real estate, for Columbian
University had several moves before settling where it now is in
Washington and becoming George Washington University. The land
meant a great deal to Gallaudet and he eventually invested several
sums of money in land and property for himself. He had one great
dream which went unfulfilled in his lifetime, and that was to convert
the property adjoining Kendall Green into a beautiful park: a second
"Hampstead Heath." He had first tried to buy Brentwood as an
addition to Kendall Green but the Patterson heirs would not sell it.
Finally, he worked long and hard to get the city Commissioners to
ask Congress for it. He would be happy to know that it is now
officially Brentwood Park and is used by the neighborhood children
for games. The list of his activities is legion and he lived the role
of a devoted citizen while in Washington.

The Ethics of Friendship

The capacity for making friends was one of Gallaudet's finest qualities; his ability to keep them, his most enviable possession. He worked at cementing friendships and endowed his friends with the very essence of their better qualities, so that these glowed for others as well. He created around himself an existence which furthered the gentle mixing of the groups he moved among as he went about his business and his pleasure.

His devotion to the theatre, which included the dance, gave him diverse interests and although he did not "approve" of all that went on he nevertheless allowed such experiences to enter his horizon, making him better qualified to pass judgment than if he had rejected these experiences through prejudice. He maintained an open mind and never did he play ostrich.

From his first writings one can follow his interests as he grew in stature as an educator and devotee of the arts. He had an intense desire to express himself through the written word. His philosophy, by the very nature of his work, was based on expedience; if one method did not bring results, try another. He admitted this quality himself. His writings show that they were not the work of a man of leisure. They took on the tone of reporting rather than creativity, although when he first began writing as a boy of 14, in 1851, he started as a poet! He kept a small composition book of poetry and by 1856 he was seeing himself in print, although under a pen name of E. D. Veer.

He wrote a play when he was 19 that had the dramatic title of *Maniac's Revenge,* which he hoped to sell but never did.

When the summons came from Amos Kendall that took the youthful Edward to Washington his aspirations for a "literary" career were abandoned for the more realistic life ahead. His writing talent then went into reports, articles, lectures, Sunday sermons, precise letters, and communications with Congress. Seldom did he step into a new field of thought but continued to build each successive article on preceding works, chiefly related to the education of the deaf and the methods best fitted to teach them. He became a prodigious writer and wrote for many periodicals other than those pertaining to the deaf, although the subject matter did not differ. His legal thinking finally achieved a goal when he rounded out his *Manual on International Law* in 1877. It became a textbook and went into five editions, with numerous revisions. Ten years later he published a biography of his father.

He actually tried a novel in 1891, naming the book *Bob Erwin de Quiescas.* He destroyed this manuscript in 1911 when he cleared out his office desk at retirement. This book might have revealed the dark days he spent during 1866 of which he wrote in his *Occasionals.* Oddly enough he chose the name of a cousin, Robert Erwin, the grandson of his Uncle James in Georgia. He alluded to a second novel begun in 1893 which he called *The Fortunes of Percival.* Evidently he destroyed this too, although he never mentioned it but the one time.

It was the Literary Society that gave Gallaudet an opportunity in his later years to express himself in a literary way. Even then his papers were not fully and beautifully written but were often in outline form which he referred to as he talked, especially about his travels. He composed a small amount of music to which he wrote lyrics. He composed a song to Susy called "The Sunshine of Love," and his island home caused him to write "My Garden Far Out at Sea." He had the song to Susy played as a surprise at one of the Literary meetings and it ended up by embarrassing her, much to Gallaudet's chagrin. However, one of the most unnerving moments of Gallaudet's association with the Literary Society came the evening of January 21, 1882. The hostess was Frances Hodgson Burnett, of *Little Lord Fauntleroy* fame, who was known for her soirées and for her personal eccentricities. On this particular evening, before a brilliant gathering of artists, writers, actors, and eccentrics, Mrs. Burnett introduced her surprise guest, Oscar Wilde, who had just arrived in the States 19 days before. Gallaudet's one comment was that, "The famous or rather notorious Oscar Wilde was present, a good deal to my disgust." Gallaudet kept active membership in the Literary Society until his retirement, remaining an associate member when he left Washington.

In always going to the source for his material Gallaudet was fortunate in meeting many famous men of the day who became interested in his work and his writing and gave him advice that was invaluable. While doing his work on international law he met, through his friend Thomas F. Bayard, the eminent authority on international law, Dr. Francis Wharton, and he talked with Sir Wilfred Laurier, the Canadian Premier. When he needed points he got in touch with Admiral Dewey, and when his study called for maps he called on General Adolphus Greely, the scientist and Arctic explorer, and borrowed some. When William Beach Lawrence lectured at Columbian University Gallaudet became acquainted with him. But it was to the Library of Congress that Gallaudet went most often to do his work, and Mr. Spofford, the Librarian, was always eager to help. The justices and jurists knew Gallaudet as a student and a scholar and they were always ready to give a word of advice or help him on some legal point. He missed Garfield deeply and followed him in office as President of the Literary Society, but he had really found good companionship among artists, musicians, journalists, scientists, historians, and diplomats. He could imagine himself E. D. Veer again, and dream with the heroes of the fiction he loved.

Books Over the Years

Gallaudet's writings and his reading enjoyed different climates. He was a devotee of the novel, using it as "escape" literature. Among the men writers he admired F. Marion Crawford and S. Weir Mitchell. However, he read more stories and books written by women than by men, which might be laid to the fact that he read many magazines and monthly periodicals, and many women wrote prolifically during the 1890's under masculine pseudonyms. He rejected stories with low talk, unfaithfulness, triangles, or unhappy endings. He saw no reason why the author could not contrive a happy ending. He might even finish a book he felt commonplace, then begrudge the time he gave it! Once in a while he finished a story "with regret." Such a book was Hugo's *Les Misérables*. He hated to part with the interesting personalities, and felt that Jean Valjean was a sinner sanctified into a saint of the highest rank, and that many passages in the story were of rare beauty. Susy once caught him reading a story named "Guenn" which she claimed was "a story of man's inhumanity to woman."

Gallaudet often thought in poetry, and a sunset or a moonlit night had him jotting down bits from a familiar poem in his diary. Once at Indian Neck the lines from James Gates Percival's poem, "Coral Grove," which he had known as a boy, flashed through his mind:

Above is a photo of members of the Gallaudet College faculty in 1885. Seated, left to right, are Edward Allan Fay, E.M.G., Noah Porter. Standing left to right, are Joseph Gordon, John J. Chickering, J. Burton Hotchkiss, Charles Ely, and Amos G. Draper.

In picture below, taken in 1890, seated from left to right are Chickering, Fay, Draper, E.M.G., Hotchkiss, and Porter. Standing is Joseph Gordon.

Dr. Nathan S. Lincoln,
College physician.

Miss Mary T. G. Gordon,
teacher of speech in 1890's.

A photograph of co-ed students at Gallaudet College in the spring of 1900.

"Deep in the wave is a coral grove, where the purple mullet and gold-fish rove. . . ." Longfellow was a favorite, and he recalled lines from that poet while on the sound in Portland, Maine, when the "Deeping oaks" brought to mind "A boy's will is the wind's will . . ." Charles Kingsley was still another favorite.

His interests ranged from Lawrence Sterne to Bulwer Lytton; from Hawthorne to Thomas Hardy, turning suddenly to Dr. Lord's *Beacon Lights of History*. He would explore Francis Parkman, then read *The Nation*, a weekly devoted to politics, literature, science and art. During the 1880's spiritualism came into vogue and a number of books and stories with mystical settings flooded the market. Gallaudet knew Sarita M. Brady, an "advanced thinker" in spiritualism. He preferred, however, the actual mystery or mystic background, such as George Eber's *Narda*, a story of Egyptain life, or a story in Scribner's called "A Study of Apparent Death," about fakirs of Persia and Hindustan. Washington Irving's *Alhambra* had its turn as did Bryant's transla-tions of Homer's *Iliad*. Tolstoi's *Kreutzer Sonata* intrigued him, and Thackeray's *Burlesque Novelettes*. He read Meredith and Howells, Warner and Rider Haggard, George Eliot and Mrs. Humphrey Ward, Julia Ward Howe and William Black. He read the works of Con-necticut writers such as Rose Terry Cooke and Annie Slosson (a Trumbull relative) and the Washington writer, Mary Imlay Taylor. He liked Annie Besant, the theosophist, and Mary Mapes Dodge, editor of *St. Nicholas Magazine* and author of *Hans Brinker, or the Silver Skates*. They were correspondents.

Robert Ingersoll's articles fascinated him, and the works of Mark Twain. Booth Tarkington and Joseph Vance came under his eye. He read Coppet's *Les Vrais Riches*, "a sweet healthful book," and Benson's *Relentless City*—"lurid glimpses into English and American 'high life'. " Daudet and Zola he considered "heavy reading." Much of this reading had no direction: Mary Johnston, Frances Hodgson Burnett, Mrs. Dolaro, Sarah Jewett, Mary Yonge, Blanche Howard, Mary E. Wilkins, Mrs. Juliana E. Ewing, and Clara Morris, the actress who wrote about the stage, were typical of the women writers he read. He enjoyed the new writer, Robert Louis Stevenson, but after such diversions he invariably turned to a book like Sir Henry Maine's *On International Law*, or John Fiske's *Excursions of an Evolutionist*. He liked Bliss Perry's *The Amateur Spirit*, and while travelling on shipboard often caught up with books like Irving's *History of New York* and Balzac's *Catherine de Medici*, or perhaps Bacon's *Novum Organum*. William James' *Pluralistic Universe* was read while he visited at Glenmore, New Hampshire, attending the summer school of philosophy founded by Thomas Davidson. F. Hopkinson Smith's *Tides of Barnegate* was "a painful and unsatisfactory story. All the fine people come to grief and the villain does not get *her* due recompense at all." *The Rosary* was better reading: "a remarkably fine story, and ending happily."

Several well-known writers of the day wrote about Gallaudet's work. Sarita M. Brady published an article in the October, 1875, issue of *Harper's* on the deaf-mute College. Adophus Greely wrote on the sign language an article published in *American Annals of the Deaf*, and also one about the College in the *Review of Reviews* in 1897. Gail Hamilton publicized the Institution, and the press in Washington was always cooperative.

Gallaudet met Helen Hunt Jackson while she was on a mission to Washington in 1881 in behalf of the Indians in Colorado. *Ramona* was a result of this investigation of their needs. Washington writers he knew included Horatio King, once Postmaster General, and Thomas Nelson Page who had moved to Washington from Richmond, Virginia, and was later Ambassador to Italy.

He heard all the prominent lecturers who visited the city, and corresponded with Phillips Brooks and Oliver Wendell Holmes. While abroad in 1900 he met Hendrik Willem Van Loon at Belle Rive, and when this young Dutchman, who later turned to writing, came to the United States to enter Cornell in 1903 he visited Gallaudet during April of that year. But aside from literature and authors Gallaudet was devoted to the theatre. During his life-time he saw nearly all the famous actors, either in this country or abroad, and heard many well-known singers.

THE MAKE-BELIEVE WORLD

As early as 1880 Gallaudet saw Joseph Jefferson perform in the "new version" of *The Rivals*. This was in contrast to his most famous characterization, Rip Van Winkle. He saw Mary Anderson play the part of Julia in *The Hunchback* and of Pauline in *The Lady of Lyons*, before she retired in 1889. In 1890 he saw *Richelieu*, starring Edwin Booth and Modjeska, but one of his favorite actors was Lawrence Barrett, who was a guest the same night he met Oscar Wilde. Gallaudet and Susy were introduced to Julia Marlowe at the home of a friend, and the same year, 1899, they enjoyed Maude Adams in *The Little Minister*, which Gallaudet thought superb.

That September they saw Katharine Kidder play both Perdita and

Hermione in *The Winter's Tale,* and he and Susy heard Deschamps speak on the revival of the heroic French drama in March of 1901. Gallaudet went alone to see the *Tale of Two Cities,* produced under the title of *The Only Way,* with Henry Miller playing the lead. While in Paris attending the Congress of the Deaf, he managed to see Sarah Bernhardt in *L'Aiglon,* and at home he never missed a William Gillette performance.

Gallaudet saw these performers over and over again as they came in new productions. Others he admired were Francis Wilson, Richard Mansfield, Frank Daniels, Eleanor Elsie Robson, who became Mrs. August Belmont, Raymond Hackett, W. H. Crane, Maxine Elliott, Henry Woodruff, E. H. Sothern, and Mrs. Fiske. As late as 1910 he saw Elsie Janis in *A Fair Co-ed,* and Sothern and Marlowe in *The Taming of the Shrew.*

He was not averse to musicals and thought Fritzi Scheff was delightful in *Madamoiselle Modiste.* He also liked the DeKoven comic opera, *The Student Prince.* The Gilbert and Sullivan operas were among his favorites, although he liked the "heavier" plays such as the Robertsons performed. He enjoyed the Ben Greet Players, and when he was 71 he saw Isadora Duncan dance to Damrosch's orchestra. He explained that as he sat watching her, barefooted and bare-legged up to her thighs, he came to a decision: "to the pure all things are pure," and while he watched this was in his mind a good deal.

The night he saw Edward Sheldon's *Salvation Nell,* Gallaudet was intrigued by the play itself because it was written by a youth of 24. Could he have been thinking about his early play, *Maniac's Revenge?*

Personal Friendships

After Gallaudet's close friendship with Garfield, and following his untimely death, it could be said that the man closest to Gallaudet in the later years was John Watson Foster (1836-1917,) prominent in the Temperance Union Society among his many activities in Washington. There was one year difference in their ages and they passed away the same year.

John Watson Foster was born in Indiana and went to the State University, later having a year at the Harvard Law School before studying in a law office in Indiana. He fought on the Union side during the Civil War thus gaining the rank by which Gallaudet usually referred to him: General Foster. Following the War he edited a newspaper in his state and in 1872 branched into politics, becoming the Chairman of the Indiana Republican State Committee. He was instrumental in bringing General Grant into office, and Grant later appointed Foster Minister to Mexico. In 1880 President Hayes appointed him to represent this country in St. Petersburg. From there he returned to practice law in the District of Columbia. In 1883 President Arthur made him Minister to Spain. Following this assignment he again practiced law in the District during Cleveland's administration. President Harrison sent Foster on a special mission to Madrid to work on a reciprocity treaty, and he also acted as agent for the United States in the Bering Sea or fur-seal arbitration. For one year during this time he was Secretary of State, and although he negotiated a treaty for the annexation of Hawaii it was not approved by the Senate. Foster also acted on the "Baltimore" incident which occurred under Captain W. S. Schley,[1] and in 1894 helped to bring about the peace treaty with Japan after the Chino-Japanese War.[2] Foster prepared the case for the Alaska-Canada boundary in 1903, and in 1907 represented China at the Second Hague Conference, the Conference to which Gallaudet so longed to be appointed.[3]

As a lawyer in Washington, Foster represented various governments, notably the Mexican. He lectured widely on international relations, and his courses at George Washington University covered the salient features of American diplomatic history from 1776 to 1876. One source points out that the rules and procedure of Foster's lectures of diplomatic intercourse developed into the best work of its kind written by an American. He wrote his autobiography in his work, *Diplomatic Memoirs,* published in two volumes in 1909.

This man had lived the kind of life Gallaudet dreamed about. It is not to be wondered that Gallaudet admired him deeply. Gallaudet attended the marriage of Foster's daughter Edith to the Reverend Allen Macy Dulles, Presbyterian minister whom Gallaudet had heard in Washington on several occasions. He later held the pastorate at Watertown, New York, before going to teach at the Auburn Theological Seminary. His father had been a minister and another relative had served as United States Minister to Great Britain in 1879. A child of this union was John Foster Dulles, born in 1888, who is at present the United States Secretary of State and carries on the tradition of being an expert in international law. At 19 he attended the Peace Conference in 1907, acting as his grandfather's secretary when John W. Foster represented China.

Gallaudet imagined he would have been fitted for the arduous life of arbitration. This, in all probability, was true; but he sometimes forgot that he excelled in his own field of arbitration, and that few could have taken his place. He controlled his ambitions admirably, however, and made no ill-advised move to alter his hard-earned standing. One can point to the manner in which he handled the campaign to obtain civil service benefits for the deaf as the ultimate in diplomatic strategy. For this successful undertaking he enlisted the help of Taft and Theodore Roosevelt.

Gallaudet had journalist friends like Wilhelmus Bogart Bryan of the Washington *Star*; Charles Nordhoff, Washington Correspondent for the New York *Herald*; Mary Katherine Keemle Field who edited a paper called *Kate Field's Washington;* Donn Piatt who edited *The Capitol;* Theodore W. Noyes, editor of *The Star*, and Francis Preston Blair, an early journalist and politician. George Kennan was an outstanding journalist. He was selected by Western Union to be a member of its Siberian expedition which surveyed a route for the extension of the telegraph system from America to Europe. His books on Russia made him famous. Gallaudet knew him in the Literary Society and the two families exchanged calls.

There were others over the years who inspired Gallaudet to continued study and a re-dedication to his own life work, and he never ceased to write about the subject dearest to his heart: that of improving the mental vision of the deaf. At the age of 73 he wrote a paper on "The Mind of the Deaf Child," and at 75 he finished the article about his father, "A Philanthropic Hartford Man," which was published in the Hartford *Courant* of April 9, 1912.

"MY CHILDREN"

In writing about Gallaudet's friends one would never exclude his friendships among the deaf, or the educators of the deaf. From the time the young College awarded its first honorary degree to the deaf John Carlin at the special convocation on June 28, 1864, Gallaudet sought outstanding deaf persons he could so honor. Carlin, a brilliant writer, social worker for the deaf, and a successful miniature portrait painter of New York, had for years advocated a higher education for the deaf. It was a source of great pleasure to Gallaudet to have deaf friends scattered over the land, and he often went out of his way while travelling to visit with them. In Chicago was Lester Goodman; in St. Louis James Henry Cloud; in Minnesota Jay Cooke Howard and Howard L. Terry; and the Washburn family would welcome him because of their son Cadwallader. In 1871 every section of the country was represented at the College except the Pacific Coast. By 1896, however, Winfield Scott Runde, a Californian, had entered, and by 1901 three other Californians had joined the ranks.

Many deaf persons are still living who were taught by Gallaudet; many more are alive who knew him before he died. Those who later learned about him revere the name that for over a hundred years has stood as a symbol for the advantages extended to the deaf of this country and abroad in their educational and cultural development. It was a deaf man who first suggested, in 1924, that a biography should be written about their benefactor. James H. Cloud wrote to Grace Gallaudet in that year to inquire why such a book had been neglected. Plans were begun but not finished. Eleven years later another alumnus, H. Lorraine Tracy, tried to start the ball rolling again in behalf of a biography. The Memorial Fund, begun on Gallaudet's seventieth birthday had been added to, and by 1930 had reached the total of $39,000 under the Chairmanship of Harley D. Drake, '04. World War II intervened, and after Katharine Gallaudet's death in 1942 her nephew, who was Gallaudet's oldest grandson, came into possession of all papers, and the plan for a biography was considered again. He chose a biographer, and when the work got under way the alumni again rallied and offered their aid, proposing to send reminiscences to the author and to place their orders for a copy of the book.

One of the first letters to come was from the original California student, Winfield Scott Runde. He sent a copy of a eulogy he had written at Gallaudet's death, which was published in the *California News* in November of 1917. In this account Mr. Runde spoke of having sat for two years in Gallaudet's classes and said, "He made us all understand uninteresting studies. His lectures were forceful and were delivered in signs that were beautiful and fascinating." Mr. Runde emphasized the fact that the educated deaf hailed Gallaudet as their champion in their efforts to compel the schools throughout the land to continue to employ the combined system of instruction and to preserve the sign language. He thought of Gallaudet as the greatest benefactor of all time, and called him "the uncrowned king of the profession of teaching the deaf . . . a staunch friend and a man of sterling character whose influence was uplifting and irresistible."

Gallaudet's last trip to Washington was in February of 1916. President and Mrs. Hall gave up their room so that Gallaudet might stay in the room that was "Susy's and mine in the old days. It was like awaking from a long dream." He attended part of the afternoon Chapel exercises. In the audience sat Benjamin M. Schowe, a senior, who captured the spirit of the scene in an article he wrote for the *Buff and Blue,* the literary quarterly of the College. He wrote that this last message from the lips of Gallaudet "was conceived in his heart, built in his imagination, long before the architects first began to make their preliminary sketches on paper." Gallaudet's personal appearance showed clearly that he was not strong, but "his complexion was still smooth and clear with a spot of pink glowing in either cheek . . . he was still a distinguished figure of a man." When he mounted the rostrum on President Hall's arm he turned and looked at the audience a long time "as if he would recapture all at once the experiences of a lifetime of work and service in these halls"—then raised his hand to speak as though he were lifting a heavy burden. The gist of the message was that they in their Garden of Ideals should plant the seed of discontent—"not a futile, fault-finding seed of dissatisfaction, but a wholesome seed of discontent with worldy success." He cautioned them that there was nothing they might do in this life that might not be done better, and he quoted the scripture of a good and faithful servant. The silence that followed was strained—but finally Gallaudet seemed to have absorbed the scene to his satisfaction and turned to leave with President Hall. A young lady student handed him a bouquet of red roses and Gallaudet's face lighted up. He turned to his audience and said, "I am tempted—I am tempted to be content."

Of an older generation was a deaf man who was awarded an honorary master of arts degree by the College in 1896. George Morris McClure, from Kentucky, is now 97 years old, but in 1950 he flew to Hartford to speak at the birthday anniversary of Edward Gallaudet. "I had a great respect and admiration for the Doctor Gallaudet," he remarked. He spoke of how Gallaudet stood up against great odds at times for his belief in the Combined System, and quoted the words: "Unshaken, unseduced, unterrified, his loyalty he kept." In recent years Gallaudet College has bestowed the doctor of pedagogy on Mr. McClure, and Centre College the doctor of literature. He can he called the Dean of the Deaf of the United States.

The list of accomplishments of the deaf graduates is long. One would like to honor each individual young man and woman who passed under Gallaudet's guidance and then proceeded to make his contribution to the community. Many have had sons and daughters to carry on their names: James Henry Cloud, George M. Teegarden, Ethel Zoe Taylor (who became Mrs. Percival Hall, wife of the second

President of the College,) Horace D. Lee Clarke, and Paul Lange, among many others.

The Gallaudets, the Peets, and the Fays became a triumvirate in the profession of teaching the deaf. From Thomas Hopkins Gallaudet (1787-1851) and Harvey Prindle Peet (1794-1873,) through their sons Edward Miner Gallaudet (1837-1917) and Isaac Lewis Peet (1824-1898,) the teaching of the deaf was guided in this country by men carrying these names. No less illustrious was Edward Allen Fay (1841-1923) who came into the profession through the interest of his father, the Rev. Barnabas Fay, who was the first Principal of the Michigan School. Edward Fay had a son and a daughter to follow him in the work, as did Isaac Lewis Peet whose daughter Elizabeth was the first woman to sit on the College Faculty at Gallaudet College. The record of these three families probably has no equal in the annals of education.

In subsequent issues of the *Buff and Blue* former students have paid tribute to Edward Gallaudet. Thomas Francis Fox, '83, remarked: "Looking at it in the perspective of time, the fame which rightly attaches to the name of Edward Miner Gallaudet was the outcome of constant, thoughtful tending, pushing, waiting, yet never losing faith in his main purposes—the advancement of the cause of the higher education of the deaf." All acknowledged his love and respect for human dignity.

XVI

The Rewards of Love

While winding up the various details preparatory to leaving Washington the following June, Gallaudet sat down to his dairy on December 22, 1910, and made the following entry: "Forty-two years ago today, Susy Dension and I were made husband and wife. It was a day of great joy to me, and I hoped to have the dear girl as my companion to my dying day. And she has left me lonely more than 7 years. Oh! how lonely at times, in spite of the presence of loving children and grandchildren."

Gallaudet's life with Susy was one long love story. He always thought of his romance with her as his manhood's first love. "Never was man more devotedly in love with woman than was I with my wife Susy," he wrote in his *Occasionals* four years after his marriage. But this young wife ten years his junior had not undergone the hardships that Edward had, and found it difficult to understand his moods and to meet his great demands for personal love. A most maternal woman, she found her nature well satified with her babies and their care, and she was possibly less ardent by nature than Edward. She was happy with her relatives and from the first days of her marriage managed to have someone related to her near at hand. The first photograph taken of her and Edward shows his two little daughters leaning against Susy's lap, and leaning against her shoulder is her nephew Will Denison. This Brady picture shows Edward standing guard at the rear.

Susy was a fearless person to have assumed two young daughters at the outset of her marriage, besides moving to Washington to become mistress of the President's Home. It was a large order for a 21-year-old girl; as large as the order expected of Edward when he first ventured to Washington, a green youth of 20. In his second marriage he was an experienced man of 31 who had lived in the nation's capital nearly 11 years, had been abroad, and had gained the poise of experience. He naturally expected a great deal from his bride, although she had just left her home for the first time.

Within four years' time, however, Edward came to feel insecure in Susy's affections and wondered if she could ever really love any one save those in whom her own blood coursed! In 1872 he had put Susy on "probation" the year they spent abroad, when he took his niece along to act as Susy's companion. In his state of mind he could easily have thought Susy was at fault. However, while they were at Lake Como visiting the Villa d'Este something like a "revelation" came to Susy as to the "folly" of her course. Gallaudet allowed her to make a complete "acknowledgment" of her errors, and they were both entirely happy, for his love for her had never altered during all the estrangement.

There would be similar occurrences throughout the years. Susy could hurt Gallaudet and he could "punish" her—and it grew into a kind of game. Under the same roof they wrote notes and letters to each other, then the tensions would clear and all was serene. When she felt ill or was enduring one of her blinding headaches he would read to her, play a game of whist to "amuse" her, just as parents put a child to bed before slipping out into their adult world. Susy loved cards and was particularly fond of backgammon. He called it that "innane game Susy loves and I have come to despise." He seldom won at cards. Once she did not deal him in the game when guests were present. He was crushed, but Susy never noticed it.

Another time at Quinipi Lodge during vacation she said something that so disturbed Gallaudet he ran off to Branford, took the train, and spent the next two days visiting relatives in Guilford and Durham. No one knows what Susy thought, and Gallaudet never referred to the incident again. He was probably woefully ashamed of himself. His great craving for love and devotion, for respect and regard, dominated his days. Even his handwriting changed with his emotions and health. A discipline case invariably upset him. Once Marion giggled when he said grace, and into the diary went his feelings. Another time when he wanted to conduct a family "sing," which was a ritual with him, he struck a tune for a hymn and Marion said, "Not *that*." He felt they had lost all respect for him.

Susy's youth often made her vulnerable in the eyes of this teacher-husband, and her only weapon was a firm stand and a manner of indifference. She did not care for horse-back riding, sports, and "shop talk"; she studied water color painting, took cello lessons, and collected books. She painted a head of Gallaudet which he did not care for, but she liked his Hermitage so well she practically moved into it. Her headaches were an excuse not to be "at home," but if she wanted to plough through a downpour to an exhibition at the Corcoran Gallery she ploughed. What she did alone during his many trips without her no one knows, but when she decided to go to Europe with *her own children* Gallaudet scurried about getting tickets and seeing them off. He then spent a lonely summer at Indian Neck, feeling terribly unwanted.

After their school days Grace and Katharine were in the home, although Grace did study kindergarden work and applied herself to it diligently for a while. Katharine was happy just to be around, with occasional trips. However, when Susy's daughter Marion reached young womanhood it vexed Susy to always have the two older daughters about. She was adamant about their leaving when Marion made her debut. Gallaudet sent the sisters abroad and Susy had the run of the house for a change.

Gallaudet tried to think of ways in which to please Susy that would reveal originality and thought. Once he took a heavy gold chain he had owned for a long time, sold it, put the money with some he had saved, and had an orange blossom pin made for Susy, using two stones in a setting that had been left to her by a relative. However, the day she came to him with the idea of buying a farm in Virginia he was thunderstruck. This was an emergency he had never dreamed of, and his diary got the results of his wonderment. "Susy knows I cannot afford to buy a farm in Virginia," he ruminated. However, that fall she had him on a train headed for Bluemont, Virginia, only several hours from Washington, and they looked for a farm. When he later resisted the sales talk, and tried to make Susy "see sense," she decided to sell some stock she owned and buy the farm herself. Gallaudet ended up by selling the stock for her, worrying about the clear deed of the property and getting the final sale completed. Often after that he and Susy would take a run over to Bluemont to see "our" farm. But Susy had an idea in the back of her head: she wanted something to leave her children! It was none other than her husband who had put the real estate idea in her head.

Father Fessenden had died on January 4, 1888. When his will was probated it was learned that he had divided almost equally with Gallaudet and his two granddaughters. In 1888 $57,000 was a nice sum, and this amount he had left to the three. It was the first time that Gallaudet had ever had that much money at one time. Some of his salary he had always managed to save, investing it in insurance bonds, but when the Fessenden money came to him he began thinking about real estate in Washington. Here was an apportunity to make some investments for his daughters that would eventually give them a degree of financial independence. Washington was a growing city and real estate was valuable.

Beginning in 1880 Gallaudet began to keep financial accounts in his diaries. These show that he owned some stock in the Aetna Life Insurance, in the Hartford Fire and Phoenix Bank Insurance Companies, the Phoenix Life, and the Charter Oak Bank. He also held some Columbia railroad stock, as well as mortgages on property. His salary otherwise was supplemented only by royalties on his books and sales on his articles.

In February of 1883 he spoke of having called at the bank and finding the Cookes had sold his railroad stock, the amount yielding exactly what he had expected. In March of 1885 a Mr. Strong paid him $1,700 on his mortgage and it was about this time Gallaudet built his Indian Neck Lodge. While he was building this summer spot the Washington papers came out with the news that Gallaudet had built "a fine place on the beach near Pine Orchard." He was horrified at such publicity and hastened to his newspaper friends.

It was at this zero hour that Susy chose to talk about buying the Tayloe House in Washington, an idea she held on to for the next five years. This home, known as the Octagon House, had been the home of Colonel John Tayloe, a wealthy Virginia planter and friend of George Washington. It had housed President Madison and wife Dolly when the British burned the Executive Mansion in 1814. When Susy had her eye on it, it was in a sad condition, but had she been able to persuade Gallaudet she would have owned a valuable piece of property. She lived to see the house taken over by the American Institute of Architects in 1903 and restored for their occupancy.

Gallaudet estimated his Hartford home, Quiescas, cost about $11,000 which included the $3,000 lot. This building had been completed before he came into the Fessenden money. However, in February 1889 he thought of buying a lot with a small house on 12th, near G, and he continued his real estate investments in the District, buying a lot on the corner of S and 19th Streets, through his agent Mr. C. Early, for which he paid about $5,000. Since Gallaudet was buying with the idea of selling and making a profit, the turnover in his property was quite fast—and although he never stated what fees he paid his agents, it is assumed that the profits he showed, and called "net," discounted any fees he must have paid.

At first he was offered an advance of $300 over what he paid for the S and 19th Street property, but he held out for $500 advance. Such an offer came in April. However, he had bought property on 15th Street at $4,100 for his daughters the year before which he managed to sell at a profit of $1,100. In July he was offered an advance of $1,000 for his 12th Street property for which he had paid $7,200. He transacted this deal in August with Harding and King, and the following month chose a property through the same firm on 11th Street, valued at $10,000, as an investment, but which he bought later in December for $9,500. Through the advice of a lawyer, J. W. Thompson, he was advised not to sell at a $1,000 advance, but in two days' time he was offered an advance of $1,500 and accepted it, clear-. ing a net of over $1,000. In the meantime he had received a remit- tance of a sum over $10,000 for the stock he, Grace, and Katharine had in the Phoenix Mutual Life Insurance Company, which he thought was realizing a very handsome sum for the amount of money originally invested. "At this rate," he wrote, "the accident of wealth may yet happen to me."

During December he had looked at some property on 9th Street, and also on 15th, both between L and M Streets, but later in the month decided on the 9th Street house only, buying it for Grace through Early for $6,200. Through Harding's firm he bought one for himself on G Street at $10,000. Several days later he gave some time to the consideration of a possible purchase on G Street of two houses and lots, costing $30,000, which he felt was a large thing for him to think of. He met and consulted with Henry Strong and B. H. Warner, neither of whom were very enthusiastic in advising the pur- chase. After thinking it over he went to two other friends. Both agreed that the price was the top of the market, but both said he could lose nothing on the property, "and had quite a show for making a good thing." He began to hope the increase of riches would not lead him to set his heart on them. He made a pact with himself to increase his "give away" decidedly.

He received a check from Early for the sale of the 11th Street lot on Christmas Eve of 1889 and that evening he had a call from Early saying that $30,000 was the best he could bargain for the G Street homes, and Gallaudet authorized him to get them. Up to then it was the largest personal transaction he had ever been a party to, should it carry through. It seemed as though Early had not laid all his cards on the table, but Gallaudet claimed not to be disturbed. "I find," he said, "it very distasteful to me to have my mind too much on the making of money—there are other games much better worth the candle."

In the early part of 1890 while walking up the avenue with Senator Henry L. Dawes they talked of real estate matters, and Dawes asked Gallaudet to make an investment of $8,000 for him. A few days later Gallaudet learned that Early had been trying to overreach both the owner of the $30,000 property and Gallaudet as well. The owner was now asking $35,000, and Gallaudet stated frankly it was more than he could pay. Yet, when this fell through, Gallaudet immediately began to think of purchasing the 13th Street Baptist Church property, at $36,000. He asked Senator Dawes his thoughts and Dawes was willing to go along with Gallaudet if he thought it a good investment. Gallaudet regarded this as a mark of great confidence. Dawes, however, later decided not to go into the purchase of the church property with Gallaudet and Gallaudet made up his mind to buy the property at 12th and G Streets, first contemplated in 1889, at $7,775. But when the owner jumped his price to $12,000 Gallaudet hesitated. In the meantime he walked over to the 13th Street Baptist Church with one of his Directors and talked with his friends J. W. Thompson, Robert C. Fox, and John W. Foster. Though they held the property to be cheap at $36,000 Gallaudet did not decide at once to buy, but the next day, after a final consultation with Thompson and Fox, he bought the church property agreeing to pay $20,000 cash on the 31st and assume the debt of $16,000. Fox's partner prophesied that the property would sell before Gallaudet obtained the deed.

Almost a week later Gallaudet made a trip to examine his 13th Street Church and found it in excellent condition for renting evenings, Sundays, and special occasions. J. W. Thompson offered to lend Gallaudet what money he needed to pay for the church, and within ten days after he had made the purchase W. F. Holtman made him an offer of $38,000. Gallaudet paid for the church on January 31, 1890, giving his $20,000 cash and assuming a debt of $16,000 at 6 percent interest. The first person to rent the church was Father Clinquy, the famous Romish priest past eighty who had renounced his faith many years before and married. He was the uncle of young Charles D. Allard of Illinois, a student at the College.

Gallaudet christened his church "Fessenden Hall," and directed a sign to be put up over the front door. He considered enlarging the place, but almost immediately a party began seeking to buy the hall for $45,000. The direct offer came in March and Gallaudet accepted it, making a splendid profit in five weeks. Gallaudet had been told that his church would probably bring $60,000 if the Great Fair was held in Washington, but events turned it to Chicago. Gallaudet closed the church transaction by March 7 of 1890, through the firm of King and Harding. He and Susy signed the deed two weeks later, celebrating by going to a concert of the Boston Symphony Orchestra. Although a later offer of $50,000 came for the hall, Gallaudet was already considering the purchase of the corner of 13th Street and New York Avenue and H for $56,000.

On March 24th Gallaudet completed the purchase of the property on G Street, possibly one of the two lots he had been considering in December of 1889, paying $15,000 for it. At the same time he offered $56,000 for the lots on 13th, at the corner of H and New York Avenue. Two days elapsed when he was offered $18,500 for his recent G Street purchase, but he declined it. He then completed the bargain for the lots on 13th, "Which seems," he said, "a very large thing for me to do."

Gallaudet went on a trip and his agents wired him about his G Street property being bid on for $21,000, a third promised in cash. Gallaudet replied that he preferred one-half to be in cash, but the exchange of wires caused a delay and the deal fell through. There was already a nibble for his 13th Street-New York Avenue purchase: an offer of $62,000, with an advance of $4,000 net to him. This he declined, holding his value at $66,000.

In the middle of April Gallaudet went to the bank and arranged for a loan from the National Savings Bank for $55,000 at 5 percent. It was exactly one month after this that his agent gave him the news that he had sold the property for ten dollars a foot, at an advance to Gallaudet and the girls of $10,000 over what he had paid for it. "Wonderful!," he wrote. By June he had made the final settlement on the sale of the property.

Real estate matters had a rest while he took his family to the shore, but soon he heard there was a possibility of making a good turn on F Street near 7th. He followed this up for the next several days and finally agreed to buy at $10 a foot. This particular deal fell through when the owner received a higher offer. In August a telegram reached him that there was an offer on his G Street property for a $20,000 net and he wired back to make it $20,200.

Returned to Washington, Gallaudet decided to buy a corner of 12th and E Streets at $49,424, and later looked after his sale of the G Street lot. Since the 12th and E Streets deal had not come through he turned again to 11th Street when he, Kitty and Grace decided to invest in a house and lot next to one owned by John W. Foster, which Foster rented for $1,200 per annum. Gallaudet paid $20,000 for this, completing the purchase in October. In this same month an offer was made to him of property on F Street, a whole block between 9th and 10th Streets, at $100,000—two stories with offices above, renting for nearly $5,000 per annum. This seemed a large purchase, but the price of $19.79 per foot was not high. His friends who knew property values advised him to buy, and he gave a $1,000 check to close the purchase. This was his largest transaction to date, and he offered a little prayer hoping God would give him grace not to set his heart on riches as they increased. This property was owned by a Mrs. Coyle.

Gallaudet had a note discounted for $8,000 at the bank, left one of the 13th Street church mortgage notes for the same amount as collateral, and took up a note of $3,000, as the first step towards making payment on his F Street purchase. At this time he also sent a check of $500 for Faith Chapel from the girls and himself, and $100 to Henry Barnard who was in straitened circumstances. These many transactions had given Susy notions. Her next proposition was to establish a $10,000 book fund. Gallaudet had a talk with her as to her "impracticable project." He was forlorn because his words and judgment seemed to her but the "idle wind,"—in spite of the fact that he assured her they were living at a rate of more than $1,000 per annum beyond their income. "Her attitude and speech made me wish I had never made a cent in real estate," he moaned. "It is strange that so much unreason is mingled with her generally reasonable spirit." He always believed that a sweet disposition was better than brains in a woman.

Gallaudet spent quite some time raising the money for the purchase of the Coyle block. Money was "tight" and the bank refused to lend him all he needed. He sold $10,950 of his real estate notes at a discount, and this, with the amount taken in the sale of his G Street house, made it possible to meet his commitments to Mrs. Coyle. After paying her the sum of $25,000 he then mortgaged the property to her for $75,000. A friend, George Dudley Seymour, congratulated him upon the purchase, saying he would take it off Gallaudet's hands any time he wanted to be rid of it. Gallaudet felt reasonably sure that his daughters would have some property and a fair income to make them independent.

Over the years Gallaudet reduced the mortgage on the Coyle block, then continued to renew the loan of the $50,000 balance, paying interest twice a year from the rents on the property. He eventually invested $18,000 for himself and daughters in Aetna Insurance. In 1905 he decided to build a house on the 18th Street property of Grace and Katharine, which later sold for $24,226.48, and the money was sent to Hartford to the girls' account. They did not fare so well when he sold their 11th Street property in 1908, since it brought only $15,500, after holding it 12 years. He remarked that it had always been a poor investment.

It was Susy's dislike of Hartford that caused her husband to give up the idea of retirement at 50. He began to rent his lodge Quinipi and finally sold it because Susy was tired of the family moving upheavals twice a year. All of this gave Gallaudet a "great pang," but he did it. He asked $7,000 for the lodge and grounds, and finally sold it to Mr. Fellowes, with insurance, for $6,664.41 in 1889. But he never sold Quiescas. With the real estate he now owned Susy felt confident that Washington would remain their home.

But Susy had only four more years to make an earthly home. Gallaudet took her to many well recommended physicians to see if they could diagnose her trouble: headaches, abdominal pain, and a general feeling of illness. Gallaudet was never to know how lonely he could be until his "dear girl" really left him alone on November 4, 1903. On the 7th, with Susy's body lying in the library of their Kendall Green home, he wrote in his diary: "Flowers, notes, cards and telegrams continue to pour in for dear Susy's last 'Saturday at Home'." She had enjoyed her farm only two years before she died and willed it to her children and her husband. Gallaudet sold his part and divided the money between Grace and Katharine, who were not included in the will.

As his full retirement neared Gallaudet thought it best to withdraw his money from Washington real estate and make other investments. He sold the F Street property for $115,110, and after paying his debt of $50,000 to the Coyle estate he had realized a profit of $15,110. He was satisfied with the sale for he learned that real estate values were beginning to move from 9th to the vicinity of 15th Street.

XVII

New Outlets

It was the latter part of 1898 that Susy began to encourage Gallaudet to look into diplomatic work. She felt that he could still keep his position as President on the Green and be sent on Government missions. Perhaps he might like it well enough to leave the Green. Dutifully, Gallaudet called on John W. Foster "and had a good talk with him as to Susy's ambitions for me to do some diplomatic work," he recorded. The next day he made a call on Secretary of State John Hay. He was received cordially and stayed 10 minutes. For the third day in a row he made a similar trip, this time calling on President McKinley at the White House by appointment. Gallaudet referred to the incident of his name having been given to McKinley the summer before as a possible Peace Commissioner. "He was courteous and complimentary to me about this," he later said, "and spoke of other important matters that were to receive attention in the near future."

It was not Gallaudet's role to ask favors for himself: begging for the school was his job, but to seek office made him feel out of his element. His consequent reticence made it possible for the political men of the day to become evasive when he went to see them on legitimate business. He recalled several times when he sensed their impatience and lack of cooperation. But he would make these attempts for an appointment for Susy's sake. Maybe she was right: hadn't his friend Henry L. Dawes surprised him by inquiring why he did not run for the Connecticut Legislature, since his voting privileges were in Branford, near Quinipi? Another friend B. H. Warner told Gallaudet in 1890 that he might have the presidency of a bank or insurance company in Washington if he desired it.

At the age of 60, with a truly monumental achievement behind him and still in good health and ambitious, it is likely that at times he found life somewhat monotonous. His remaining energy needed to find an outlet. Susy was dissatisfied with the routine of success

Gallaudet represented, and she communicated her unrest to him.
With their children seeking interests elsewhere they found life flat.
In November of 1898 he had said as much in his diary. The new point
of view that a special mission would bring might make him forget
that his finger joints were becoming crooked, and he would have less
time for reflections on life after death. The disciplinary problems in
the school were wearing to his nerves: he could not understand why
persons who had reached college age had so little self-discipline. He
was forgetting for the moment how he wrote in his early *Occasionals*,
asking for guidance!

Gallaudet's great need to feel "needed" was uppermost now. He
had become so used to attending to every detail of the home, during
Susy's frequent indispositions, that when his family dwindled and
took over their own adult duties he began to doubt his own worth
to them. He expressed the fear that his presence gave little pleasure,
and that all he was needed for was for writing checks! As his social
activities decreased and he remained more often at home he began
to crave more of an intellectual intercourse. Into 1901 he was still
seeking a special appointment of some kind. He asked his minister,
Dr. Teunis S. Hamlin, what he thought of some diplomatic work for
him, and then he went to see Justice David Brewer, leaving him a
copy of his *International Law*. Susy had definitely planted the idea
in Gallaudet's mind. A year after her death he was still trying to
attach himself to a special mission.

The summer of 1907 he was not well at all, finally taking to bed with
a case of pneumonia while in a summer hotel at the shore. Friends
returned him to his Hartford home to recuperate, and he was able
to attend his first faculty meeting in September, of which he said,
"It was not unpleasant to feel that my hand was on the helm again."
He was now beginning his fiftieth year on Kendall Green, at the age
of 70. There might be a few more thoughts to cross his mind about
diplomatic work, but the future of life on earth seemed very short
and he was resigned to the thought of its termination. After 50 years
of being a diplomat to his deaf friends all over the United States
and Europe, how could a short term as a government diplomat compare? His years of work would leave impact of a thousand-fold value
compared to many another man whose work had seemed more spec-
tacular during its course.

Gallaudet attended, in turn, three Presbyterian churches during his
years in Washington. He was first a member of the First Presbyterian Church whose minister, Dr. Byron Sunderland, held a grudge

against Gallaudet long after he had changed to the New York Avenue Church, where Lincoln had attended. This misunderstanding was referred to in earlier pages while Sunderland sat on Gallaudet's Board of Directors. Gallaudet remained at the New York Avenue Church until the pastor was called to New York. His last choice was the Church of the Covenant, where he was with his friends W. E. Curtiss, Commissioner McFarland, John W. Foster, and Gardiner Greene Hubbard. On March 26, 1905, he joined their ranks as an Elder. His only criticism was that they used individual wine cups when the prayer was to bless "the cup."

In 1908 he began to write of resigning his Presidency, or request some material dimunition of his duties and responsibilities. There were a number of disciplinary troubles with the boys involving hazing, that carried over into 1909 and were unpleasant and depressing to Gallaudet. He talked with Kitty about resigning and about their future. In February of 1910 he took action, encouraged by Professor Fay who advised him to resign at an early date and lay down his burdens. He made a call on John W. Foster and unfolded his plan, and he named the professor he wanted to succeeed him. Gallaudet's only stipulation was that he should remain President of the Board of Directors one more year, while living in the home. When the Board met in Senator Francis Cockrell's office its members unanimously accepted his resignation. His duties and his salary would cease during the summer and his Presidency of the Board would continue while he occupied the house. "So now it is settled when I shall be 'down and out'," he said. "I'm glad and sorry." [1]

On March 31 of 1910 he talked with Percival Hall and told him he had tendered his resignation and that it was his wish that he succeed him. Hall was overcome and expressed the wish that Gallaudet could stay longer.

Percival Hall, right out of Harvard College, had been a member of the second Normal Class to train under the new program. A son of Asaph Hall, prominent astronomer of the U. S. Naval Observatory, he had taught briefly at the New York School for the Deaf after training at the Columbia Institution, and was called back to Kendall Green in 1894 to teach Latin in the College, and to head the Articulation work. A young wife had died earlier but in the years at the College the young professor had fallen in love with one of the co-eds from Denver, Ethel Z. Taylor; and when they married, Gallaudet opened his home for the wedding, having the rehearsal on June 18, 1900, and the wedding the afternoon of the 20th.

Gallaudet gave the bride away, and Allan Fay, the Hotchkiss children, and Kitty were in the wedding. Professor Hall's young family had grown up on the Green with Gallaudet's grandchildren. Percival Hall was one of the first of the Fellowship men to have his children follow in the profession, and his two sons eventually taught at the College.²

The summer of 1910 Gallaudet and daughter Katharine went abroad. He went to his usual haunts and visited with friends in England and Switzerland. They went over on the *Berlin* and returned on the *Finland,* and he received a royal welcome back to the campus on October 18. He was back in his office the 20th, approving a lot of vouchers, saying, "These will stand as my last approvals." Professor Hall took over the duty October 1. Gallaudet signed contracts for the repair of damage done by a fire during the early part of 1910, and spent time taking the new President to the Capitol and introducing him. When Gallaudet told Secretary of the Interior Richard A. Ballinger that he had signed the First Report, Ballinger remarked, "You are quite an old stager."

Gallaudet and Katharine gave a tea for President and Mrs. Hall on November 1 and invited all campus dwellers and many who had moved off the Green, about 80 in all. He took time off in November to travel to Branford and vote "the straight Republican ticket." He could scarcely wait to return to his "dear Quiescas" in Hartford. He went to Boston from Branford to ask President Lowell of Harvard to speak at Presentation Day exercises, then visited son Herbert and his lovely wife Elizabeth who took him up Bunker Hill Monument. Gallaudet walked up the 300-foot monument and his only comment was, "The view was rather poor." He then visited his sons Denny and Edson on his way back, at their aeroplane plant in Norwich.

The winter was an interesting one, and in the spring of 1911 Gallaudet made plans to attend the convention in Delavan, Wisconsin. He then resigned his Trusteeship at the George Washington University.

XVIII

Making An Exit

Gallaudet began to pack his belongings in October of 1910. He had an interview with his cousin Wallace, the Institution's Supervisor and Disbursing Agent, to balance his accounts. They showed quite a handsome credit. He consulted banks and business offices and learned that the time was not promising for investment in real estate loans, and so he held onto his money for a while. Gradually he went through his papers and letters and read once more those he had kept because of sentiment. He tore up some of his father's and his mother's letters and some from Jane and Susy. A few he kept and they were left with his travel journals and diaries among his papers.

One of the most interesting things he did in the latter part of 1910 was make a movie. Roy Stewart, '99, consulted him about this project on October 22. He suggested the making of a film depicting a lecture by Gallaudet in the sign language. Gallaudet immediately thought of the story of *Lorna Doone*, perhaps because he had recently visited the Doone country the month before while in England. He thought it would lend itself excellently to drama and pathos, both of which could be so well depicted in signs. They made a test, and in January of 1911 he went to the film company's place on 11th Street where President Hall, Professors Hotchkiss and Draper, and Mr. Ballard and Mr. Stewart awaited him. They were shown the working of the "film moving picture," and all were satisfied with the experiment film. It worried Gallaudet that his performance might not justify expenditure of $400—the amount of money the deaf were investing in this film. But he went ahead with his lecture. It was a tedious operation. He had to stop five times for changes of film. It took 50 minutes to get through what could have been given in 29 minutes of continuous sign lecturing. It was January 30 before they saw the completed film. Everyone pronounced it a success. The film was shown at the College. Helen Nicolay came out to see it with an artist friend, and the Fanwood School of New York put on a military drill for the occasion.

Gallaudet next turned this thoughts to helping Edson and Denison get started in the airplane company. Edson had been interested in inventions since he was 14, and Gallaudet was pleased to see this talent finding an outlet. Edson subsequently taught physics at Yale following his graduation, and later received a Ph. D. in applied electricity at Johns Hopkins University. His aim, however, was to become an aeronautical engineer. He had worked on a device for aiming large guns, in which the Navy had become interested. He had studied rotary engines, and in September of 1900 he began work at Cramp's Ship Company. When the Technical Department opened at Gallaudet College he was offered the Chairmanship but refused it because it would not give him time for his inventions. The officers in the Navy Department were most encouraging and finally tested his device on a seven-inch gun. After his marriage to Marion Cockrell in 1903 he gave more time to his inventions, working on his kite, or "flying machine" as Gallaudet termed it. He borrowed writings on aerodynamics from Samuel Pierpont Langley, and in 1906 went abroad at a request from the German emperor to test the air compressor at Kiel.

Edson, with his brother Denison, who had been in railroad work, got together to form the Gallaudet Airplane Company at Norwich, Connecticut, and their father invested sums in this company several times. Frank Julian Sprague, the engineer and inventor, became affiliated with the company. Gallaudet became quite air conscious, and he and Katharine went out to Benning's Race Course in Washington to see Glenn Curtiss and others display their flying machines. Edson said at this time that his machine would be ready by April of 1912. Edson held license No. 32 in the United States, and was also brevetted in France. His firm built a seaplane for the army in 1913. Edson held advanced ideas in aviation and had he sought a patent early enough his model would have preceded Wright's.

Within six weeks of leaving Washington Gallaudet went to his brokers and invested considerable sums in railroad bonds and in United States Steel. He had paid out $20,000 on such investments by January 11, 1911, and $30,000 before the month was over. A few weeks earlier, when he received the balance on his F Street property, he had confided to his diary that "It seemed like a fairy tale for me to be walking the streets of Washington with $65,000 in my pocket."

He got through Presentation Day, although Lowell did not come,

and had time on his hands to think about the move he was about
to make. There would be no more ice skating around the Washington Monument with Herbert, which he had done when he was 70!
He was now to become "Edward-sit-by-the-fire" and no longer hear
men like Ambassador Bryce make addresses, or act as a judge for
debates at Georgetown. There would be no more wonderful drives
with dear Susy over the streets of Washington. He would have to
leave his horses, valued servants, and all that had meant life on
Kendall Green. Another life would be his now, and he must accept
the conditions that would come with his Hartford existence. He
would still be able to balance his accounts, however; which was a
diversion for him. New friends just entering his horizon he would
have to leave: the Pinchots, Mrs. Galt and Miss Bolling, the Robert
Lansings, the incoming Secretaries, and members of the Literary
Society. He had enjoyed the John Hays and the Henry Cabot Lodges.
It had often been remarked how much Gallaudet, Lodge, and Henry
Adams resembled each other. Had Gallaudet inherited the means
for more freedom he might have taken his place with these as a
known scholar.

Gallaudet accepted many invitations before he left, and continued
to take President Hall on calls. He presided for the last time at
Presentation Day, donning his white flannels and preaching his fare-
well sermon. The Officers of the Institution presented him with a
fine gold watch.

The packers were soon at hand and Katharine urged her father
to go to Marion Cockrell's Washington home and rest during this
time, but Gallaudet was reluctant to take his final leave of "dear
Kendall Green," calling it "a pretty poor day for poor Edward." A
rather strange thing happened late in that day: a heavy thunderstorm
came up and a severe bolt of lightning shattered the flagstaff on
the Chapel. After a cool night Gallaudet slipped away the next day
and made a solitary trip to Bluemont, Virginia, going to bed that
evening in a quiet room. He did not tell his thoughts to his diary.

Gallaudet had many interesting events to relive after settling in
Hartford. He could look back on the reception to the Archbishop
of Canterbury at the Corcoran Art Gallery, where he had seen his
old schoolmate "Pip" Morgan. An affair to remember was Gifford
Pinchot's reception to the state governors and waterways commissioners, at which he had spotted William Jennings Bryan. He could
recall the Yale Alumni dinner at Rauscher's and the fine speeches of
Justice Brewer and Secretary of War Taft, even then being boomed

for President; and the magnificent parties at the Westinghouses'. He had met Woodrow Wilson at one of the John W. Foster receptions. When again would he ever attend a reception at the Vice President's in honor of members of the High Joint Commission? He would miss talks with men like these. Once he and Susy had attended a notable dinner at Justice Brewer's when they were the only guests other than the members of the Supreme Court. This was when Justice Harlan had predicted that the end of 1900 would see accomplished an African Republic.

He had had his own share of famous visitors on the Green. Mrs. George (Phoebe Apperson) Hearst, mother of William Randolph Hearst, had called on them; the Queen of Hawii had visited him in 1887, en route home from a visit to England with her sister-in-law who became Queen Liluokalani, the last monarch of Hawaii. Representatives from China, Japan, France, and England, and other dignitaries had crossed his threshold and were to become the symbols of his accomplishment as well as the reminders of his happier days— for they were gone now, and he would experience distress that the era had ended. He was not one to delude himself that better days were ahead. He might welcome the release of duties, but he faced his retirement stoically, as a general faces a truce.

He settled down to his life at Quiescas and began to renew his friendships. An old servant of the Twichell's saw him and said, "You've failed wonderful. You used to be round and plump." His friends rallied round, but there were animal friends he missed: the horses were going from the scene. "Very few of these old friends," he wrote. He visited his bank and consulted with H. K. Taylor about Wabash Pittsburgh Terminal Bonds, and invested $4,000 for his girls. He attended the Convention at Delavan, Wisconsin, and received an ovation.

For another six years he went through his routine, fixing up his study and planning to write. "I have really had a wonderful experience and have done an amount of work of which I am not ashamed," he wrote after going through his papers and keepsakes.

His ambition was to live for the Centennial Celebration of the American School which his father had founded. As late as January of 1915 he continued to use his chest weights and take his walks. He remembered Susy again in December of 1916 when he wrote on their anniversary: "This is the 48th Anniversary of my marriage with Susy, in the cold of Vermont mid-winter. It was a joyous day for me.

I felt much younger than my years. How sad it is for me Susy is not here to mark time for me."

His 1917 entries were few and short. He worried because his friends were passing, and he felt he *must* get engaged in some writing if nothing more than reminiscences of Prospect Street. He began to re-read his diaries. But mostly they were "dull days for Edward." Kitty was his companion at Quiescas. Grace had married again in 1907, her first husband having died six months after their marriage in 1893.

Superintendent Wheeler of the American School called on Gallaudet in March. Plans were under way for the Convention in June. Gallaudet hardly expected to live that long but he thought he might "hold out." He visited in town and saw Yvette Guilbert in her remarkable dramatic representations, and declared her "a remarkably well preserved woman of 60." The American School's Board President, Professor Henry A. Perkins of Trinity College, called in relation to the Convention. Too many things seemed to be happening: Herbert's going into the army; Liberty Bond sales; the Ringling Circus in town—and he wanted to go; his Convention Address to write. He decided that he would ask President Hall to read it for him; he knew he would not be able to do so.

President Hall and Professor Fay called on June 28th. Gallaudet envied them their strength. He let it be known that friends could call on him between 4 and 6 o'clock—and then the 29th dawned with good weather for the Convention. The Program proceeded according to plans. Gallaudet's friends called on him during the appointed hours. They stayed in the yard and only waved to him. He was too weak to invite them into his home. On the page in his diary allotted to June 20, 1917, he entered this note: "I am writing on this page on the 25th of July, having neglected my diary shamefully. I cannot hope to 'make up.' The Conventions were eminently successful, and continued cool weather most unexpected. Those who look for satisfaction from the following July record will be disappointed." The rest of the little book is blank, and for the first time in many years he failed to balance his accounts. His object had been achieved: he had lived to witness the 100th celebration of the founding of his father's school. Edward Miner Gallaudet died on September 26, 1917.

Seldom is the soul of a dreamer and a doer combined in the same man, but certainly Edward Miner Gallaudet's person embodied both these qualities. Where his father had been a pioneer in introducing the education of the deaf into America, Edward became an innovator in this field of specialized work. His aim, when he landed in Washington, was to plant the roots of a college for the deaf, and as soon as he had a sturdy elementary school he began to draw from it college material, train it, and then ask Congress for the power to confer degrees. He literally built a college from an elementary school, and became a messenger between the deaf to the public, keeping the needs of the deaf ever within view of those who could help. In time he became the ambassador of the deaf from this country to foreign nations, gaining ideas to introduce into his own school and endeavoring to plant a seed that would inspire higher education for the deaf abroad. However, when he died September 26, 1917, he was, and has remained, the only person in the world to accomplish this aim. Gallaudet College in Washington is the only college for the deaf in the world today. It remains an enduring memorial to the two men who devoted their lifetime to freeing the minds and breaking the silence of a minority group of citizens who have much to contribute to their community.

Although convinced of the value of the language of gestures in the training of the deaf, Edward Miner Gallaudet was one of the first in the United States to advocate giving all deaf children instruction in speech and lipreading, and when he called the principals of the schools for the deaf in the nation to Convention in Washington in 1868 he swung the tide toward the acceptance of oral teaching in all the state residential schools for the deaf. He insisted on keeping academic standards high, and introduced co-education, teacher training, and technical instruction in his college as the needs rose. Above all, he listened to the voice of the deaf.

References

CHAPTER I

[1] The Prioleau name is traceable to Pruili, an Italian name prominent in Venice during the sixteenth and seventeenth centuries. See "The Family of Pruili," a paper by Edward Miner Gallaudet, read before the Huguenot Society of New York, April 13, 1894.

[2] Information through research of Eric P. Newman of St. Louis, expert on American coins and currency.

[3] This statement was made in Edward Miner Gallaudet's diary for January 7, 1895.

[4] See *Life of Thomas Hopkins Gallaudet*, by Edward Miner Gallaudet; New York: Henry Holt and Company, 1888.

[5] The Abbé Roch-Ambroise-Curron Sicard (1742-1822) is credited with adding a more philosophical method of work built on the Abbé de l'Epée's principles, recognizing the importance of language to the deaf. De l'Epée had established the Royal Institution for Deaf-mutes in Paris between 1755 and 1760.

[6] Jean Massieu (1772-1846), born at Semens, near Bordeaux, was one of six deaf children.

[7] Laurent Clerc (1785-1869), born in La Balme, near Lyons. His great-great grandson, Guy Holt, is the present President of the Board of Directors at the American School for the Deaf in Hartford.

[8] See the Hartford *Courant*, July 1, 1817. Also *Famous Visitors and Distinguished Guests of Hartford (1645-1936)*, by Merrill H. Dooey. M.A. Thesis, Trinity College, 1938.

[9] The first six Principals of the American School were Yale graduates: Thomas H. Gallaudet, 1805; Lewis Weld, 1818; William W. Turner, 1819; Collins Stone, 1832; Edward C. Stone, 1862; Job Williams, 1864. Dozens of Yale men were trained under these Principals.

[10] Gallaudet's books for children on Natural Theology and Scripture Biography were reprinted in fourteen or more languages and filled a great need in the 1830's, when little literature existed for children.

[11] John Dewey, when speaking at the 100th Anniversary of the American School in 1917, remarked that Thomas Gallaudet was, so far as he knew, the first person to speak of an *experimental* school.

[12] Yung Wing (1828-1912) was the first Chinese student to graduate from Yale. He became the Assistant to the Chinese Minister in Washington between 1878 and 1881. He spent his late years in Hartford.

[13] See the Seventh Annual Report of the Columbian Institution for the Deaf and Dumb and the Blind, p. 17. Laurent Clerc was present on this occasion and made an address.

CHAPTER II

[1] Edward did not state in his diary that he received no diploma at Trinity, although he had expected to win a B.S. degree. The President withheld it because of Edward's irregular attendance. It was not until 1885 that he was presented this diploma—after he had won several honorary degrees: M.A., Trinity, 1859, LL.D., 1869; Ph.D., George Washington University (then Columbian University,) 1869. In 1895 he received the LL.D. from Yale.

[2] This old house was razed during March of 1895 when the new dormitory for boys was built on the spot, called Dawes House, in honor of Senator Henry L. Dawes, of Massachusetts, who worked in Congress for the support of the Institution.

[3] This building was on G Street, west of the War Department building.

[4] Details are to be found in pamphlet form in the Gallaudet Papers. Early minutes of the Board also reveal pertinent facts.

[5] The Government Hospital for the Insane, now known as St. Elizabeth's Hospital, was founded by an Act of Congress in 1852 to "provide the most humane care and enlightened curative treatment of the insane of the Army and Navy of the United States and of the District of Columbia." The measure was written by Dorothea Lynde Dix (1802-1887), outstanding social reformer who became superintendent of women nurses during the Civil War. She visited the campus of the Columbia Institution several times.

[6] The temporary assistant was Mr. J. Orville Olds, who was paid $75 between April 16th and July 1st. Miss Alice Adams was secured for the girls. Edward's salary began at $1,000; his permanent assistant's was $500. Mrs. Thomas Gallaudet received $300 and her assistant the same.

[7] Mr. Fessenden gave them the family bible in which Edward recorded the dates of marriage, children, and deaths. This Bible was presented to the College in 1958 by Mrs. Edson F. Gallaudet of Pine Orchard, Connecticut, widow of Edward's second son.

CHAPTER III

[1] Edward had been given permission in the beginning to plan toward a national institution. The Board had not stipulated a set time.

[2] Robert Gould Shaw (1837-1863), commanded the first Negro troops, Union Army.

[3] Robert A. Anderson (1805-1872), was a Kentuckian whose sympathies were with the South preceding the secession, but whose responsibilities bade him do what he was ordered to do as a West Point man. He was made a Brigadier-General in the Union Army in 1862, retired, and was succeeded by W. T. Sherman.

[4] See J. C. Stevenson, *The Mind and Art of Henry Adams*, Boston: Houghton Mifflin Co., 1957. Chap. 1, p. 10.

CHAPTER IV

1. Gardiner Greene Hubbard (1822-1897), wealthy Boston lawyer, was well-known for his interest in welfare movements. His deaf daughter married Alexander Graham Bell, to whom he gave needed financial backing in his invention of the telephone. Hubbard led the movement in oralism in Massachusetts.

2. Jeanie Lippitt (Weeden) (1854-1940), daughter of Henry Lippitt (1818-1891), manufacturer and Governor of Rhode Island; and sister of Henry F. Lippitt (1856-1933), industrialist and Senator from Rhode Island. This information was furnished by Henry F. Lippitt, II, great-nephew of Jeanie Lippitt Weeden. His mother, Marion Almy Lippitt, wrote a book about Jeanie, *I Married a New Englander*. Boston: Chapman and Grimes, Inc., 1947. Revised edition 1949.

3. Henry Winter Syle (1846-1890) was born in Shanghai, China, of mis-

sionary parents. His mother was a sister of Henry Winter Davis of Maryland.
Deafened by scarlet fever at 6, Henry was brought to America and put in a
private school at Poughkeepsie, N.Y., under David Ely Bartlett. He entered
Trinity College, Hartford, in 1868; suffered eye trouble, and later won a scholar-
ship to St. John's College, Cambridge. After a breakdown he return to the
United States and taught at the New York School for the Deaf before taking all
examinations for the four-years course at Yale, which he did in three weeks. He
received an A.B. from Yale and later won an M.A. Subsequently he studied at
the Columbia School of Mines and worked in the Philadelphia Mint. Determined to become a minister, he was ordained to the priesthood in 1883 and
founded All Soul's Church for the Deaf in Philadelphia.

4. Line drawings of these symbols, written on tissue—like paper, are pasted
in Edward's notebook. The symbols, or characters, resemble the "Visible Speech"
symbols invented by Melville Bell and taught by his son Alexander Graham
Bell during the 1870's and later.

CHAPTER V

1. A resolution was passed in the Board meeting of December 31, 1867,
to admit into the Institution speaking persons of suitable age and attainments to
fit themselves to teach the deaf. At first it was thought they would be charged
for maintenance, but scholarships were developed. Women were admitted as
well as men.

2. The Rev. John W. Chickering of New Hampshire became the professor
of articulation at the Institution the fall of 1870, teaching both the primary pupils and the college students, twenty in all this first year.

3. These proceedings and papers were printed in the 1868 Annual Report,
this Conference really proving a turning point in the progressive affairs of the
Columbia Institution.

4. Elihu B. Washburne (1816-1887), Maine born, was one of four brothers,
but the only one to add an "e" to his surname. His brother, William Drew
Washburn, was a Senator from Minnesota whose son, Cadwallader Washburn,
was a deaf boy who later went to the National Deaf-Mute College. His uncle
Elihu, who did so much to oppose the College, lived to see his nephew go there,
as well as Amos G. Draper, whose application from Illinois he had turned down.

5. Rufus Paine Spalding (1798-1866), Representative from Ohio though born
in Massachusetts. A graduate in law he became an Ohio State Representative,
a State Supreme Court Associate Judge, then a United States Representative.

6. On February 12, 1868, it was announced in Board meeting that the Committee on Appropriations of the House of Representatives, in pursuance of the
suggestion in the Report of the Secretary of the Interior, agreed: "That in addition to the Directors whose appointment has heretofore been provided by law,
there shall be 3 other Directors appointed in the following manner, viz: One
Senator by the President of the Senate and two Representatives by the Speaker
of the House, these Directors to hold their office for the term of a single Congress
and to be eligible to a reappointment." (Referred to: Hon. Rufus P. Spalding,
a member of the Committee on Appropriations). The Smithsonian Institution
had worked under a similar ruling.

7. A copy of this Report is attached to Gallaudet's *Memoirs*. The debate

itself is copied out in his handwriting *in toto*. Washburne's Minority Committee was composed of Benjamin F. Butler of Massachusetts, James G. Blaine of Maine, and F. C. Beaman of Michigan.

8. Thaddeus Stevens died August 11, 1868. His interest in the Columbia Institution had early been aroused when he had wanted to send a constituent from Pennsylvania to Washington, only to learn that he could not because of the limited scholarships. He determined then to remedy that situation and began at once his fight for the rights of the Institution.

9. Washburne later told Spalding that he "would get even with that d-d little Frenchman yet."

CHAPTER VI

1. See *Representative Deaf Persons in the United States of America—Portraits and Character Sketches*. Edited by James E. Gallaher, Chicago, 1898. Amos Draper sketch pp. 33-36.

CHAPTER VII

1. Spalding had been Associate Judge in the Ohio Supreme Court from 1849 to 1852, before coming to Washington for the 38th, 39th, and 40th Congresses, having been elected as a War Democrat. His term expired on March 3, 1869, which made this bill's passage his last day in the House as a Representative from Ohio.

2. Baker's rare collection on the education of the deaf in early times, in different countries, is now in the Edward Miner Gallaudet Memorial Library at Gallaudet College. A catalogue of the books is in the appendix of the 1875 Report.

3. Henry L. Dawes (1816-1903) served for 34 years on Gallaudet's Board. He became United States Senator in 1875 and served until 1893.

4. Jacob Dolson Cox (1828-1900), American lawyer and army officer, was Governor of Ohio from 1866-1868; Secretary of the Interior from 1869-1870, and Dean of the Cincinnati Law School from 1881 to 1897, acting as the University's President during 1885-1887.

5. Gallaudet took Amos Draper on this trip, knowing he would make an excellent impression at the dinner.

6. Joseph Harrison (1810-1874) a self-taught mechanical engineer who later designed locomotives, and was under contract to the Russian government between 1843 and 1851, and was later decorated by Russia.

7. The interest on the note, $5,000, was payable July 1, 1870. Due the first of each succeeding January were the following payments: $10,000 in 1871, $25,000 in 1872, $25,000 in 1873 and the balance of $20,000 in 1874. The original asking price for Kendall Green was $90,000, but Gallaudet and his Directors had it reduced to $85,000 which included improvements.

8. James Abram Garfield (1831-1881) was not only a friend of the Institution but became a warm friend of the Gallaudet family. His first visit to the Institution was in the winter of 1865-1866. See *President Garfield's Connection with the Deaf Mute College*, the *American Annals of the Deaf*, January 1882.

9. George Franklin Edmunds (1828-1919) helped dedicate the Main Building in 1871.

10.   Cornelius Cole (1822-1924) was a New Yorker who went west and made his fortune in the gold mines. He served in the Senate from 1867 until 1873. When nearly 100 years old he visited Washington and addressed the House of Representatives. Roscoe Conkling (1821-1888) of New York served from 1867-1888. William Windom (1827-1891) of Minnesota, who served from 1870 to 1883, was Secretary of the Treasury under Garfield. William Sprague (1830-1915) served from 1863 to 1875, after being Governor of Rhode Island; he was the son-in-law of Chief Justice Chase.

11.   The text books and reading requirements for the Columbian Institution compare favorably with the highest ranking colleges and universities of the period. Research was made into the studies pursued in leading eastern universities of the same years, and many of the same textbooks appeared.

12.   This was the public recognition of the plan to erect, in New York's harbor, a colossal Statue of Liberty as a memorial to men "from every clime" of the alliance between France and the United States.

13.   When J. Randolph Tucker came on the Board by Congressional appointment in 1882 he expressed his views at nearly every meeting of the Board on the point of federal beneficiaries, and when he had "cleared his conscience" he would go ahead and give his adhesion to what the Board decided to ask of Congress.

14.   Those acting as clerks for Gallaudet during his tenure of office were: Emma J. Speaks, of Washington, who was in the Intermediate Class in 1865; Roswell Parish, Jr., of Hartford, an Instructor; James C. Balis, '75, who acted as Gallaudet's Secretary from 1875 to 1877; James H. Logan, '69, private secretary; Amos G. Draper, '72, private secretary; John B. Wight of Washington; Wallace G. Fowler, a cousin from Connecticut; several of the Normal students at different times; Albert C. Gaw, an Instructor; and his first and only woman secretary, Julia A. Hayden, who came in September of 1901 and stayed until he left in 1911.

15.   The full list of guests is in the 1878 Annual Report, pp. 7-8. Gallaudet would not have introduced people in such a manner, since it is not acceptable, but in his journals and diaries he related people to their work and placed them in their environment politically.

16.   Mgr. de Haerne received the honorary degree of L.H.D. from Gallaudet College in 1889, in absentia. The certificate was taken to him by Amos Draper when he went abroad to attend an International Convention for the Deaf in Paris.

17.   By 1893 there would have been twenty-nine graduates of Yale College to teach at the American School alone.

CHAPTER VIII

1.   Melville Ballard received a bachelor of science degree in 1866 after pursuing two years of study while teaching in the Primary Department, thus becoming the first graduate of the National Deaf-Mute College before the graduation of a class.

2.   Joseph Roswell Hawley (1826-1905) lived in Hartford and had known the American School a long time. He was a newspaperman and Governor of

his state before becoming a Congressman from 1873-1875; 1879-1881. He served in the Senate from 1881 to 1905, and was on Gallaudet's Board from 1883 until his death in 1905.

3. Gallaudet summed up this Department's actions at one time by saying: "The Department people act like Satan."

4. Joseph Gurney Cannon (1836-1926), a native Carolinian, moved to Illinois and was elected to Congress from there. He later became famous as "Uncle Joe."

CHAPTER IX

1. Susannah Hull, the daughter of a London doctor, played a prominent part in the regeneration of work for the deaf in England, working with children who had been left deaf by fevers. Alexander Graham Bell did his first teaching with the deaf in her school—trying Visible Speech.

2. See Kenneth W. Hodgson, *The Deaf and Their Problems*. New York: Philosophical Library, 1954. Chap. 13, pp. 244-245.

3. This resulted in the Royal Commission of the United Kingdom for the Deaf and Dumb and the Blind, held in London 1886-1888, to which Gallaudet would be called in 1886.

4. This "Message" is published in full in Gallaudet's 1897 Annual Report, in the Appendix. This gives an accurate account of the expenditures made by the College up to that year and of the various schools for the deaf throughout the county.

CHAPTER XI

1. While abroad in 1886 Gallaudet purchased some columns which he used in the entrance hall of "Quiescas." The eight-foot overhead spacing carried the carved motto: "18 - Pax - Interantibus - Salus Exeuntibus - 87." This he carved with the help of his son Edson, then sixteen years old. A stained glass window adorned the landing.

CHAPTER XII

1. Daniel Chester French (1850-1931), sculptor of the Lincoln Memorial in Washington, D.C., among many fine pieces.

2. Edwin Allan Hodgson was given an honorary master of arts degree by the College in 1883.

3. French's daughter, Margaret French Cresson, devotes parts of two chapters in her biography of her father, *Journey Into Fame*, to the Gallaudet statue and the selection of the site. Published by Harvard University Press, 1947; chapter 9, pp. 148-149; chapter 10, pp. 156-157.

XIII

1. Dr. Campbell was knighted in England and was otherwise highly honored. He tried to induce Gallaudet to establish a college for the blind at Kendall Green, but Gallaudet's Board of Directors did not take to the idea.

2.   It was at this Milan Conference that the Abba Tarra had almost "incited" the delegates to a "Evviva la parola" riot. The vote for speech led. In Brussels in 1883, at the third international Congress, speech did not fare so well. The Nationalistic feeling was uppermost, and the French had not taken to the ruling of the Italians.

3.   This evidence is all printed in the *American Annals of the Deaf,* and also collected and edited by Joseph C. Gordon, 1892 (Volta Bureau, Washington, D.C.) This includes the evidence of Alexander Graham Bell who gave evidence before the Commission in 1888, although he had told Gallaudet in December of 1886 that he had decided not to appear before the Commission, but would send a communication in writing.

4.   Benjamin Butterworth (1837-1898) was a lawyer from Ohio. After serving as a Member of Congress from 1879-1883, and again from 1885 to 1891, he practiced law in Washington, D.C. He was a Regent of the Smithsonian Institution and a Commissioner of Patents. In 1892 Harrison appointed him President of the Commission to European Governments. His grandson, Paul Butterworth, now serves on the Board at the American School.

5.   Bell's secretary, A. W. McCurdy, had appeared before the Committee on Appropriations on the day before.

6.   Bell also explained that oral schools financed their schools through private enterprise, and asked why combined schools and the College could not do likewise.

7.   The Convention of American Instructors of the Deaf, founded in 1850, was incorporated by an act of Congress in 1897.

XIV

1.   Founded in 1821 as Columbian College, Congress authorized the change from College to University in 1873. In the year 1904 the name was again changed, this time to George Washington University.

XV

1.   Winfield Scott Schley (1839-1911,) a United States Naval officer of Bavarian ancestry whom Gallaudet spoke of as his "double."

2.   This war between China and Japan, often referred to as the Sino-Japanese War, 1894-95, ended by China paying a heavy indemnity; giving Japan Formosa.

3.   Gallaudet attended the Arbitration Conference in January of 1904. Foster put him on the Committee to hand in the Resolutions to the Senate Committee on Foreign Relations.

XVII

1.   Gallaudet went into the Johns Hopkins Hospital in Baltimore in 1908 for surgery and had a successful operation.

2.   Percival Hall, Jr., and Jonathan Hall are professors in the College now.

Index

A

A.A.P.T.S.D. (American Association to Promote the Teaching of Speech to the Deaf), 126, 136-138
Academy of Sciences, 128
Ackers, St. John, 106, 107, 109, 130
Adams, Charles Francis, 53, 54
Adams, Henry, 46, 54
Adams, John, 35
Adams, John Quincy, 4
Adams, Maude, 148
Adams, Nehimiah, 45
Aetna Insurance, 163
Allen, J. M. 119
Allison, William B., 101, 134
American Annals of the Deaf, 67, 128, 129, 130 (Chap. 13, fn 3), 135 148
American School, 7, 13-14, 16-19, 43, 50-51, 77, 94, 96 (chap. 7, fn 17), 97, 105, 125, 132, 171-172
Anderson, Duncan, 63
Anderson, Mary, 148
Anderson, Robert A., 45 (Chap. 3, fn 3)
Andover Theological Seminary, 2
Andrews, E. F., 120
Angell, James Burrill, 105
Anthropological Society, 138
Archaeologcial Society, 105
Archbishop of Canterbury, 170
Argus of Western America, 22
Arthur, Chester, 150
Articulation, 5, 12, 49, 51-53, 55-57, 59-63, 65-67 (Chap. 5, fn 2), 126
Astor, John Jacob, 7, 32
Ayres, Jared, 16, 18, 19

B

Bacon, Sir Francis, 147
Bailey, Gamaliel, 21
Baird, Spencer, 103
Baker, Charles, 62, 63, 81
Baker, Mrs. Charles, 81, (Chap. 7, fn 2)
Baker Library, 62, 63, 81 (Chap. 7, fn 2), 89
Balis, James C., 94 (Chap. 7, fn 14)

Ballard, Melville, 94, 97 (Chap. 8, fn 1), 168
Ballin, S., 121
Ballinger, Richard A., 167
Baltimore and Ohio Railroad, 143
Balzac, Honoré de, 147
Banerji, Jamini Nath, 141
Barnard, Frederick A. P., 58
Barnard, Henry, 8, 162
Barrett, Lawrence, 148
Bartlett, Joseph J., 62
Baumgras, Peter, 43
Bayard, Thomas F., 129, 146
Beaman, F. C., 69 (Chap. 5, fn 7)
Beecher, Catherine E., 8
Beecher, Henry Ward, 45
Bell, Alexander, 122
Bell, Alexander Graham, 92, 103, 105, 106, 122-126, 129, 132, 133, (Chap. 13, fn 6), 134-138
Bell, Mrs. A. G. (Mabel Hubbard), 124, 126
Bell, Alexander Melville, 122
Bell, David Charles, 122
Belle Rive, 107
Benedetto, Conte, 59
Benson, A. C., 147
Bernhardt, Sarah, 149
Besant, Annie, 147
Biebuyak, the Abbé, 55
Biddle, Clement, 84
Bigelow, John, 58
Black, Charles Edward Drummond, 130
Black, William, 147
Blaine, James G., 21, 69 (Chap. 5, fn 7), 82, 84, 104-105
Blaine, Mrs. James G., 110
Blair, Francis, 22
Bliss, Cornelius, 100
Blount, James, 94, 99
Bone, A. E., 84
Bonney, Rev. Samuel W., 16
Booth, Edmund, 105
Booth, Edwin, 148
Borges, A. P. de Carvalho, 92
Boselli, Signor, 59
Boyden, Hon. N., 84
Brady, Sarita M., 147, 148
Braidwood family, 5, 51
Brentwood Park, 113, 143

181